The Concept of Validity

Revisions, New Directions, and Applications

The Concept of Validity

Revisions, New Directions, and Applications

edited by

Robert W. Lissitz
University of Maryland

INFORMATION AGE PUBLISHING, INC.
Charlotte, NC • www.infoagepub.com

Library of Congress Cataloging-in-Publication Data

The concept of validity : revisions, new directions, and applications /
edited by Robert W. Lissitz.
    p. cm.
  Includes bibliographical references.
  ISBN 978-1-60752-227-0 (pbk.) – ISBN 978-1-60752-228-7 (hardcover)
1. Examinations–Validity. I. Lissitz, Robert W.
  LB3060.7.C66 2009
  371.26'013–dc22

                                                    2009037250

Printed in the United States of America

CONTENTS

PART III

APPLICATION ORIENTED

CHAPTER 1

INTRODUCTION

Robert W. Lissitz

It is my honor to be the editor of this volume on Validity. It is the result of work by ten of the eleven presenters who began this effort at the conference titled "The Concept of Validity: Revisions, New Directions and Applications," October 9 and 10, 2008 and wrote a chapter for this book. The conference was sponsored by the Maryland State Department of Education and produced by the Maryland Assessment Research Center for Education Success (MARCES) at the University of Maryland, where I am the director. The chapters in this book are probably best read after having looked at some more basic material on validity, at least at the level presented in introductory textbooks such as that by Crocker and Algina (1986). In any case, I hope that this book gives the reader a chance to develop a wider perspective on what I believe to be the most important foundational area in Assessment. Validity becomes an issue whenever we ask: How can we assess a concept that we have? If the concept is 7th grade algebra, the question might be relatively easy to answer. If the concept is something like truth or beauty or internal locus of control, the question becomes much more difficult to answer.

A student reading the typical introductory measurement book about content validity, criterion validity, and especially construct validity may not see the inherent difficulties contained in that typically abstract and sim-

The Concept of Validity, pages 1–15

Copyright © 2009 by Information Age Publishing

plified presentation. Sometimes we are faced with the complexities only when we try to work on an application and we suddenly see that what we have been taught does not translate so well. In around 1915, our profession began to consider the problem of validation. The early work in this area focused on what we now call criterion related validity and that gradually was supported by a realization that how we developed the test (content validity) was also important. As the field became more sophisticated, we began to think about what we like to call construct validity.

While Messick (1989) attempted to unify the concept of validity by presenting construct validity as a conceptualization that includes the others, many people continue to be confused, particularly if they are trying to apply their newfound knowledge. As Gorin (2007) said, in reaction to the paper by Lissitz and Samuelsen (2007), "Despite my best attempts to describe the holy trinity, the unified framework, or argument-based approaches to validity, few students emerge from class with confidence that they could evaluate validity when developing, using, or even selecting tests" (p. 456). Sireci (2007) contributed the following quote about the unitary theory: "Paramount among these imperfections is that the unitary conceptualization of validity as construct validity is extremely difficult to describe to lay audiences" (p. 478).

Conversations with students and even more important, with sophisticated professionals working on state and other large scale testing projects, especially in performance assessment in education, have compelled me to draw the same conclusion. As Einstein reportedly once said, "You do not really understand something unless you can explain it to your grandmother." Construct validity, as it is currently articulated, seems to flunk the grandmother test. The authors of these chapters have taken the time to contribute to the literature in an attempt to clarify the concepts within the study of validity and their chapters provide considerable food for thought. My own brief comments contained in this introductory chapter were written without the benefit of the authors' reactions, but I hope they may still help the reader as he or she struggles to reason through this area and to advance their level of understanding.

The paper by Lissitz and Samuelsen (2007) contains a brief history of some of the high points of the validity literature starting with work that dates back to 1915. This introductory chapter will not attempt to repeat or even summarize that literature, although our authors make extensive reference to many of the most important papers. In fact they contributed some of these, themselves. What is more important here is the variety of conceptualizations and reactions to the current state of affairs in the field of validity study. The purpose of this book is to bring together in one volume a collection of papers that present the richness of diversity that still exists in the modern literature on validity. Unlike some intellectual areas that seem to become more and more settled as scholars pursue the intricacies of ideas, that is not the case here. While there are authors who feel that validity is a somewhat settled concept others clearly disagree with that position. The primary purpose of this book is to organize a confrontation of these two viewpoints. The reader will decide if they agree that the field is largely settled or if they agree with the antithetical viewpoint that the conceptualization of validity needs to be radically changed. Some attempt to resolve the contradictions and confusions that are seen in the literature is presented by authors in this volume, but I suspect that many readers will finish this book with the feeling that validity is still in great need of intellectual advancement. Perhaps some of the readers will be challenged to contribute to this literature and I certainly hope that is the case.

In my introductory remarks to the conference I attempted to motivate the meeting by providing two classes of examples of concerns that are confusing from a classical mainstream validity standpoint. Each example might be debatable, but I hope that they will help motivate the reader, just as I was motivated to hear more about this subject. One class concerns the confusion between reliability and validity. For example, there is the case of an accountant who wants to establish the validity of the results obtained in his spreadsheets. There is a variety of evidence that might be gathered to support such a claim but perhaps the simplest and most basic argument is the verification that the sum of the rows equals the sum of the columns. In other words, there is internal consistency, i.e., reliability, in the spreadsheet. If the accountant can get the same result by approaching the problem in two different ways, that is taken as evidence that the accounts are at least calculated correctly and hence is, in an important sense of the word, valid. Contrary to common instruction in measurement in which a somewhat sharp distinction between validity and reliability is drawn, it is often the case that reliability is taken as direct evidence of validity and there is even an equivalence of the two.

A second example of this issue comes from the well-known classic chapter by Lindquist (1951) in which he suggests that one of the best ways to develop a test that is valid is to develop a test that is as much like the criterion it is intended to predict as possible (see pages 152 and 154 for his presentation on this matter). In other words, Lindquist encouraged us to convert the validation paradigm (model, metaphor, theory or whatever you wish to call it) to that of a classic test-retest or equivalent forms reliability paradigm in which the test and the criterion are equivalent or nearly so. Again, reliability and validity can become confusingly similar to each other and essentially a reliability argument becomes substantiation of the existence of validity.

A third example of this confusion is when we validate the cut score set by a standard setting exercise. One approach to this problem in the field is to split the standard setters into two groups and see if they get similar cut points. If they do so, in my experience at least, state assessment profession- als and state education specialists take that as evidence that the exercise was a success and by extension as providing a valid determination of the cut point. Another set of data that is important to standard setters is that the judgments of the panel become more homogeneous across rounds. Again, homogeneity is really a measure of what we call reliability, although it is in- terpreted as an indication of validity. These examples and many more sug- gest that the validity literature is confused and not just confusing, as Sireci (2007) and Gorin (2007) said.

Another class of concern has to do with terminology. For example, just what do we mean by the term construct? This is a term that appears fre- quently in the literature on validity and within the pages of this book. The paper by Borsboom et al., which discusses this issue at some length, helps us. As they indicate, and I believe, it is not easy to figure out what we mean by the term construct and I would add that other terminology in the field is not well defined either. For example, it is not particularly clear what we mean by a latent construct. Related to this confusion is the definition of construct validity, itself. Should we continue to define construct validity in the sense that Cronbach and Meehl (1955) presented the term? Their concept introduced a very complex model involving both nomothetic span (development of theory relating multiple constructs) and the process of establishing construct definitions and anchoring at least some of them to observables. Perhaps we should adopt what is proposed as a more modern definition (Gorin, 2007) in which "... it is the internal theories of the con- struct (i.e., the relationships between subprocesses and dimensions com- prised by the construct), not those of the nomological network, that are the focus of construct validity in contemporary measurement" (p. 457).

The establishment of a construct and the assessment device through evidentiary procedures such as those advanced by Mislevy, Steinberg, and Almond (2003) and Kane (2006) are among the most respected of modern approaches to validity and these approaches seem to emphasize the estab- lishment of a device to measure the construct rather than the nomologi- cal span of the construct as it relates to other constructs. So perhaps the definition has morphed into a more useful form, although this is, at best, debatable. This simplification seems to me to render construct validity as very similar, if not identical, to content validity, which also concerns the process of establishing a device as an adequate measure of a construct (of- ten referred to as a domain or in some fields as a trait). Whether this more modern view of construct validity is confused with that of the traditional view of content validity is also debatable, as some see a distinction and some do not. Unfortunately, what appears to me as less debatable is that a lack of clarity about even the most basic terms in a field is not a good sign of an intellectually successful field of study. The reader will see that some of these authors share the view that clarity is not there and some do not, but everyone agrees that it should be present.

A number of issues such as these arise whenever one begins to think about applying validation to real applications. As a former president of NCME and senior author of the intermediate level standard text (Crocker & Algina, 1986) on assessment stated in her presidential address (Crocker, 2003) "When scores are used for educational accountability, the 'load-bearing wall' of that (validity) argument is surely content representativeness (p. 7)." In other words, the table of specifications that defines the coverage of the subject matter (i.e., the domain) of the test becomes paramount, as it does when establishing content validity. The problem in my opinion is that the modern unified approach to validity, as defined by Messick (1989) has denigrated content validity to such an extent that the end user trying to apply unified concepts of validation has been left with little that is useful.

Sadly, in my opinion, the unified field of validity as articulated by Messick (1989) is not just historically unsettled at a theoretical level, but it offers little in the way of usable advice to people working on test construction efforts in the field. Fortunately, there has been developing a body of work including the very applied (evidence centered) side of the work by Mislevy, Steinberg, and Almond (2003) and Kane (2006), for example, which attempts to provide method to validation concerns. Please note that it was not an accident that both authors were asked to write for this volume. One can argue that the field is finally moving toward a state in which useful procedures will be available to the practitioner trying to develop a test that meets some standard for test development and test validation. The reader will have to make his or her own judgment of whether there is improvement in the field. If they decide that there is, they might then decide if that improvement is a function of ignoring the emphasis on a unified theory of validity and instead looking more closely at the procedures for developing and justifying the instruments that are based on evidence of their adequacy of defining a construct. It is my perception that these methods actually owe more to content validity than they do to construct validity, but that is not the viewpoint of their originators. It has been my experience that application often precedes useful theory and I argue that is the case here. The emphasis upon evidentiary procedures seems to me to largely ignore the unified theory of construct validity, but the reader can see what the authors say and more importantly see with whom they agree.

This book is an attempt to explore the various conceptualizations of validity. The authors are a collection of outstanding contributors to this literature as well as many other areas within the psychometric/assessment/testing field. The reader will see that the chapters of this book can be divided, somewhat arbitrarily, into three sets of papers. I will give you my sense of how the chapters can be usefully clustered, although clearly not everyone reading them will agree with my perception. In all fairness to the authors and the readers, I must admit that the papers are complex ones that do not easily fit into any simple categorization. After listening to the papers as they were presented and reading the chapters that were finally submitted for the book, I maintain my belief that there are three somewhat distinct sets of papers, although admitting that there are imperfections in my classification. I will next talk briefly about the nature of the three sets and offer some brief comments on the papers within this volume. Finally, I include a list of suggested questions that the readers might try to answer for themselves as they read this book.

I have called the first set of papers *Relatively Mainstream*. This, and the other categories (*Relatively Divergent* and *Application Oriented*) are not meant to be judgments of the quality of these papers, in any negative (or positive) way. As I said, I selected presenters who are widely regarded in very favorable light by our profession. As Editor, I am trying to encourage the reader to see comparisons and contrasts that may be made among these papers, as well as identifying fundamental issues that underlie these papers. These mainstream papers are not limited in their scope or complexity at all, but they do strike me as essentially within the thrust of many of the historical and especially the most modern work that we have seen on validity, as epitomized and fostered by Messick (1989). In fact, these papers can be seen as extensions of that work in a way that maintains a consistency with the traditions of the field of validity study. When the reader gets a chance to read the papers in the set that I have chosen to describe as "Relatively Divergent," the reader will see better what I mean. The mainstream papers are largely supportive of the literature on validity. While the authors certainly have their own opinions about these matters and their opinion, in many cases, extends the ideas of other authors or even differ on some important matters, they are not even remotely nihilistic or even discouraging about the current state of affairs in validity research. These authors have themselves contributed a great deal to that literature and are committed to improving the clarity of the concepts and their usefulness. In other words, while I believe they are largely supportive of the current state of the literature, I do not mean to imply that they do not see the need for better organization and greater clarity. For the most part, they do seem to think that the literature is on the right track and provides the foundational guiding principles for validation in the field of assessment.

The first of these papers is by Steve Sireci, who has been quite involved in the current effort at codification of validity in a revised Test Standards to eventually replace the 1999 version. This series has always represented the "official" position of the American Educational Research Association (AERA), National Council on Measurement in Education (NCME) and the American Psychological Association (APA) (1999). His chapter in this book is particularly good as the first chapter in this section because he provides a very nice overview of the history of validity by largely focusing on this series of compendia (beginning in 1954) of our field's test standards and providing a perspective on the cyclical nature of the treatment of this field. He presents a view that validity had become overly complex and that precipitated an effort of simplification to the point of perhaps becoming overly simplified and that was followed by an effort to deal with the need for greater coverage that inevitably arose. He indicates that he feels that the field of validity study is in a good place today. As the reader will see later, not everyone would characterize this evolution as resulting in an improvement in validity theory. This chapter is very helpful to gaining a sense of the historical nature of this field as very distinguished members of our community tried to deal with a topic that is central to our field. Sireci calls this a cycle between unpacking and packing and I believe that perspective to be quite helpful to appreciating the literature and what appears to be its somewhat unsteady past. Sireci clarifies the interpretationist position that is dominant in the field that validity is not a characteristic of, nor does it lie within, the test, even the test development phase, but instead has to do with the interpretation of the test scores. He also helps introduce us to the argument-based approach to validity that Kane has developed, (along with the work by Mislevy) and is further presented in this book in chapters authored by each. Sireci notes that this model is an approach to the problem of practical validation and not a new theory or type of validity.

The second paper in this section is by Michael Kane, whose many contributions have to be considered one of the primary sources in this field since Messick's (1989) own work. He draws a clear distinction between validation for "observable" attributes or what I might have called manifest variables and contrasts the validity argument needed for that case with the case for measurement to determine "traits and theoretical constructs." The latter might be called latent traits or latent constructs, although standardization of the terms in this field has still not yet occurred, as I indicated in my initial remarks above. He, as did Sireci, goes on to consider the test interpretation as the essential issue for validation and makes a number of important claims, cautions and arguments with respect to that orientation. As Kane indicates, this differs from a belief that the validity of the test lies largely in the test itself and its construction process, as argued by Lissitz and Samuelsen (2007). The dedicated reader could skip forward and see what the application papers are doing or what they indicate that others are doing or should be doing with respect to validation, but I suggest that the reader control his or her curiosity and proceed in the current sequence of the book chapters. Kane's paper goes on to present the argument-based validation model involving Toulmin's (1958) work. This orientation is also represented in the evidence-based validity approach advocated by Mislevy et al. (2003). Kane does an excellent job providing a response to those who challenge the traditional approach, while clarifying and extending the approach in ways that are potentially quite helpful to the practitioner.

The third paper is that by Bruno Zumbo, whose focus is first upon a diagnosis of the problems with the concept of validity as usually presented and then with an approach to validity that he feels will provide a better conceptualization. His emphasis on theory as critical to relating observables to unobservables will sound very much like the approach suggested by Borsboom et al., although he does draw distinctions. I left Zumbo's chapter in the section of mainstream papers because he sees himself as very much in the tradition of Messick and so I will honor that claim, although I am not sure that he is not saying something much more important than a simple extension or clarification of that work. Zumbo's emphasis is upon explanation of the underlying processes that give rise to the manifest observation, while acknowledging that there are different ways to view the explanation. In that sense his approach sounds somewhat like that by Mislevy and his notion of multiple metaphors for understanding "explanation." The reader will see that Zumbo's emphasis on context, although not developed to the same extent, is consistent with Chalhoub—DeVille's paper on the same matter.

The fourth and last paper in this section is by Bob Mislevy. This paper could almost be put into the next category, since he raises so many fundamental issues regarding how we ought to think about validity. But, since he clearly supports validation as articulated by Kane (2006) and more importantly by Messick (1989) and that much of his work, as I indicated above, involves an evidence centered argument for validation it seems best to place this chapter in the section I have labeled mainstream. Of course, perhaps I should just take his own assurance of his position since Mislevy characterizes his own work as within the "currently dominant view of validity..." The reason I hesitate to list his paper in this section is because, as the reader will note, it is an attempt to look at validity as a conceptual issue that depends upon the perspective and the psychometric model that are chosen and from which the validation emanates. In many ways he is raising really serious issues regarding validity while presenting it as a conditional enterprise dependent upon the modeling metaphor that is selected.

In other words, Mislevy's view, in part at least, seems to be that different, yet legitimate, validation arguments might exist depending upon the model (what Mislevy calls the metaphor) that has driven the testing in the first place. The Borsboom et al. paper also discusses the role of the model that guides ones approach to validity, although they come to a very different conclusion. As one reads all the papers in this book, this question of what is the dominant metaphor (in Mislevy's terminology) and whether validation should be seen as a different enterprise depending upon the metaphor selected seems to arise repeatedly, although not always explicitly. Mislevy's chapter is trying to come to grips with a series of questions that have bothered validity experts for years. They include, for examples, What exactly are we validating?, What do our models mean?, and What is their role with respect to the validation enterprise? The reader will want to refer back to this paper, over and over, especially as they read the paper by Borsboom et al. which seems almost to be responding to and might even be seen as a conversation with the ideas that Mislevy has presented.

I have called the second set of papers *relatively divergent* and both of them may even be considered radical in their orientation. It seems safe to say that the two papers present a belief that nearly the whole of the field of research on the concept of validity is taking us in a direction that is just plain wrong. That is not to say these authors have not learned from the literature, but what they seem to have learned is how wrong the field of validity is. They take the position that the weaknesses and errors need to be addressed and remediated by radical change in our conceptualization, rather than relatively simple clarification or even complex extension of the basic ideas.

The first of the two divergent papers from the conference is by Joel Michell. Other papers in the broader literature exist that are equally (or nearly as) nihilistic. Lissitz and Samuelsen (2007), for example, provided suggestions for substantial change to the field of validity. Their discussion of validity and possible solutions were rejected by the responders in that edition of the *Educational Researcher* and even precipitated another critical paper in a subsequent issue (Kane, 2008). Their views of our paper might safely be characterized as negative. I suspect that those reactions would be extremely mild compared to what the reactions would have been to this paper by Michell. Elements of his argument are not altogether unrelated to that of the paper by Mislevy and the last paper in this section, which is by Borsboom et al. Mislevy's work is quite related but he seems to be quite comfortable with the notion that many metaphors might exist for a particular problem and presents the idea that "In applied work, the issue is not a simple question of truth or falsity of a model, but of aptness for a given purpose." This comment strikes me as quite important and insightful, as well as very tolerant, perhaps even a bit too much so. It appears that Dr. Michell is not nearly as tolerant when he indicates that assessing validity is difficult if one questions whether a "test measures something..." at all. His paper raises considerable doubts about whether a trait is being measured when we test, and within the trait model metaphor, to use Mislevy's term, that indeed is an important debate to have and Michell does a really nice job presenting the doubts that arise with the claim that a test does measure something, let alone measures what it is supposed to measure.

Mislevy indicated that various models might not be strictly true, but still useful, while Michell and, next, Borsboom et al. are raising the issue of whether we should continue to talk about measurement the way we do if the models are in fact quite demonstrably false. The reader will notice that Michell seems to limit measurement to what S. S. Stevens refers to as interval measurement. N. R. Campbell (1946) made this same argument many years ago. Interval level measurement does appear to be a goal that many of us have and Michell makes clear that many psychometricians operate as though they were convinced that they are measuring at that level. Further he indicates that this assumption, which he believes to be patently false, is critical to the work that we pursue in psychology and education. Other models (metaphors) do exist and some question may be raised about their appropriateness and adequacy for the questions that we are trying to answer, particularly for those who are trying to develop theory. Examples of such efforts might include cognitive models of learning as well as measures of IQ, and an effort to characterize functional independence. The latter occupies much attention by Michell. One can debate whether ordinal or at least ordered difference scales are functionally so very different from scales that require linearity. For, example, what does the reader think if the focus is upon practical applications such as determining the order of the objects of some assessment (e.g., students in a classroom being ordered by performance) as a result of the measurement process and its dependency upon the assumption of interval scaling? Michell, Mislevy, and Borsboom et al. each appear to me to be wrestling with the same issue but coming to quite different conclusions. The reader will want to think about that, I suspect, and, perhaps at best, come to only a tentative judgment on the issues raised in these two divergent papers. Of course, the opinion of the reader toward these two papers will have great impact on their perception of the papers in the mainstream grouping.

The last chapter in this section is by Borsboom, Cramer, Kievit, Scholten and Franic and titled "The end of construct validity." I chose to repeat the title here to make the point that the conference really did present a wide variety of viewpoints toward validity and some have raised serious issues with what has been written about in the name of validation. While these authors certainly argue that the interpretationist view of construct validity needs to be rejected, they do offer an alternative to that mainstream approach to validity theory. Their chapter is particularly important as a way of understanding how validity evolved and became what is currently known as construct validity. Tying the validity of a test to the nomological network in which it functions is a sensible, and at one time, traditional idea. The problem, as they point out, is that there does not seem to exist in education and psychology such networks defined to any sufficient level that can justify or support the construct validity of a test. Perhaps Michell would say this is in part due to the lack of satisfactory measurement in the first place and that is largely due to the nature of the phenomenon that is being measured. Gorin

(2007) might respond that the nomological network is not really relevant to the determination of construct validity, as currently conceptualized, although as we have seen, that is not a universally held opinion.

This paper by Borsboom et al., without using the same terminology, stresses the importance of understanding the metaphor that is being employed (a' la Mislevy). They spend considerable time trying to clean up the vocabulary used in mainstream "construct theory." Similar to the paper by Lissitz and Samuelsen, Borsboom et al. seem, in the end, to believe the field as it currently exists is hopeless and then offer their own terminology and conceptualization. Clarifying the difference between the way practitioners relate to validity and the way theoreticians present validity is an important part of their paper and a particularly useful discussion, in my opinion. Perhaps the most strident difference from the mainstream theorist is their belief that what makes the interpretation true is a property of the test. That happens to be a position that I favor, so it does not surprise me, although it would certainly be rejected by mainstream theorists. Further, they argue that the truth or falsity of the claims regarding the phenomenon in question is of critical concern for the measurement process and outcome. As they analyze the field, they conclude that the focus should be on whether the test works to reflect these latent properties. Their view of these matters is quite critical of the current state of affairs in validity theory and their solution to this problem, if it could even be called a solution since it is so difficult to achieve, has to do with the development of theory. This is the same "theory" which is sorely lacking in education and psychology, as they claim, and I strongly agree with them on this matter. Perhaps the day will come when we study phenomena that we can show some evidence of understanding in a formal way, but in most areas of education and psychology this would seem to be a long time in the future.

The last set of four papers were put together into a class by themselves because their authors are attempting to provide coherent summaries of actual validations and, perhaps even more important, they are trying to provide advice for those involved in specific application efforts. Therefore, this section is called *application oriented*. It is my feeling that ending the book with these examples will help provide a context for the papers that have spent more of their time trying to summarize, analyze and revise various ideas that might be a part of validity theory. Obviously, there are many other areas of application beyond these three (two papers deal largely with the same area—No Child Left Behind), but hopefully they will provide the reader with a chance to apply the ideas they have gained from the prior mainstream and divergent papers on validity. They offer a chance in a single book to read about validations that might illustrate or even contradict or perhaps be irrelevant to the various ideas presented in the first two sections. These papers also provide real problems that help the reader (I hope you agree with me about this) to understand the reasons for the existence of such an extensive literature on validity and the continued motivation to improve on the concepts found therein.

Now that the reader is familiar with at least a large variety of the ideas and concerns and advice in the literature on validity, they might ask themselves some questions as they read the following four papers that talk about applications. The following are overlapping questions, but in any case, the reader might consider them:

1. Did the validity literature clearly guide these application efforts?
2. What issues were not addressed, but should have been, based on the literature?
3. What issues were addressed, but are really irrelevant to establishing validity?
4. How did the author's know what was critical to their validation and what was not?
5. Is there a conceptual system that is guiding their validation? In other words, would they have done the same thing if all they knew about validity was that they should validate?
6. Since test score interpretation is the critical focus of mainstream validity theory, did the applications focus upon that? Did they offer a correct interpretation of the tests they discuss and perhaps illustrate with interpretations that are not correct or should be avoided?
7. Did the previous papers provide any special meaning or insight when you read these application papers? For example, the paper by Mislevy discussed metaphors. Can you see a metaphor exhibiting itself in each or at least some of the various applications? The papers by Kane and Sireci summarized a good bit of the largely established validity theory. Do you see that work illustrated in these applications? How do you think Borsboom et al might have approached the problem addressed in each application? Do you think Michell would have become convinced by their work?

The first of these papers is by Schafer, Wang, and Wang. This paper is looking at the problem of establishing the validity of a state-testing program for the purposes set by No Child Left Behind (NCLB). As the reader may know, NCLB requires peer review of all state testing as part of the compliance process with which states must adhere. The Schafer et al. chapter reviews the processes that states utilized and extracts the "most salient elements of validity documentation in actual use." This paper illustrates what states do when faced with the task of supporting their testing program with validity evidence. State assessments are certainly an important application and a challenging one, too. The reader will see that the paper considered

5 categories of evidence regarding state validation—test content, student response processes, internal structure, relation to other variables, and the consequences of the testing.

The second and related paper is by Bob Linn. His chapter is another excellent source for the reader interested in validation in the context of NCLB. Dr. Linn's chapter complements that by Schafer et al. and together the reader will see how states are currently trying to comply with federal mandates as well as how several experts encourage them to comply. Dr. Linn's discussion of the "Validation of School Quality Inference" is particularly worth reading as well as his comments on the consequences of testing. Dr. Linn argues that consequences are very much an important part of such an effort and the federal government seems to agree by encouraging states to engage in studies that explore the reactions from schools. Whether consequences are relevant to validity is another subject that has enjoyed some difference of opinion.

The third of these application papers is by Mattern, Kobrin, Patterson, Shaw, and Camara and focuses on the validation of the 2005 revised Scholastic Aptitude Test for college admission. This test is, as the reader will know, a very widely known test that is not without controversy. The paper takes a broad view of the College Board validation effort including basic issues ranging from selecting a validity sample to considering how to communicate the results. They place their validation effort into a wider context of a test that is used to supplement practical decision-making and thus incurs broader ethical concerns along with the more usual issues regarding validation. In other words, the validation issues become quite complex and the implications of test use become a part of the concern with validity, as Linn and Schafer, et al indicated with regard to NCLB testing. They also spend some time discussing the issue of interpreting the results of the validation efforts and providing ways that communication might be improved.

The fourth paper in this set of application papers is by Michelline Chalhoub-DeVille and concerns the validity of language testing. This area presents a particularly complex validation task and the paper does an excellent job of looking at the issue of validating language tests while also relating the specific task to the general literature on validity. Dr. Chalhoub-DeVille uses as her examples one assessment from the U.S. and one from Europe and stresses the importance of context upon the problem of validation. While context may be an especially important problem for language testing it is certainly not just relevant there and her comments are worth thinking about for anyone interested in validation at a practical or a theoretical level. Her chapter closes with a reference (Moss, 2007) to a request to the Standards (1999) revision committee to compile concrete examples of the application of testing and the development of validity support for these applications. This is a suggestion for the Standards (1999) Committee to which the Editor of this volume on validity would like to add his support. I would also hope that the collection of such examples would support some theoretical constructions regarding validity and not just be stand-alone examples of what was done in particular applications.

Reading these application papers teaches us a lot about the complexity of validation and the difficulty of developing a supporting theory. All the authors in this book have certainly done a thoughtful job while wrestling with a very complex and challenging field. They have not answered every question since that is a goal impossible to achieve, but they have certainly pushed our understanding much further along. For this I am personally quite grateful and I hope the reader shares my appreciation for their work.

REFERENCES

American Educational Research Association, American Psychological Association, & National Council on Measurement in Education (1999). *Standards for educational and psychological testing.* Washington, DC: American Psychological Association.

Campbell, N. R. (report published in 1946) and referenced in S. S. Stevens (1946). On the theory of scales of measurement. *Science, 103*(2684), 677–680.

Crocker, L. (2003). Teaching for the test: Validity, fairness and moral action. *Educational Measurement: Issues and Practice, 22*(3), 5–11.

Crocker, L., & Algina, J. (1986). *Introduction to classical and modern test theory.* New York: Holt, Rinehart, and Winston, Inc.

Cronbach, L. J., & Meehl, P. E. (1955). Construct validity in psychological tests. *Psychological Bulletin, 52,* 281–302.

Gorin, J. S. (2007). Reconsidering issues in validity theory. *Educational Researcher, 36,* 456–462.

Kane, M. (2006). Validation. In R. L. Brennan (Ed.) *Educational measurement* (4th ed., pp. 17–64). Washington, DC: American Council on Education/Praeger.

Kane, M. (2008). Terminology, emphasis, and utility in validation. *Educational Researcher, 37*(2), 76–82.

Lindquist, E. F. (1951). Preliminary considerations in objective test construction. In E. F. Lindquist (Ed.), *Educational measurement* (pp. 119–184). Washington, DC: American Council on Education.

Lissitz, R. W., & Samuelsen, K. (2007). A suggested change in terminology and emphasis regarding validity and education. *Educational Researcher, 36,* 437–448.

Messick, S. (1989). Validity. In R. Linn (Ed.), *Educational measurement* (3rd ed.). Washington, DC: American Council on Education.

Mislevy, R., Steinberg, L., & Almond, R. (2003). On the structure of educational assessments. *Measurement: Interdisciplinary Research and Perspectives, 1,* 3–62.

Moss, P. A. (2007). Reconstructing validity. *Educational Researcher, 36,* 470–476.

Sireci, S. G. (2007). On validity theory and test validatioin. *Educational Researcher,* *36*, 477–481.

Toulmin, S. E. (1958). *The uses of argument.* Cambridge: Cambridge University Press.

PART I

RELATIVELY MAINSTREAM

CHAPTER 2

PACKING AND UNPACKING SOURCES OF VALIDITY EVIDENCE

History Repeats Itself Again

Stephen G. Sireci

ABSTRACT

Validity has taken on many different meanings over the years, and different "types" or "aspects" of validity have been proposed to help define and guide test validation. In this chapter, I trace some of the history of test validity theory and validation and describe validity nomenclature that has evolved over the years. The historical review focuses on the *Standards for Educational and Psychological Testing* and its predecessors. Although the concept of validity has been described in various ways, there has long been consensus that validity is *not* an inherent characteristic of a test and what we seek to validate are inferences derived from test scores. The argument-based approach to validity as articulated in the current *Standards* provides sound advice for documenting validity evidence and for evaluating the use of a test for a particular purpose. Suggestions for further research and practice in test validation are provided.

The Concept of Validity, pages 19–37

INTRODUCTION

Validity has often been described as the most important concept in psychometrics, but its meaning is elusive because it has been given so many definitions over the years. This chapter, like the other chapters in this book, emanates from a conference where validity theorists presented different perspectives on validity theory and test validation. In this chapter, I trace some of the history of the concept of validity and I summarize what I believe to be the fundamental characteristics of validity theory and test validation. I end by pointing out some of the limitations of contemporary validity theory, but I argue that the current consensus definitions of validity theory and test validation provide sufficient guidance for helping us gather and document evidence to support the use of a test for a particular purpose.

Let me state from the outset that I believe validity:

1. is *not* an inherent property of a test,
2. refers to the interpretations or actions that are made on the basis of test scores, and
3. must be evaluated with respect to the *purpose* of the test and how the test is *used.*

These fundamental tenets of validity are not new, but there are some theorists who do not agree with some or all of them. To explain their criticality, and to respond to the critics of this point of view, I will first provide some history on the concept of validity to illustrate why we have arrived at the consensus opinion that (a) validity refers to the interpretations of test scores, not the test itself, and (b) what we strive to validate are *interpretations* (and actions) based on test scores, not a test per se. Since 1952, consensus opinions regarding validity theory and test validation have been put forward by various professional associations, particularly the American Educational Research Association (AERA), the American Psychological Association (APA), and the National Council on Measurement in Education (NCME). Thus, the definitions and validity frameworks provided by these associations are highlighted in the historical review.

A BRIEF HISTORY OF VALIDITY THEORY

Validity theory and the practice of test validation are almost as old as the practice of testing itself, but not quite. Wainer (2000) refers to the biblical story from the Book of Judges (12:4–6) as perhaps the earliest high-stakes test.[1] In this story, the Gileadites developed a one-item test to identify the enemy Ephraimites who were hiding among them. The test was to pronounce the word "shibboleth." Although the stakes associated with passing this one-item test were high (i.e., all those who failed the test were killed), the Bible does not mention any validity studies conducted to support its use. Talk about test anxiety and performance under pressure! Seriously though, the modern era of educational assessment most likely began with Alfred Binet who developed a battery of 30 brief subtests designed to ensure that no child could be denied instruction in the Parisian school system without formal examination. Binet's purpose was laudable, since the goals were inclusion of children who were being excluded and identification of students who would not benefit from the school system. More important, the key characteristics of standardized testing were in place—children were tested with the same instrument, under the same conditions, and were scored uniformly.

The Binet-Simon scale was published around the turn of the last century (Binet, 1905; Binet & Henri, 1899) and so it is hard to find validity studies for it. However, a review of the early psychometric literature indicates that the earliest definitions of validity were largely pragmatic, defining validity primarily in terms of the correlation of test scores with some criterion. Given that Pearson had only recently published his formula for the correlation coefficient (Pearson, 1896), it makes sense that validity was initially defined in this manner. There was an exciting new statistical index that could be directly applied to the issue of how well examinees' scores on an assessment related to other manifestations of the attribute tested. For this reason, by the 1920s, tests were described as valid for anything with which they correlated. Such a description was found in the most influential works of the early 20th century including Kelly (1927), Thurstone (1932), and Bingham (1937). This view endured into the middle 20th century as is evidenced by Guilford's definition that "a test is valid for anything with which it correlates" (1946, p. 429).

The empirical view of validity was extended with the emergence of factor analysis as developed by Spearman (1904).[2] Early psychometricians saw factor analysis as a tool for understanding unobservable "traits" or "constructs" that underlie test performance. Many psychometricians such as Thurstone (1932) interpreted the factors derived from analysis of item and test data as representing latent psychological attributes, whereas others such as Anastasi (1938) argued that factors were ". . . only a mathematical summary or conceptual simplification of the observed relationships among concrete tasks" (p. 335). Guilford (1946) was a strong proponent of using factor analysis to define validity and validate tests. He classified validity into two categories: factorial validity and practical validity. Practical validity referred to the correlations between test scores and relevant criteria, while factorial validity referred to the factor loadings of the test on "meaningful, common, reference factors" (p. 428).

This pragmatic and empirical view of validity dominated research and practice in test development and validation as is evidenced by the work in military testing for World War I and World War II where the Army Alpha and Beta[3] tests were administered to millions of recruits to help classify them into the most appropriate units of service. As Jenkins (1946) described, tests for military personnel were added to batteries based solely on incremental validity (i.e., the ability to account for more variance in performance on a criterion).

In addition to the empirical view of validity based on correlation and factor analysis, a theoretical definition of validity was also proposed during the early 20th century. This theoretical view was simply that validity is the degree to which "*a test measures what it is supposed to measure*" (Garrett, 1937, p. 324). Although largely refuted today as an incomplete definition, this simplistic view is still seen in textbooks and some psychometric literature, because it is an important requirement to support the use of a test for a particular purpose. That is, one cannot properly interpret a test score if what the test measures were not known. However, the definition is insufficient and has been criticized as such for quite a long time. Consider, for example, Rulon (1946) who stated,

> Validity is usually described as the extent to which a test measures what it is purported to measure. This is an unsatisfactory and not very useful concept of validity, because under it the validity of a test may be altered completely by arbitrarily changing its "purport." (p. 290)

To summarize the earliest conceptions of validity, validity theory emerged in a manner congruent with the philosophy of science and statistics that were popular during the time educational and psychological tests first emerged. Theories that unobservable psychological attributes existed and could be measured (e.g., Fechner, 1860) promoted the idea that validity is the degree to which a test measures what it is supposed to measure. The "new" statistical methods of correlation and factor analysis provided a framework for evaluating whether the observed test scores and item responses were congruent with prevailing notions about what the test was "supposed to measure." Although the initial theories and validation strategies were straightforward, it did not take long for dissatisfaction with the theory and practice of test validation to emerge.

1940s: Validity Theory Evolves Beyond Test/Criterion Relationships

Although many of the early 20th-century psychometricians were excited about the new science of psychological measurement and the statistical procedures of correlation and regression for "validating" tests, others were thoroughly dissatisfied with the notions that validity referred merely to "what the test measured" and that tests could be validated solely through correlational and factor analytic studies. With respect to what we would now call criterion-related validity, many researchers pointed out that the criteria against which tests were correlated were often imperfect at best, and often had questionable reliability and validity. Jenkins (1946) in particular underscored the need to establish the reliability and validity of criteria used to validate tests and criticized earlier psychometricians for not fully considering the appropriateness of the criteria against which test scores were validated. As he put it, "... psychologists in general tended to accept the tacit assumption that criteria were either given of God or just to be found lying about" (p. 93). Jenkins listed four reasons why criterion data are likely to be unreliable and five reasons whey they "may not be adequately valid" including "failure of the criterion-measure to comprise a large and significant part of the total field of performance desired" (p. 95).

Criticisms regarding the correlational approach to validation encouraged psychometricians to consider more carefully the attributes intended to be measured by a test as well as those reflected in criterion performance. Such considerations required analysis of how the attributes intended to be measured by the test were operationally defined, as well as analysis of the test content, and analysis of what the criterion measured. By focusing on the content of tests and the criterion against which they were correlated, a new perspective on test validation emerged, one that would eventually come to be known as content validity.

An early proponent of this newer perspective was Rulon (1946), who noted that in some circumstances, such as in educational achievement testing, it did not make sense to approach test validation through test-criterion relationships. He argued there were:

> ... two general ways of asking about the validity of achievement tests ... The first is, Are the materials on this test, and the processes called for on these materials, the same things and processes we are trying to teach children? The other is, if they are not, do we have evidence that scores on this test go hand in hand with those we would obtain with a test about which the answers to our first questions were in the affirmative? Thus we see that the direct observation of the things and processes which are the aims of instruction is the final proof of validity, as compared to the correlation coefficient of validity, which is at best secondary. (p. 292)

Rulon's approach encouraged test evaluators to compare the content of a test with the objectives of instruction—a concept which remains critically important in contemporary educational assessment with respect to content validation and test-curriculum alignment. However, his argument was more against a purely correlational approach to validation than it was for a content-based approach. He was ahead of his time in that he argued tests would require different types of evidence depending on their purpose and that we should not rely on a single type of evidence when evaluating the use of a test for a particular purpose. These are important concepts that are widely accepted today and are characterized in the current *Standards* (AERA et al., 1999). It is interesting to see how Rulon phrased these important points in 1946:

> Thus the validity of a test may be high for one use and low for another, and the whole question of validity boils down to the question whether the test does what we are trying to do with it. Accordingly, we cannot label a test as valid or not valid except for some purpose... The thing to ask for is a proof that the test does its job, but not to ask always for the same kind of evidence that it does. (pp. 290–291)

Rulon (1946) is one example of many psychometricians near the middle of the 20th century who called for a more comprehensive treatment of validity theory and test validation. Others include Ebel (1956), Gulliksen (1950), Mosier (1947), and Cureton (1951).[4] Given different notions of what validity referred to and how tests should be validated, the time was right for professional associations in the fields of educational and psychological measurement to provide some consensus. An early development in this area was the *Technical Recommendations for Psychological Tests and Diagnostic Techniques: A Preliminary Proposal* (APA, 1952), which resulted from a panel commissioned by APA to offer a formal proposal of test standards to be used in the construction, use, and interpretation of psychological tests. This committee, the APA Committee on Test Standards, dramatically changed the conception and terminology of validity and described four "categories" of validity: predictive validity, status validity, content validity, and congruent validity. This preliminary proposal led to the formation of a joint committee of the APA, AERA, and NCME, which published the *Technical Recommendations for Psychological Tests and Diagnostic Techniques* (APA, 1954).[5] These *Technical Recommendations* represent the first version of what today is the *Standards for Educational and Psychological Testing* (AERA et al., 1999) and it changed the four "categories" of validity to "types" or "attributes" of validity. "Congruent validity" was renamed "construct validity," and "status validity" was renamed "concurrent validity."

With the publication of these *Technical Recommendations* in 1954, the concept of "construct validity" was born. However, the concept was further described and elaborated by two key members of the Joint Committee—Lee Cronbach and Paul Meehl. Cronbach and Meehl's (1955) seminal article stated:

construct validation is involved whenever a test is to be interpreted as a measure of some attribute or quality which is not 'operationally defined.' The problem faced by the investigator is 'What constructs account for variance in test performance?' (p. 282)

The notion of a latent construct that was the target of measurement long existed within the factor analytic approach to validation, but Cronbach and Meehl developed this notion into a formal validity theory, and one that guided test validation. An important part of their formulation was the concept of a nomological network (i.e., the system of laws and relationships that define a theory), which is used to define the construct, defend its existence, and provide a framework for gathering validity evidence. In developing this concept they extended the thinking of how to approach validation and stimulated further developments in validation such as Campbell and Fiske's (1959) multitrait-mutlimethod matrix.

A close reading of Cronbach and Meehl suggests they initially proposed the concept of construct validity primarily for tests of a more psychological nature as opposed to those measuring educational achievement. The following two excerpts illustrate this point.

1. Construct validity must be investigated whenever no criterion or universe of content is accepted as entirely adequate to define the quality to be measured (p. 282).
2. Construct validity was introduced in order to specify types of research required in developing tests for which the conventional views on validation are inappropriate (p. 299).

Given that the 1954 *Recommendations* listed four "types" of validity, it makes sense that construct validity would be described as most pertinent to psychological testing and content validity was described as most pertinent to educational testing. In any case, it seems clear Cronbach and Meehl were hesitant to ascribe construct validity as relevant to all educational and psychological tests. Soon after, however, several validity theorists quickly concluded construct validity *was* applicable to *all* educational and psychological tests. Loevinger (1957), for example, claimed "since predictive, concurrent, and content validities are all essentially ad hoc, construct validity is the whole of validity from a scientific point of view" (p. 636). Loevinger, Messick (1989), and others forcefully argued there is never an acceptable criterion universe of content, which meant all validity is construct validity. This notion of validity became known as the unitary conceptualization of validity and remains popular to this day.

Angoff (1988) provided a concise definition of construct validity and illustrated why it put an end to the notion that validity merely referred to a test measuring what it purported to measure as evidenced by a correlation coefficient or the results of a factor analysis.

> In construct validity...Cronbach and Meehl maintained that we examine the psychological trait, or construct, presumed to be measured by the test and we cause a continuing, research interplay to take place between the scores earned on the test and the theory underlying the construct. In this way, the theoretical conception of the construct...dictates the nature of the data...collected to validate the scores on the test and used to interpret the results of the testing. In turn, the data resulting from the test administration are used to validate, reject, or revise the theory itself. Viewed this way, we see that all data that flow from the theory, including concurrent and predictive data—but not exclusively so—are useful for construct validity. Indeed, virtually all properly collected data are legitimately validity data, including ethnic and sex distributions...internal correlations matrices among items and subtests...and finally data resulting from studies of content analyses. (p. 26)

This unitary conceptualization of validity deserves further discussion, which I return to in a subsequent section. Before doing so, however, it is instructive to consider how validity and its various aspects were characterized in all of the iterations of the *Technical Recommendations* or *Standards* that resulted from the joint AERA/APA/NCME committee. These characterizations are listed in Table 2.1. Although it is not evident in Table 2.1, a close reading of these various iterations suggests the shift from separate types of validity to a unitary conceptualization became explicit in the 1974 version. An excerpt from these *Standards* illustrates the shift, as well as the notion

TABLE 2.1   A Summary of Validity Nomenclature Used in the *Technical Recommendations* and *Standards*

Publication	Validity Nomenclature
Technical recommendations for psychological tests and diagnostic techniques: A preliminary proposal (APA, 1952)	*Categories:* predictive, status, content, congruent
Technical recommendations for psychological tests and diagnostic techniques (APA, 1954)	*Types:* construct, concurrent, predictive, content
Standards for educational and psychological tests and manuals (APA, 1966)	*Types:* criterion-related, construct-related, content-related
Standards for educational and psychological tests (APA, AERA, & NCME, 1974)	*Aspects:* criterion-related, construct-related, content-related
Standards for educational and psychological testing (AERA, APA, & NCME, 1985)	*Categories:* criterion-related, construct-related, content-related
Standards for educational and psychological testing (AERA, APA, & NCME, 1999)	*Sources of evidence:* content, response processes, internal structure, relations to other variables, consequences of testing

that validation is a comprehensive effort requiring multiple sources of evidence that support the use of a test for a specific purpose:

> A thorough understanding of validity may require many investigations ... called validation. There are various methods of validation, and all ... require a definition of what is to be inferred from the scores and data to show that there is an acceptable basis for such inferences ... It is important to note that validity is itself inferred, not measured ... It is ... something that is *judged* as adequate, or marginal, or unsatisfactory ... The kinds of validity depend upon the kinds of inferences one might wish to draw from test scores. Four interdependent kinds of inferential interpretation are traditionally described to summarize most test use: the *criterion-related validities ... content validity,* and *construct* validity ... These aspects of validity can be discussed independently, but only for convenience. They are interrelated operationally and logically; only rarely is one of them alone important in a particular situation. A thorough study of a test may often involve information about all types of validity. (APA, AERA, & NCME, 1974, pp. 25–26)

This excerpt also points out that the 1974 *Standards* explicitly stated validity referred to interpretations of test scores, rather than to an inherent property of a test itself. The following excerpt indicates how explicit they were in making this point:

> Statements about validity should refer to the validity of particular interpretations or of particular types of decisions ... It is incorrect to use the unqualified phrase "the validity of the test." *No test is valid for all purposes or in all situations or for all groups of individuals.* Any study of test validity is pertinent to only a few of the possible uses of or inferences from the test scores. (APA et al., 1974, p. 31)

This point and its emphasis were carried over into the next version of the *Standards*, which stated,

> Validity ... is a unitary concept. Although evidence may be accumulated in many ways, validity always refers to the degree to which that evidence supports the inferences that are made from the scores. The inferences regarding specific uses of a test are validated, not the test itself. (AERA, APA, & NCME, 1985, p. 9)

CURRENT CONCEPTUALIZATIONS OF VALIDITY

The conclusion that validity is not an inherent property of a test, but rather a concept that refers to the appropriateness of inferences derived from a test is supported in the current version of the *Standards* (AERA et al., 1999) as well as in the other seminal validity writings since 1974 including Messick (1975, 1989); Kane (1992, 2006), and Shepard (1993). In fact, Messick's (1989) definition of validity as "an integrated evaluative judgment of the degree to which empirical evidence and theoretical rationales support the *adequacy* and *appropriateness* of *inferences* and *actions* based on test scores and other modes of assessment," (p. 13), is very close to the definition provided in the most recent version of the *Standards*, which state "Validity refers to the degree to which evidence and theory support the interpretations of test scores entailed by proposed uses of tests" (AERA et al., 1999, p. 9).

Based on the historical review of validity, and its more current definitions, it is clear the consensus is that validity is not something to be attributed to a test, but rather to the *use* of a test for a particular purpose and the defensibility of such use. Since at least the 1940s, psychometricians have cautioned about referring to validity as a property of a test and instead have reserved the term for interpretations and decisions based on test results (e.g., Rulon, 1946). Similarly, validation focuses on the "...accuracy of a specific prediction or inference made from a test score" (Cronbach, 1971, p. 443). To claim that validity refers simply to demonstrating that a "test measures what it purports to measure" or that it is an inherent property of a test is to ignore at least 70 years of research on validity theory and test validation as well as the consensus *Technical Recommendations* and *Standards* that have existed since 1954.

Are there weaknesses in the current view that validity is not a property of a test and that validation needs to focus on inferences derived from test scores? I do not think so. There are weaknesses, or at least frustrations, associated with the act of validating score inferences because it can be seen as an endless task, but that does not require that we return to the simplistic notion of validity that existed in the very early 20th century. A compromise between an overly simplistic view of validity and one that presents validation as an unobtainable goal, is the *argument-based* approach to validity articulated by Kane (1992, 2006) who cites Cronbach's earlier work on validation as an evaluation argument (Cronbach, 1988). The argument-based approach is congruent with the approach to validation suggested by the most current version of the *Standards* (AERA et al., 1999) and so its logic and its relation to the *Standards* are described next.

Argument-Based Approach to Validation

Kane (1992) proposed an argument-based approach to validation to make the task of validating inferences derived from test scores both scientifically sound and manageable. In this approach, the validator builds an argument that focuses on defending the use of a test for a particular purpose and is based on empirical evidence to support the particular use. The approach involved first determining the inferences to be derived based on test scores, coming up with hypotheses or deciding on the sources of evidence that would support or refute those inferences, gathering the appropriate data, and analyzing the evidence. Kane suggested the argument explicitly include analysis of competing interpretations of test scores.

Kane (1992) described this interpretive argument as an "approach to validity rather than a type of validity" (p. 534) and thus avoided the historical problems of validity nomenclature. He also acknowledged that validity could never be proven in an absolute sense, but rather the task was to present a body of evidence based on the proposed use of the test and empirical evidence that would provide a reasonable case to justify the interpretations that were made. Thus, the argument-based approach is a compromise between sophisticated validity theory and the reality that at some point, we must make a judgment about the defensibility and suitability of use of a test for a particular purpose. As Kane (1992) put it,

> it is not possible to verify the interpretive argument in any absolute sense. The best that can be done is to show that the interpretive argument is highly plausible, given all available evidence. (p. 527)

Although this validation framework acknowledges that validity can never be established absolutely, it requires evidence that (a) the test measures what it claims to measure, (b) the test scores display adequate reliability, and (c) test scores display relationships with other variables in a manner congruent with its predicted properties. Kane's practical perspective is congruent with the current *Standards*, which provide detailed guidance regarding the types of evidence that should be brought forward to support the use of a test for a particular purpose. For example, the current version of the *Standards* state:

> A sound validity argument integrates various strands of evidence into a coherent account of the degree to which existing evidence and theory support the intended interpretation of test scores for specific uses... Ultimately, the validity of an intended interpretation... relies on all the available evidence relevant to the technical quality of a testing system. This includes evidence of careful test construction; adequate score reliability; appropriate test administration and scoring; accurate score scaling, equating, and standard setting; and careful attention to fairness for all examinees.... (AERA et al., 1999, p. 17)

This perspective is also congruent with Messick's (1989) seminal chapter on validity, where he comments:

> Validation is a matter of making the most reasonable case to guide both current use of the test and current research to advance understanding of what the test

scores mean...To validate an interpretive inference is to ascertain the degree to which multiple lines of evidence are consonant with the inference, while establishing that alternative inferences are less well supported. (p. 13)

The Current Standards Five Sources of Validity Evidence

As illustrated by the preceding excerpt, the current version of the *Standards* embraces an argument-based approach to validation. They are also pragmatic with respect to validity theory because although they state validity is a unitary concept, they avoid describing all validity as construct validity. For example, rather than refer to "types," "categories," or "aspects" of validity, it proposes a validation framework based on five "sources of validity evidence" (AERA et al., 1999, p. 11).

These sources of evidence may illuminate different aspects of validity, but they do not represent distinct types of validity. Validity is a unitary concept. It is the degree to which all the accumulated evidence supports the intended interpretation of test scores for the proposed purpose. (p. 11)

As illustrated in Table 2.1, the five sources of validity evidence are evidence based on (a) test content, (b) response processes, (c) internal structure, (d) relations to other variables, and (e) consequences of testing. Evidence based on test content refers to traditional forms of content validity evidence such as practice (job) analyses and subject matter expert review and rating of test items and test specifications (Sireci, 1998a, 1998b), as well as newer "alignment" methods for educational tests that evaluate the link between curriculum frameworks, testing, and instruction. Evidence based on response processes refers to "evidence concerning the fit between the construct and the detailed nature of performance or response actually engaged in by examinees" (AERA et al., p. 12). Such evidence can include interviewing test takers about their responses to test questions, systematic observations of test response behavior, evaluation of the criteria used by judges when scoring performance tasks, and analysis of item response time data. Evaluation of the reasoning processes examinees use when solving test items, such as those described by Mislevy (this volume) or Emberetson (1983), would also fall under this category. Evidence based on internal structure refers to statistical analysis of item and sub-score data to investigate the dimensions measured by an assessment. Procedures for gathering such evidence include factor analysis (both exploratory and confirmatory) and multidimensional scaling. Evidence based on relations to other variables refers to traditional forms of criterion-related evidence for validity such as concurrent and predictive validity studies, as well as more comprehensive investigations of the relationships between test scores and other variables such as multitrait-multimethod studies (Campbell & Fiske, 1959). Finally, evidence based on consequences of testing refers to evaluation of the intended and unintended consequences associated with a testing program.[6] Examples of evidence based on consequences of testing include adverse impact, evaluation of the effects of testing on instruction, and evaluation of the effects of testing on issues such as high school drop out and job applications.

In my opinion, the five sources of evidence put forward in the current *Standards* provide a useful framework for evaluating the use of a test for a particular purpose, and for documenting validity evidence in a coherent way.[7] This framework encourages us to use multiple lines of evidence to support the use of a test for a particular purpose, but it is not overly prescriptive. The lack of strong, prescriptive rules for what needs to be done to "validate" an inference has frustrated some researchers and test evaluators because it is not clear when sufficient evidence has been gathered. That is a valid criticism of the current *Standards*, but it is a criticism that can never be satisfied in a scientific manner. The science of educational and psychological measurement is too complex to boil down to a single statistical test or cookbook-like procedure for determining when sufficient validity evidence is obtained. It is simply not that simple. Perhaps the best question to guide test validation efforts is "If the use of this test for the purpose I am using it for were challenged in court, do I have sufficient evidence to persuade the judge or jury and win the case?" If the answer is yes, the evidence will comprise a solid validity argument (see Phillips, 2000, or Sireci & Parker, 2006, for the use and interpretation of validity evidence by the courts). If not, more evidence is needed, or use of the test cannot be defended.

Packing and Unpacking the Components of Validity

I titled this chapter "Packing and Unpacking Sources of Validity Evidence: History Repeats Itself Again," because a review of validity theory indicates that from the beginning, validity theory and practices have wavered between simple and complex notions, and multiple types of validity and associated modifiers have been proposed. Although the unitary conceptualization of validity is currently prominent, the various aspects or types of validity persevere, and are still used by test developers and practitioners (Sireci, 1998b). As illustrated in the historical review, and summarized briefly in Table 2.1, there are several basic notions of validity theory and practice that appeared during the earliest days of modern measurement, and have continued to reappear and persevere, even though the words we use to describe them have changed. It appears that what validity is has been "unpacked" (into various types or aspects) and "packed" (into a unitary conceptualization) many times and this metamorphosis will likely continue for the foreseeable future.

Regardless of the packaging, several fundamental notions about the appropriateness of tests will persevere. Specifically, that tests should (a) measure what they purport to measure, (b) demonstrate predicted relationships with other measures of the intended constructs and unintended constructs, (c) contain content consistent with their intended uses, and (d) be put to purposes that are consistent with their design and are supported by evidence. These persevering notions are needed to protect us from more simplistic notions that tests are somehow inherently valid or invalid, or that consideration of test use is not important in evaluating test quality. They are also consonant with emerging notions of how to promote validity through constructing tests based on evidence-centered design (e.g., Mislevy, Steinberg, & Almond, 2002) and other principles based in cognitive psychology (Emberetson, 1983; Mislevy, this volume).

CONCLUSIONS

In this chapter, I reviewed some of the classic and seminal literature related to validity theory and practice, emphasizing the various editions of the *Standards for Educational and Psychological Testing*. The review highlighted early conceptualizations of validity and how they were extended to explain how we currently think about validity today, and current thinking regarding the process of test validation. Is all well within the field of test validation? Do the *Standards* give us everything we need to properly validate tests? Unfortunately, the answer is no. Many validation efforts continue to be unsystematic, avoid exploring hypotheses that might provide evidence of invalidity, and there is no governing body or professional association that will "certify" tests as sufficiently appropriate for one or more applied purposes. Nevertheless, our task in evaluating or demonstrating the utility and appropriateness of a test for a particular purpose is clear. We need multiple sources of evidence, some based on theory and subjective judgment, and some based on statistical analysis, to justify test use and score interpretations.

Although not covered in this chapter, statistical techniques and research methods for gathering and analyzing validity data are readily available. Such techniques are mentioned in the *Standards*, but there are not specific examples, nor citations to exemplary validation practices. It is hoped future versions of the *Standards* will provide examples of or references to successful validation efforts. Perhaps such examples could be provided in a companion volume, one that is meant for test developers and evaluators. Thankfully, examples of applied validation techniques are plentiful in the literature, including books and book chapters (e.g., Holland &

Wainer, 1993; Nunnally, 1967; Pedhauzer & Schmelkin, 1991; Wainer & Sireci, 2005; Zumbo, 2007; etc.) and measurement journals (e.g., Campbell & Fiske, 1959; Crocker, Miller, & Franks, 1989; Pitoniak, Sireci, & Luecht, 2005; Zwick & Schlemer, 2004; etc.).

A Look to the Future

Our review of the history of test validity and of current validity theory and practices illustrates techniques for gathering and analyzing validity data are available, but there is much work to be done. There are criticisms of the current version of the *Standards*, some of which were raised here. However, I believe the *Standards* are extremely helpful to those who build and evaluate tests, and I believe it is easier to work with them, than against them. It will be interesting to see how the forthcoming version of the *Standards* will describe validity.[8] One prediction is safe—validity will continue to be described as pertaining to inferences derived from test scores, rather than as an inherent property of a test. My hope for the future is that we see more validation activities. We have the theories, we have the methods, but most validation practices still fall far short of providing a convincing, comprehensive validity argument.

In closing, history has seen different perspectives on validity theory, and differences will likely continue into the future. However, there are some fundamental tenets of validity that are widely accepted and will not change. Psychometricians are scientists and statisticians and so we prefer objective data and rules, such as those involved in hypothesis testing or in evaluating an effect size. Thus, it is frustrating that whether a test is valid for a particular purpose will always be a question of judgment. Nevertheless, a sound validity argument makes the judgment an easy one to make. That is, anyone looking at the evidence will come to the same conclusion—the test is appropriate for its use.

With respect to the validity of scores from educational achievement tests, about 70 years ago it became clear that validity evidence based on test content is a fundamental requirement for such tests. Without confirming the content tested is consistent with curricular goals, the test adequately represents the intended domain, and the test is free of construct-irrelevant material, the utility of the test for making educational decisions will be undermined. However, it is also clear that validity evidence based on test content is insufficient for confirming the appropriateness of test use. As Messick (1989) described, validity is "an integrated evaluative judgment of the degree to which empirical evidence and theoretical rationales support the *adequacy* and *appropriateness* of *inferences* and *actions* based on test scores and other modes of assessment" (p. 13). Any one study, or any one form of validity evidence, is not "integrative" and probably does not sufficiently address the theory underlying the test or how test scores are used. Therefore, the task for test developers and validators is to create a body of evidence sufficient to inform potential users of the strengths and limitations of a particular test for particular purposes. If we do that, and it is within our power to do so, we will not only advance the practice of psychometrics, we will promote more sound educational and psychological assessment policies.

NOTES

1. However, it could also be argued that the stories of Adam and Eve and Abraham (when God asked him to sacrifice Isaac) in the Book of Genesis represent earlier tests than this one. Refer to Bob Dylan's *Highway 61 Revisited* for an insightful retelling of the story of Abraham's test.
2. Another interesting historical note is that Spearman is also credited for developing the technique to correct correlations for attenuation (Spearman, 1907).
3. The Army Beta test was an intelligence test for illiterate recruits who were not able to read, whereas the Army Alpha was the written version.
4. See Sireci (1998b) for further discussion of the history of test validity during this time period.
5. The next year, AERA published a companion version that focused on educational achievement testing (AERA, 1955).
6. Readers interested in learning more about evaluating testing consequences and the debate over whether "consequential validity" is a legitimate term and whose responsibility it is to investigate it are referred to the two special issues of *Educational Measurement: Issues and Practice* on this topic that appeared in 1997 (Volume 16, number 2) and 1998 (Volume 17, number 2).
7. For an example of a technical manual that uses these five sources of evidence to organize validity data, see Sireci et al. (2008).
8. At the time of this writing, a new Joint Committee has been assembled to revise the 1999 version of the *Standards*.

REFERENCES

American Educational Research Association (1955). *Technical recommendations for achievement tests*. Washington, DC: Author.

American Educational Research Association, American Psychological Association, & National Council on Measurement in Education. (1985). *Standards for educational and psychological testing*. Washington, DC: American Psychological Association.

American Educational Research Association, American Psychological Association, & National Council on Measurement in Education. (1999). *Standards for educational and psychological testing*. Washington, DC: American Educational Research Association.

American Psychological Association, Committee on Test Standards. (1952). Technical recommendations for psychological tests and diagnostic techniques: A preliminary proposal. *American Psychologist, 7,* 461–465.

American Psychological Association. (1954). Technical recommendations for psychological tests and diagnostic techniques. *Psychological Bulletin, 51,* (2, supplement).

American Psychological Association. (1966). *Standards for educational and psychological tests and manuals.* Washington, DC: Author.

American Psychological Association, American Educational Research Association, & National Council on Measurement in Education. (1974). *Standards for educational and psychological tests.* Washington, DC: American Psychological Association.

Anastasi, A. (1938). Faculties Versus Factors: A Reply to Professor Thurstone. *Psychological Bulletin, 35,* 391–395.

Angoff, W. H. (1988). Validity: An evolving concept. In H. Wainer & H. I. Braun (Eds.), *Test validity* (pp. 19–32). Hillsdale, NJ: Lawrence Erlbaum.

Binet, A. (1905). New methods for the diagnosis of the intellectual level of subnormals. *L'Année Psychologique, 12,* 191–244.

Binet, A., & Henri, B. (1899). La psychologic individuelle. *Amiee Psychol., 2,* 411–465.

Bingham, W. V. (1937). *Aptitudes and aptitude testing.* New York: Harper.

Campbell, D. T., & Fiske, D. W. (1959). Convergent and discriminant validation by the multitrait-multimethod matrix. *Psychological Bulletin, 56,* 81–105.

Crocker, L. M., Miller, D., & Franks E. A. (1989). Quantitative methods for assessing the fit between test and curriculum. *Applied Measurement in Education, 2,* 179–194.

Cronbach, L. J. (1971). Test Validation. In R.L. Thorndike (Ed.), *Educational measurement* (2nd ed., pp. 443–507). Washington, DC: American Council on Education.

Cronbach, L. J. (1988). Five perspectives on the validity argument. In H. Wainer & H. I. Braun (Eds.), *Test validity* (pp. 3–17). Hillsdale, NJ: Lawrence Erlbaum.

Cronbach, L. J., & Meehl, P. E. (1955). Construct validity in psychological tests. *Psychological Bulletin, 52,* 281–302.

Cureton, E. E. (1951). Validity. In E. F. Lindquist (Ed.), *Educational measurement* (1st ed., pp. 621–694). Eashington, DC: American Council on Education.

Ebel, R. L. (1956). Obtaining and reporting evidence for content validity. *Educational and Psychological Measurement, 16,* 269–282.

Embretson, S. (1983). Construct validity: Construct representation versus nomothetic span. *Psychological Bulletin, 93,* 179–197.

Fechner, G. T. (1860). *Elements of psychophysics.* (Trans. by H. S. Langfeld, first appearing in B. Rand (Ed.) (1912), *The classical psychologists.* Boston: Houghton Mifflin.

Garrett (1937). *Statistics in psychology and education.* New York: Longmans, Green.

Guilford, J. P. (1946). New standards for test evaluation. *Educational and Psychological Measurement, 6,* 427–439.

Gulliksen, H. (1950). Intrinsic validity. *American Psychologist, 5,* 511–517.

Holland, P. W., & Wainer, H. (Eds.). (1993). *Differential item functioning*. Hillsdale, NJ: Lawrence Erlbaum.

Jenkins J. G. (1946). Validity for what? *Journal of Consulting Psychology, 10*, 93–98.

Kane, M. T. (1992). An argument-based approach to validity. *Psychological Bulletin, 112*, 527–535.

Kane, M. (2006). Validation. In R. L. Brennan (Ed). *Educational measurement* (4th ed., pp. 17-64). Washington, DC: American Council on Education/Praeger.

Kelley, T. L. (1927). *Interpretation of educational measurement*. Yonkers-on-Hudson, NY: World Book Co.

Loevinger, J. (1957). Objective tests as instruments of psychological theory. *Psychological Reports, 3*, 635–694 (Monograph Supplement 9).

Messick, S. (1975). The standard problem: meaning and values in measurement and evaluation. *American Psychologist, 30*, 955–966.

Messick, S. (1989). Validity. In R. Linn (Ed.), *Educational measurement*, (3rd ed.). Washington, DC: American Council on Education.

Mislevy, R. J. (2009). Validity from the perspective of model-based reasoning. In R. Lissitz (Ed.,), *The concept of validity: Revisions, new directions and applications* (pp. xx–xx). Charlotte, NC: Information Age Publishing Inc.

Mislevy, R. J., Steinberg, L. S., & Almond, R. G. (2002). On the role of task model variables in assessment design. In S. H. Irvine & P. C. Kyllonen (Eds.), *Item generation for test development* (pp. 97–128). Mahwah, NJ: Lawrence Erlbaum.

Mosier, C. I. (1947). A critical examination of the concepts of face validity. *Educational and Psychological Measurement, 7*, 191–205.

Nunnally, J. C. (1967). *Psychometric theory*. New York: McGraw-Hill.

Pearson, K. (1896). Mathematical contributions to the theory of evolution. III. Regression, heredity and panmixia. *Philosophical Transactions of the Royal Society A, 187*, 253–318.

Pedhazur, E. J., & Schmelkin, L. P. (1991). *Measurement, design, and analysis: An integrated approach*. Hillsdale, NJ: Lawrence Erlbaum.

Phillips, S. E. (2000). *GI Forum v. Texas Education Agency*: Psychometric evidence. *Applied Measurement in Education, 13*, 343–385.

Pitoniak, M. J., Sireci, S. G., & Luecht, R. M. (2002). A multitrait-multimethod validity investigation of scores from a professional licensure exam. *Educational and Psychological Measurement, 62*, 498–516.

Rulon, P. J. (1946). On the validity of educational tests. *Harvard Educational Review, 16*, 290–296.

Shepard, L. A. (1993). Evaluating test validity. *Review of Research in Education, 19*, 405–450.

Sireci, S. G. (1998a). Gathering and analyzing content validity data. *Educational Assessment, 5*, 299–321.

Sireci, S. G. (1998b). The construct of content validity. *Social Indicators Research, 45*, 83–117.

Sireci, S. G., Baldwin, P., Martone, A., Zenisky, A. L., Kaira, L., Lam, W., Shea, C. L., Han, K. T., Deng, N., Delton, J., & Hambleton, R. K. (2008). *Massachusetts Adult Proficiency Tests technical manual: Version 2*. Center for Educational Assessment Research Report No. 677. Amherst, MA: University of Massachusetts,

Center for Educational Assessment. Available at http://www.umass.edu/remp/CEA_TechMan.html.

Sireci, S. G., & Parker, P. (2006). Validity on trial: Psychometric and legal conceptualizations of validity. *Educational Measurement: Issues and Practice, 25*(3), 27–34.

Spearman, C. (1904). General intelligence: objectively determined and measured. *American Journal of Psychology, 15,* 201–293.

Spearman, C. (1907). Demonstration of formulae for true measurement of correlation. *American Journal of Psychology, 18,* 161–169.

Thurstone, L. L. (1932). *The reliability and validity of tests.* Ann Arbor, MI: Edwards Brothers.

Wainer, H. (2000). Epilogue. In H. Wainer (Ed.), *Computerized adaptive testing: A primer* (2nd ed., p. 249). Hillsdale, NJ: Lawrence Erlbaum.

Wainer, H., & Sireci, S. G. (2005). Item and test bias. *Encyclopedia of social measurement* (Vol. 2, pp. 365–371. San Diego: Elsevier.

Zumbo, B. D. (2007). Validity: Foundational Issues and statistical methodology. In C. R. Rao & S. Sinharay (Eds.), *Handbook of statistics, Vol. 26: Psychometrics* (pp. 45–79). Amsterdam: Elsevier Science B.V.

Zwick, R., & Schlemer, L. (2004). SAT validity for linguistic minorities at the University of California, Santa Barbara. *Educational Measurement: Issues and Practice, 23*(1), 6–16.

CHAPTER 3

VALIDATING THE INTERPRETATIONS AND USES OF TEST SCORES

Michael Kane

ABSTRACT

In most discussions of educational and psychological measurement, *validity* has been defined broadly, to cover the evaluation of interpretations and uses of test scores. If the proposed interpretation of test scores is limited, as it is for some observable attributes, the requirements for validation can be very modest. If the proposed interpretations are more ambitious, as they are for traits and theoretical constructs, more evidence and more kinds of evidence are required for validation. Because validity addresses the wide range of issues associated with the interpretation and uses of test scores, it is viewed as the most fundamental consideration in evaluating testing programs. We can redefine validity as a more specific, technical property of tests or test scores, but if we do so, we should probably not think of it as the most fundamental consideration in evaluating testing programs.

The Concept of Validity, pages 39–64

INTRODUCTION

It is generally reasonable to expect that a person or organization that makes public claims should be prepared to justify these claims if they are challenged, and in some contexts, justification may be expected, even if the claims are not challenged. The authors of the Declaration of Independence took it as a given that, in breaking from England:

> a decent respect to the opinions of mankind requires that they should declare the causes which impel them to the separation. (In Congress, July 4, 1776)

Similarly, a decent respect for the opinions of various stakeholders suggests that support be provided for the claims based on test scores. And if decent respect is not sufficient motivation, some court or state agency may intrude.

OVERVIEW

In the first part of this chapter, I intend to make four general points about validation. In the second part, I will make the discussion more concrete by examining how these general points apply to three content- based interpretations of test scores—those for observable attributes, operationally defined attributes, and traits. The analysis of these closely related interpretations provides an indication of how the general principles play out in practice. The first two points reflect basic assumptions about validity.

First, it is the interpretations and uses of test scores that are validated, and not the tests themselves. Although, it can be quite reasonable to talk elliptically about the "validity of a test," this usage makes sense only if an interpretation/use has already been adopted, explicitly or implicitly.

Second, the evidence required for validation depends on the test and the interpretation/use, and therefore, different interpretations/uses will require different kinds and different amounts of evidence for their validation.

Given, these basic assumptions about validation, two additional points can be made about the practice of validation.

Third, validity is conceptually simple, but can be complicated in practice. The devil is in the details. Such is life.

Fourth, a failure to pay careful attention to what is being assumed in the proposed interpretations and uses of test scores can lead to miscommunication and to fallacious reasoning (e.g., "begging the question").

VALIDATING PROPOSED INTERPRETATIONS AND USES OF TEST SCORES

Validity has traditionally been defined in terms of the accuracy and/or appropriateness of the interpretations assigned to test scores and the uses made of test scores (Sireci, 1998, 2006). The possible interpretations and uses to be considered have evolved and expanded over time, but the focus has been on interpretations and uses throughout this development. In reaction to Messick's (1989) work, there has been debate about whether the social consequences of test-score uses should be evaluated as part of validity (Popham, 1997), but until recently (Borsboom, 2006; Borsboom, Mellenbergh, & van Heerden, 2004; Lissitz & Samuelson, 2007) there has been little debate about the conceptualization of validity as an evaluation of proposed interpretations and uses of test scores.

Borsboom et al. (2004) think of validity as a property of the test, and they define validity in terms of a causal relationship between the attribute being measured and performance on the test tasks:

> A test is valid for measuring an attribute if and only if (a) the attribute exists and (b) variations in the attribute causally produce variations in the outcomes of the measurement procedure. (Borsboom et al., 2004, p. 1)

Lissitz and Samuelsen (2007) also treat validity as a property of the test, but associated it with the representativeness of its content relative to some domain (e.g., algebra):

> ... meaning that the test is a combination of tasks and these tasks are the operational definition that is captured ... by the name and description of the domain to be measured by the test. (Lissitz & Samuelsen, 2007, p. 441)

Lissitz and Samuelsen (2007) take content-based validity evidence, along with reliability, as the focus of validation, and as is also the case for Borsboom et al. (2004), they see many of the issues traditionally considered under validity (e.g., relationships to criteria, relationships to other variables or constructs, and the impact, or consequences, of the testing program) as external to and separate from validity.

The approaches taken by Lissitz and Samuelsen (2007) and by Borsboom et al. (2004) are distinct in many ways, but they share several features. First, they reject what they see as overly complicated validity frameworks (particularly those based on Cronbach and Meehl's (1955) formulation of construct validity) in favor of a simple approach based on a particular interpretation of test scores. Second, they recognize that many of the issues traditionally considered under validity (e.g., relationships to criteria) can be important, but choose to have them considered under some other heading (e.g., utility). Third, they see validity as a property of the test, and not of the interpretations and uses of the test scores. As indicated below, I disagree with all three of these suggestions.

In the next section, I will examine how the evidence to be included in a validity argument depends on the proposed interpretations and uses of the test scores, but in this section, my goal is to make the case that, in educational and psychological measurement, the terms, "validity" and "validation" have been consistently defined in terms of the interpretations and uses of test scores.

In the first edition of *Educational Measurement*, Cureton (1951) defined validity in terms of the relevance of the test to its intended uses:

> The essential question of test validity is how well a test does the job it is employed to do. The same test may be used for several different purposes, and its validity may be high for one, moderate for another, and low for a third. Hence, we cannot label the validity of a test as "high" "moderate" or "low except for some particular purpose." (Cureton,1951, p. 621)

Cronbach and Meehl (1955) organized their seminal paper on construct validity around interpretations:

> the logic of construct validity is invoked whether the construct is highly systematized or loose, used in ramified theory or a few simple propositions... We seek to specify how one is to defend a proposed interpretation of a test; *we are not recommending any one type of interpretation.* (p. 284) [emphasis in original]

In the second edition of *Educational Measurement*, Cronbach (1971) defined validity in terms of interpretations and a range of possible uses:

> Narrowly considered, validation is the process of examining the accuracy of a specific prediction or inference made from a test score.... More broadly, validation examines the soundness of all interpretations of a test—descriptive and explanatory interpretations as well as situation-bound predictions. (Cronbach, 1971, p. 443)

In the third edition of *Educational Measurement*, Messick (1989) defined validity as:

> An integrated evaluative judgment of the degree to which empirical evidence and theoretical rationales support the *adequacy* and *appropriateness* of *inferences* and *actions* based on test scores and other modes of assessment. (Messick, 1989, p. 13)

In the fourth edition, I followed in this tradition, and focused on validation as:

> ...the process of evaluating the plausibility of proposed interpretations and
> uses, and on validity as the extent to which the evidence supports or refutes a
> proposed interpretations and uses. (Kane, 2006, p. 17)

Similarly, successive editions of the *Standards for Educational and Psychological
Testing* (1985, 1999) have treated validity as an evaluative judgment about
the appropriateness of proposed interpretations and uses, with this focus
becoming more explicit over time. The most recent edition of the *Standards*
states that:

> Validity refers to the degree to which evidence and theory support the inter-
> pretation of test scores entailed by proposed uses of tests. Validity is, there-
> fore, the most fundamental consideration in developing and evaluating
> tests.... Validation logically begins with an explicit statement of the proposed
> interpretation of test scores, along with a rationale for the relevance of the
> interpretation to the proposed use. (AERA, APA, NCME, 1999, p. 9)

The trajectory here is quite clear, and a similar trajectory could be traced
through textbooks and journal articles. There are differences in wording
and emphases (and there are divergent strands in the literature), but the
general assumption is that validity is a property of interpretations and uses
and not a property of the test.

The evolution of validity theory has involved the development of a range
of statistical and analytic models, but more fundamentally, it has involved
changes in the kinds of interpretations and uses to be considered in validation. Early assessments tended to involve samples of performances in some
valued activity (e.g., writing) and were interpreted in terms of level of proficiency on this activity. To assess how well students can write essays, it would
be reasonable to ask them to write some essays and then to evaluate the
overall quality of these essays.

In most activities, the scores may vary from one performance to another,
and the generalizability of the scores, based on samples of performance, to
statements about overall proficiency in the activity could be of concern, but
otherwise, the legitimacy of the proposed interpretation is supported by
judgments about the appropriateness of the test format, content, scoring
rules, and testing and scoring procedures. Cureton's (1951) main concerns
about validity were relevance and reliability, and if the interpretation did
not venture much beyond claims about the observed kinds of performance,
relevance could be evaluated using judgments about the representativeness
of content sampling. Validation efforts based on such judgments about the

relevance, representativeness, and reasonableness of test content, format, and procedures were addressed under the heading of content validity.

In many testing applications, the main purpose is to predict or estimate some performance or outcome that cannot be directly observed and evaluated (e.g., some future outcome). A question then arises about the accuracy of these estimates (or predictions) of the variables of interest (e.g., subsequent performance on the job). To the extent that the test tasks are similar to the criterion performances, or involve core components of these performances, it can make sense to simply extrapolate from test scores to conclusions about the performances of interest. However, in cases where such extrapolation is questionable, and the decisions to be made have moderate to high stakes, the relationship between the test scores and more direct measures of the performance of interest can be evaluated in a criterion validity study. For example, if the test is to be used in making employment decisions, it would be reasonable to expect evidence linking test scores to a criterion measure of performance on the job. Note that the need for criterion-related evidence depends on the intended use of the test scores—to estimate or predict some non-test performance. If the test involved a sample of the performance of interest (e.g., evaluations of performance on the job), criterion-related evidence would be irrelevant.

In the 1920s and 1930s, validity coefficients were commonly used to support inferences from observed scores to various criteria (Gulliksen, 1950). The statistical models used to analyze criterion-related validity evidence are elegant, and once the data are collected, they provide quantitative answers to some questions about validity, in particular, whether it is reasonable to use test scores to draw inferences about the criterion. However, criterion-related validity evidence does not provide stronger support for an interpretation in terms of current performance or behavior in the domain of test tasks; rather, it provides support for a different kind of interpretation.

In some cases, test scores are not interpreted in terms of observable performances or as predictions of criteria, but rather, as estimates of theoretical constructs or traits. Such interpretations are ambitious, entailing as they do, theoretical models, explanations, and claims about latent variables, and therefore, they generally call for a complex mix of evidence for their validation. Efforts to collect such evidence and synthesize it into a coherent evaluation of the claims inherent in the theoretical constructs were included under the heading of construct validity (Cronbach & Meehl, 1955; Loevinger, 1957; Messick, 1989).

Again, it is not the basic idea of validity (that we should justify the claims included in our interpretations and uses of test scores) that was challenged by Cronbach and Meehl (1955), but rather the range of interpretations being entertained. If the test scores are not to be interpreted in terms of the kinds of theoretical constructs, or traits, discussed by Cronbach and Meehl, there would be no need to develop evidence supporting such construct interpretations. Just as criterion-related evidence is unnecessary if the test scores are not used to estimate any criteria, construct-related evidence is irrelevant, if the interpretation does not make claims about any construct.

In general, the evidence to be expected in a validity analysis depends on the proposed interpretations and uses of the test scores. It can make sense to talk about the "validity of a test," if the interpretation/use is fixed. For example, if an employer is thinking about using a standardized test to predict future performance on a job, the question may be phrased in terms of, "the validity of the test as a predictor of future performance on the job," or more succinctly as, "the validity of the test," but this latter usage only makes sense because we have already decided on the use to be made of test scores. If we changed the proposed use (e.g., to predicting performance on a different job), the "validity of the test" would need to be reconsidered.

Given the trajectory outlined above, in which the range of interpretations to be validated and therefore the kinds of validity evidence to be considered has consistently expanded, shifting to a definition of validity in terms of a particular kind of interpretation would be a major change. We could decide to make such a change in our terminology and usage (Borsboom, 2006; Borsboom et al., 2004; Lissitz & Samuelson, 2007), but this would not absolve us of the obligation to develop a reasonable basis for our test-based interpretations and decisions, whatever they are.

If the work required to evaluate the inferences and assumptions inherent in a proposed interpretation and use is too burdensome when included under the heading of validity (as argued by Lissitz and Samuelson, and Borsboom and his colleagues), will they get easier if moved to a section on utility or implications? Defining validity in terms of a particular kind of interpretation would certainly simplify validity theory, but it would not simplify the basic task of justifying the interpretations and uses of test scores.

Furthermore, shifting the focus to a particular kind of interpretation could lead to serious misunderstandings, unless the new definitions were clearly stated and consistently maintained. In particular, attempts to simplify validation by adopting a single kind of interpretation as the basis for validation is likely to promote miscommunication in which tests are validated by their developers in terms of a relatively narrow set of assumptions (e.g., in terms of the representativeness of test content), but the scores are then interpreted more broadly by users (e.g., in terms of "readiness for some activity) and used for various purposes without further evidential support (Shepard, 1993). For example, adopting a content-based interpretation for validation, and then using the test to make placement or employment decisions without further evaluation would "beg the question" of whether the test scores are actually related to subsequent performance. If validity is to be interpreted narrowly (e.g., in terms of content representativeness), it will be necessary to reconsider statements to the effect that validity is, "the most fundamental consideration in developing and evaluating tests" (AERA, APA, NCME, 1999, p. 9).

EVIDENCE NEEDED FOR VALIDATION DEPENDS ON THE INTERPRETATIONS AND USES

To the extent that validity is defined as an evaluation of the proposed interpretations and uses of test scores, the evidence required for an adequate validation would depend on the proposed interpretations and uses. If the test scores have a direct and simple interpretation, little or no evidence would be needed for validation. In particular, if the interpretation does not go much beyond a summary of the observed performance, it would take very little evidence to support it; for example, a teacher's report that a student did 10 pushups during a PE class would probably be accepted at face value. A stronger claim would require more evidence. If the performance is to be taken as indicating that the student is physically fit, we might be inclined to ask for a definition of fitness and for some explanation for why this kind of performance is particularly appropriate as a measure of fitness for students in general or for students of this age and gender. If the performance is to be taken as an indication of mathematical aptitude, we would probably be incredulous. In validation, the proposed interpretation matters.

An argument-based approach to validation presupposes that it is the interpretations and uses of test scores that are to be evaluated, and this approach can be applied to a range of possible interpretations and uses of test scores. To the extent that validation focuses on the appropriateness of certain interpretations and uses, it is necessarily contingent. It depends on both the test and the proposed interpretations and uses of the test scores. More ambitious interpretations will generally involve a more extended set of inferences and supporting assumptions and therefore will require an examination of more kinds of evidence for validation (Kane, 2006) than would be the case for a simple, narrow interpretation. As a result, for validation to be effective, the claims inherent in the interpretations and uses need to be clearly understood.

In the first stage of the enterprise, the *development stage*, the interpretations and uses are to be specified in terms of the inferences and assumptions required to get from the observations for each person to the interpretations of the resulting scores for the person and to any decisions based on the scores (Kane, 2006). The first stage tends to be confirmatory in the sense that it is carried out by people who are developing the proposed interpretations and uses (and, perhaps, the test) and, therefore, tend to fix any problems uncovered during this stage. The second stage, the *appraisal stage*, is intended to be more arms-length and critical: at this stage, we kick the tires (Kane, 2006).

The interpretations and uses can be explicated in different ways, but I find it useful to lay it out as a network of inferences with their supporting assumptions, because this approach makes the assumptions quite explicit. Some of the inferences may be logical or mathematical (e.g., scaling/equating), but many of the inferences and assumptions are based on judgment (e.g., the grading of essays). Most of the inferences are presumptive in the sense that they establish a presumption in favor of the conclusions, which "usually follow" or "generally follow" from the premises.

Toulmin (1958) has proposed a standard form for inferences. The inference starts from some initial assertion, the *datum*, and generates a conclusion or action, the *claim*. The inference is justified by some rule of inference, the *warrant*, which is supported by appropriate evidence, or *backing*. For example, in using a regression equation to predict college GPA from a test score, the test score is the datum, the regression equation is the warrant, and the predicted GPA is the claim. The empirical study used to develop the regression equation would typically provide the backing for its use in predicting the GPAs.

The warrants are not inferences; they are rules of inferences that justify a large number of inferences of a particular kind. For example a regression equation may be applied to a large number of test scores over many years, even thought the regression equation was based on results for a relatively small sample of students taking the test on one occasion. One can think of the warrant for each inference as a machine, with a datum serving as the input and a claim constituting the output. If the warrant is a regression equation, we have a score going in and a predicted score coming out. For construct-based interpretations, scientific theories are regularly used as warrants to justify inferences from observations to conclusions about constructs and about other variables.

Toulmin's model of inference is quite general. It allows for different inputs, different outputs, and different kinds of warrants, with the evidence needed to support the warrant depending on the nature of the warrant and the context in which it is to be used. Some warrants (e.g., the rule used to generate scores based on examinee responses) may rely entirely on judgmental, qualitative evidence, while other warrants (regression equations) may require empirical evidence. Some warrants may be considered so plausible that they do not require any specific backing, but most of the warrants involved in interpreting and using scores require some backing, especially if they are challenged.

A full statement of the inference would also include *qualifiers* (Q) that indicate a level of confidence in the claim (e.g., words like "usually" or "almost always," or quantitative indices like confidence intervals), and *con-*

ditions of rebuttal under which the interpretive argument would not hold (Toulmin, 1958). The conditions of rebuttal are exceptions to the general rule stated by the warrant.

Using Toulmin's framework, test-score interpretations and uses can be viewed as *interpretive arguments* (Kane, 2001, 2006), involving a number of inferences, each supported by a warrant. To validate the interpretive argument for the proposed interpretations and uses of test scores, it is necessary to evaluate the clarity, coherence, and completeness of the interpretive argument and to evaluate the plausibility of each of the inferences and assumptions in the interpretive argument. The proposed interpretations and uses are to be explicitly stated in terms of a network of inferences and assumptions, and then, the plausibility of the warrants for these inferences can be evaluated using relevant evidence. If the interpretations and uses are simple and limited, involving a few plausible inferences, the validation can be simple and limited. If the interpretations and uses are ambitious, involving a more extensive network of inferences, the evidence needed for validation would also be more extensive, including for example, inferences to non-test and/or future outcomes.

It is not easy to specify the interpretive argument for most high-stakes testing programs. The interpretation may seem straightforward, but, more often than not, a serious analysis of the proposed interpretations and uses will unearth a number of implicit assumptions that may or may not be justified in a particular case. For example, scores on a licensure examination can be interpreted as measures of current competency on certain critical areas of knowledge, skills and judgment (KSJs), or as predictors of performance in practice (Kane, 2006). The first interpretation, which simply assumes that the test covers some domain of KSJs, which are needed in practice, is much more modest than the second interpretation, which assumes, in addition, that test scores provide accurate predictions of success in practice. A validation of the first interpretation (in terms of current competence in a domain of KSJs) requires evidence that the test measures the KSJs, that the KSJs are critical for practice, and that the scores are reliable. A validation of the second interpretation (in terms of predictions of future performance) would, in addition, require evidence for the accuracy of the score-based predictions.

Note that there is a significant tradeoff involved in specifying the interpretive argument. A simple interpretation may be validated with a relatively modest investment in validity evidence. A more ambitious interpretation involving an extensive network of inferences and assumptions, requires more support to achieve a comparable level of validation, but the more ambitious interpretation may be more useful, if it can be justified. If we do not claim that test scores will predict future performance, we have no obligation to develop predictive validity evidence, but the resulting validity argument does not justify such predictions.

As illustrated more fully later, interpretations that appear similar (and are perhaps described in similar ways or with similar labels) may employ substantially different Inferences and assumptions, and therefore require different mixes of evidence for their validation. A common lapse in the practice of validation occurs when the evidence for a relatively modest interpretation is use to justify more ambitious interpretations and uses.

VALIDITY IS SIMPLE; VALIDATION CAN BE DIFFICULT

One of the complaints made against CV over the years and at this conference is that it is too complicated. In a sense I agree, and in a sense, I disagree. I think that expositions of validity tend to be complex, in part because many of the technical issues are complex. However, I also think that the basic questions addressed by validity theory are profoundly simple. The test developer/user gets to propose an interpretation/use and the validator (who may also be the developer/user) tries to figure out (and document) whether this proposal makes sense and can be supported by evidence.

Two factors have, in concert, tended to exacerbate the perception that validation (particularly "construct validation") is too difficult. First, discussions of validity tend to include long lists of different kinds of evidence, all of which can be relevant to validation and some of which can be difficult to develop (e.g., long-term predictions, causal inferences). Second, some statements in the literature can be interpreted as saying that adequate validation requires that every possible kind of validity evidence be developed for validation to be complete. It has generally been recognized that a single line of evidence is not adequate for the validation of typical interpretations and uses. In itself, the call for multiple lines of evidence is reasonable, but it can easily morph into a call for the inclusion of as many kinds of evidence as possible, or worse, a call for all possible kinds of evidence. This shotgun approach is clearly unwieldy, and in its extreme form, it makes validation impossible.

The argument-based approach (Kane, 2006) to validation is intended to provide a realistic and pragmatic framework for evaluating the interpretations and uses of test scores. The basic idea is to clearly identify the inferences and assumptions inherent in the proposed interpretations and uses, and develop evidence relevant to the plausibility of these inferences and assumptions. The test developer would presumably collect much of this evidence during test development, and in doing so, would develop a preliminary argument for the proposed interpretations and uses. The validator/user would develop additional evidence, particularly evidence on specific, local test-score interpretations and uses, and would examine possible challenges to the proposed interpretations and uses. By focusing the validation effort on the inferences and assumptions inherent in the interpretations and uses, the argument-based approach can avoid both extremes, the use of some convenient but limited source of evidence to justify an ambition interpretation or use, and the assumption of a very burdensome requirement that every possible kind of evidence be collected.

This view of validity is conceptually very simple, but it can be demanding in practice, because it requires that test developers, users, and validators achieve a high degree of clarity about what they are doing, and this can involve a lot of serious analysis and hard work (e.g., see Chapelle, Enright, & Jamieson, 2008). The practice of validation gets especially complicated if the test scores are used for multiple purposes and have a complex interpretation (e.g., in terms of constructs, like verbal aptitude or intelligence), with many built in assumptions and associations.

Testing programs are designed to support certain kinds of interpretations and uses. The resulting test scores have a wide variety of important uses in education, health care, scientific research, and public policy. It is therefore of some concern to society as a whole and to many stakeholders that the uses made of test scores and the interpretations assigned to test scores are appropriate and achieve their goals. Although it may be difficult to fully articulate the reasoning involved in the interpretation and use of test scores, it is important to do so.

BEGGING THE QUESTION OF VALIDITY

The fallacy known as "begging the question" occurs when we are asked (or "begged") to accept a conclusion without critical examination (Kane, 2006). The conclusion is slipped into the argument as an implicit assumption. In a validity argument, the begging-the-question fallacy occurs if a relatively modest interpretive argument is assumed for purposes of validation, but a more ambitious interpretation is employed in practice. In extending the modest interpretation that was validated to the more ambitious interpretations and uses being employed in practice, many questionable inferences may be taken for granted, or "begged."

Shepard (1993) has described one way in which the fallacy can play out in practice. A test measuring certain skills is developed to assess "readiness" for kindergarten, and is labeled as a "readiness" test. The test provides reliable and content-representative measures of the skills, and is therefore considered valid as a measure of the skills. It is then used to decide whether six-year-olds are to go into kindergarten or are to wait a year. If the conclusion that the test is valid as a measure of the skills is used to justify its use for these placement decisions, the question of whether the test scores provide an adequate basis for such decisions is begged. If the observed score differences reflect mainly differences in maturation, the decision rule might be quite appropriate. However, if the poor test scores of some children reflect the fact that the skills are simply not being developed at home, keeping the children at home and out of school for another year would probably be counterproductive.

Unfortunately, begging the question is common in the practice of validation. For example, the proponents of authentic assessments have tended to emphasize the extent to which the observed performances match the performance of interest, while taking the generalization (or reliability) of observed scores over tasks, occasions, and conditions of observation for granted, even though empirical research indicates that such generalization represents a triumph of optimism over experience. Similarly, developers of objective tests have tended to focus on content representativeness and generalizability (or reliability) over items, while implicitly extending the interpretation to non-test contexts. In both cases, we are asked to accept the more questionable part of the argument without evidence. The fact that some major inferences are being glossed over may not be noticed, especially if other parts of the argument are developed in some detail (e.g., by providing an extended discussion of the authenticity of the performance tasks, or by proving extensive evidence for the internal consistency of the objective-test scores).

Some Examples: Content-Based Interpretations

To make these ideas more concrete, we can consider three distinct, but closely related, interpretations: observable attributes, operationally defined attributes, and traits. Content-related validity evidence plays a large role in validating all test score interpretations and plays an especially large role in validating the interpretations associated with observable attributes, operationally defined attributes, and traits, all of which are defined at least in part, in terms of domains of observations (Sireci, 1998). Each of these three kinds of attributes involves a disposition to behave or perform in some way over some range of tasks or stimuli and over some range of conditions, and therefore, each depends on evidence indicating that the observations included in the test are representative of the domain of observations associated with the attribute

The validity of the test-score interpretations depends, in large part, on how the domains are defined, and in particular, on the relationship between test content and the domain content. In some cases (e.g., observable attributes and operationally defined attributes), content-related evidence can constitute most of the evidence for validity, and in some cases (e.g., traits), content-related evidence plays an essential, but more modest role.

Observable Attributes

For some purposes (e.g., describing performance), it is useful to employ attributes that are defined in terms of actual or possible observations and that are largely devoid of excess meaning. I will refer to attributes that are explicitly defined in terms of target domains of possible observations as *observable attributes*. Observable attributes purport to represent how well people perform some kinds of tasks or how they respond to some kinds of stimuli. They represent dispositions to perform or behave in certain ways, and are descriptive rather than explanatory.

An observable attribute can be defined in terms of a *target domain* of possible observations, and the *value of the observable attribute* for a person, or the person's *target score* for the domain, can be defined as the person's expected score over the target domain. Observable attributes can be defined quite broadly (e.g., in terms of all of the cognitive, motor, and interpersonal tasks, involved in a job or other activity), or quite narrowly (e.g., ability to spell the words in a vocabulary list, when the words are spoken).

Each observation in the target domain would typically involve a task to be performed or a reaction to some stimulus situation, and criteria for assigning a value to the outcome. Most of the possible observations in the target domain would not actually be observed, but they are all observable in the sense that they could be observed. As a result, the value of the attribute, the expected value over the domain cannot be directly observed, but can be estimated from a sample of observations from the domain.

There are several points to be made about the target domains for observable attributes. First, as such, the target domains are defined in terms of possible observations. As observable attributes, these attributes do not make any assumptions about possible explanatory models for the observed performances/behavior, nor do they make any assumptions about underlying, latent attributes that account for performance. I am not arguing against such assumptions, but I want to draw a distinction between observable attributes, which are basically descriptive, and traits, for which the interpretation does involve assumptions about latent attributes. If we choose to include assumptions about underlying, causal variables in the interpretation of the attribute, we are not dealing with an observable attribute, but rather with a trait.

Second, the decision to include certain observations and not other observations in the target domain may be determined by practical considerations (e.g., the skills required by a job, or developed in a training program), or they may rely on experience or prior assumptions about the underlying skills and processes involved in the observations. Certain tasks (e.g., arithmetic items) may be included in a single domain because they are thought to require the same or at least overlapping sets of skills or component performances. However, for an observable attribute as defined here, once the target domain is specified, a person's target score can be interpreted as the person's expected score over the target domain without invoking assumptions about underlying traits or explanations. In practice, it is possible to answer questions about whether a person can perform a job or about how well they can perform the job, without having any deep understanding of how they perform the job. It is always possible to add additional layers of interpretation in terms of underlying traits, explanatory models, nomological theories, etc., but to do so is to generate a different kind of interpretation.

Third, we get to define the target domains to suit our purposes. We can define our target domains, and therefore our observable attributes, broadly or narrowly. We can include a wide range of performances, but restrict the observations to a particular context (a workplace), or we can include a range of contexts but restrict the observations to one kind of performance (e.g., solving mechanical problems). The evaluation rule can emphasize speed of performance, or the quality or accuracy of the performance, or some other evaluative criteria. We can focus on cognitive, physical, social performances, or any combination of these facets of performance. Note however that we do have a responsibility to label our observable attributes appropriately. It would clearly be misleading to define the target domain narrowly (e.g., in terms of questions about basic word meanings) but label or describe it in terms that imply a broad competency (e.g., in terms of "literacy" or "fluency").

Fourth, the target domains associated with observable attributes that are of practical interest are not restricted to test items or test-like tasks, although they may include such performances. A person's ability to perform a job well could involve skill/competence on many tasks in many contexts, ranging from routine tasks like filing documents to the potentially complex activities involved in resolving a customer complaint. It would be difficult to include some of these tasks in a standardized test, but they would still be included in the target domain. The match between the target domain associated with an observable attribute and a test designed to assess the observable attribute is an issue that needs to be addressed in validating the test scores as measures of the observable attribute; to simply assume that the test scores provide an adequate indication of ability to do the job is to assume an answer to the basic question at issue in validating test scores as measures of job competence; it "begs" the question. In defining an observable attribute, the goal is to identify the range of observations associated with the attribute of interest, as that attribute label is understood in the context in which it is used.

Tests (Measurement Procedures) for Observable Attributes

Estimating the target score for an observable attribute can be difficult, especially if the observable attribute is defined broadly. For some observable attributes, it may be possible to draw random or representative samples from the target domain and simply generalize the resulting observed score on this sample to an expected score over the target domain. However, this is not generally feasible for broadly defined attributes, and therefore, most tests are developed by standardizing many of the conditions of observation. For example, although the target domain for a job or trade could include a very wide range of performances and contexts, an assessment of job competence might be limited to specific job tasks or to objective questions about job tasks and procedures administered under standardized conditions. As a result, the observations included in the test are generally drawn from a sub-domain of the target domain.

Using the terminology of generalizability theory, the domain from which the observations are actually sampled (more or less randomly or representatively) by a measurement procedure can be referred to as the *universe of generalization* for the procedure, and a person's expected score over the universe of generalization is the person's *universe score* (Brennan, 2001a,b). As a result of standardization, the universe of generalization from which observations are sampled by a measurement procedure would be different from the target domain defining the observable attribute of interest, and it is not legitimate to simply generalize from the observed score to the target score, without additional analysis and/or evidence.

Operationally Defined Attributes

Operationally defined attributes are special cases of observable attributes, in which the universe of generalization is the target domain. Operational definitions (Bridgeman, 1927) are specified in terms of the operations defining a measurement procedure and are intended to eliminate all excess meaning by interpreting the observations in terms of the operations used to generate them. Operationally defined attributes can be defined in terms of the expected value over the universe of generalization for a measurement procedure and constitute a particularly simple kind of observable attribute. They involve no implications beyond the expected score over the universe of generalization defining the measurement procedure. Scores on operationally defined attributes are interpreted in terms of proficiency on the kinds of tasks included in the test and do not go beyond this very limited interpretation.

Operationally defined attributes can be very useful for some purposes. They were originally introduced in physics to provide clearly specified outcomes in describing phenomena and in evaluating theories. In many cases (e.g., within educational and training programs) it is necessary to assess a particular skill in a particular context, and it may be possible to observe performance of the skill in the context of interest. For such performance tests, the universe of generalization for the measurement procedure can be taken to be the target domain for the attribute of interest.

Historically, some uses of operationally defined attributes in the social sciences have been misleading, particularly if the operationally defined attribute is defined in terms of a highly standardized measurement procedure with a narrowly defined universe of generalization, but the label assigned to the attribute suggests a much broader and more ambitious interpretation. For example, to define intelligence operationally as the score on a specific test but interpret it as a measure of overall cognitive functioning is to invite misinterpretation. This kind of systematic ambiguity, in which a narrow interpretation is assumed for purposes of validation, but a much broader and more ambitious interpretation is taken for granted in the operational interpretation and uses of test scores, is a classic example of the begging-the-question fallacy.

Trait Interpretations

As noted earlier, the specification of the target domain generally relies on experience or assumptions about the cognitive processes (often based on introspection) involved in responding to the tasks or stimuli included in the target domain. For *traits*, the observed performances are assumed to reflect some underlying latent attribute that accounts for the observations in the target domain. Trait interpretations are more ambitious than those for observable attributes, in that they add an explanatory component in terms of underlying, latent attributes. A trait is commonly viewed as a characteristic of a person, "which is consistently manifested to some degree when relevant, despite considerable variation in the range of settings and circumstances" (Messick ,1989, p. 15).

Traditional trait attributions tend to be somewhat tautological. We say that students who do well in math classes have high math aptitude, and we say that they have high math aptitude because they do well in math classes. However, most trait attributions do have some empirical implications. As noted by Messick (1989), trait values are generally assumed to be invariant over a fairly wide range of contexts and conditions of observation, and possibly over long periods of time. That is, the target domains are broadly defined, including observations on a range of tasks over a range of contexts and conditions of observation. The trait is taken to be a characteristic of the person and not of the conditions of observation or the context. The observations on a person may vary over contexts, but the trait is assumed to be invariant, and therefore, the variations associated with context or conditions of observation are interpreted as errors of measurement (Brennan, 2001b). In addition, traits are considered unidimensional in the sense that the rank-ordering of individuals is expected to be similar across samples of observations.

However, even if we accept the hypothesis that there really is some latent trait that accounts for the observed performance in the target domain, in most cases, we can't conclude anything beyond the fact that persons with certain levels of the trait tend to perform at certain levels of performance on the observations in the target domain. Any additional assumptions about the meaning of trait values add another layer of interpretation to the basic trait interpretation, and a validation of the trait interpretation, per se, does not justify these additional assumptions. The labels assigned to trait interpretations often implicitly import additional assumptions that need to be evaluated if they are to be included in the test-score interpretation. In some cases, trait measures are developed for a particular application (e.g., to make placement decisions) and the label may suggest that the trait measure is appropriate for the application (Shepard, 1993).

In this vein, an IRT-based estimate of a latent trait for an individual provides a summary of how well the person performs on the items used to define the ability scale (Mislevy, 1996). IRT models are applied to particular sets of test items, and assuming that the model fits the data, the estimated trait values indicate how well the individuals with those trait values tend to do on the items. The trait values provide a very limited trait-based explanation of an individual's performance, but in most cases, no model of performance is provided.

Validating Observable Attributes and Related Attributes

As noted earlier, the interpretations and uses assigned to test scores can be validated by specifying an interpretive argument that lays out the inferences and assumptions inherent in the proposed interpretations and uses, and by evaluating the plausibility of this argument using appropriate evidence. As an illustration of how this might work, I will briefly examine the relationships among interpretive arguments for observable attributes, operationally defined attributes, and traits. These three kinds of attributes have much in common, but they are also quite different in what they assume, and the implications of these differences for validation can be illuminating.

The interpretive argument for observable attributes includes three major inferences. The observed performances are scored and combined into an observed score (a raw score or scaled score of some kind), the observed score is generalized to the universe score, and the universe score is extrapolated to the target score, representing the value of the observable attribute.

The scoring inference uses a scoring rule to transform each person's performance on a sample of assessment tasks into a score. The scoring inference assumes that the rule is appropriate, that it is applied correctly, that it is free of bias, and that any scaling model used in scoring fits the data.

The generalization inference extends the interpretation from the observed score to the universe score for the universe of generalization. The score remains the same, but its interpretation is extended from a summary of performance on the observations actually made to a claim about expected performance over the universe of generalization. The warrant for this inference is a statistical generalization. This warrant depends on two main assumptions: that the sample of observations is representative of the universe of generalization, and that the sample is large enough to control sampling error.

The third inference, extrapolation from the universe score to the target score extends the interpretation from the universe score to the target score. Again, the score remains the same, but the interpretation of the score is extended from the universe of generalization to the target domain. The warrant for this inference is an assumed relationship between universe scores and target scores that generally depends on evidence that the universe of generalization is representative enough of the target domain, or has enough in common with the target domain, that the observed score can be interpreted in terms of the expected value over the target domain.

In order for the interpretive argument for an observable attribute to be plausible, all of the inferences in the argument have to be acceptable. A rejection of any link in the chain is a rejection of the interpretive argument (Crooks et al., 1996), and therefore, the structure of the validity argument depends on the structure of the interpretive argument. That is, the evidence needed for validation is contingent on the interpretation (in terms of the expected value over the target domain for the observable attribute) being proposed. Following an evaluation of the coherence and completeness of the interpretive argument as a whole, the validity argument would include an evaluation of each of the inferences in the interpretive argument.

The first inference, the scoring inference, relies on a scoring rule as the warrant. The scoring rule and procedures are generally developed and evaluated during test development, and most of the evidence for the appropriateness of the rule is generated during test development. For achievement tests, the scoring rule is generally developed by content experts, and the experts who develop the scoring rule provide the justification for the rule (Clauser, 2000). Quality control procedures and monitoring during scoring provide evidence for the appropriateness of the scoring procedures. Empirical data can be used to check on the consistency (e.g., interrater reliability) of scoring, and the statistical procedures used to scale or equate can be evaluated empirically.

The second inference in the interpretive argument for an observable attribute is a generalization from the observed score on the test to the expected value over the universe of generalization. The empirical evidence for the generalization warrant is collected in reliability studies (Feldt & Brennan, 1989; Haertel, 2006) or generalizability studies (Brennan, 2001a), some of which are presumably conducted during test development.

The third inference in the interpretive argument is an extrapolation from the mean over the universe of generalization to the mean over the target domain. The extrapolation inference can be evaluated using conceptual analyses of the overlap between the universe of generalization and target domain, and/or empirical studies of the relationships between observed scores and more direct measures of the target score (Kane, 2006, Sireci, 1998). For example, conceptual analysis might indicate that the test covers mathematical skills that are particularly important in a work setting, and the target domain consists of the corresponding work tasks. The empirical studies could evaluate the relationship between test scores and criterion measures of performance in the target domain (Cronbach, 1971; Messick, 1989).

Note that the validity evidence for an observable attribute depends on the warrants supporting the interpretive argument for the attribute. The evidence needed to validate the interpretation in terms of an observable attribute is the evidence needed to support the three main inferences in this interpretation. We do not need the wide array of possible studies needed to support a construct interpretation (Cronbach & Meehl, 1955; Messick, 1989), because the interpretation does not include a latent trait or construct.

The interpretive arguments for operationally defined attributes are considerably simpler than those for observable attributes. The interpretive arguments for operationally defined attributes involve only two inferences, evaluation and generalization. For an operationally defined attribute, there is no extrapolation to a broader target domain, and therefore, there is no need to collect evidence evaluating extrapolation. Note, however, that this simplification has a cost. The interpretation of the operationally defined attribute, as such, is restricted to expected performance on the kinds of tasks or stimuli included in the test, and any interpretation or use of the scores that requires inferences to other kinds of tasks or stimuli is not legitimate for the operationally defined attribute, as defined here. Any inference to other variables, including performance in non-test contexts would have to be evaluated separately.

Trait Interpretations

Trait interpretations assume that there is some underlying, latent attribute that accounts for the observations in the target domain, and therefore, they add an inference from the target score to the trait value to the interpretive argument. Again, the numerical value of the score remains the same, but the interpretation is extended to a hypothetical latent attribute that accounts for the observed performances.

In addition, trait labels and descriptions can carry implications that go far beyond the kind of description of performance provided by an observable attribute. A label that includes the term, "aptitude," suggests that individuals with high values of the aptitude will be successful in certain educational contexts and that individuals with low values of the aptitude will have difficulty in these contexts. A student with high mathematical aptitude would be expected to do well in appropriate mathematics courses.

Although trait interpretations add an inference from the target score to an underlying "trait" that accounts for the performances in the target domain, they do not generally specify how the trait functions (e.g., in terms of a cognitive model or other explanations of performance). The trait is taken to be a latent attribute of the person, which accounts for (i.e., produces or causes) the observed behavior or performance, but in most cases no explicit causal model is provided. Borsboom et al. (2004) have advocated the adoption of trait interpretations with a strong causal model that indicates how the trait causes the observed performances or behavior as the standard model for validity. I think of trait interpretations as one kind of interpretation that can be validated.

Initial confidence in the appropriateness of the test as a measure of a trait is likely to depend in part on the relationship between the target domain and the conception of the trait. If the target domain reflects our conception of the trait, and the most likely sources of systematic error have been controlled, it could be reasonable to interpret the test scores in terms of the trait. A test that is designed to measure a trait will employ content, task types, procedures, context, and scoring procedures that are consistent with the trait interpretation (Loevinger, 1957: Dwyer et al., 2003). To the extent that the assumptions inherent in the trait interpretation are supported, the plausibility of the trait interpretation increases. To the extent that these assumptions are violated, the trait interpretation is less plausible.

If the trait is assumed invariant over some range of contexts, occasions, and conditions of observations, data supporting these invariance assumptions would support the interpretation, and contrary results would undermine it. On the other hand, if the attribute values are expected to change over contexts, data that is consistent with these expectations would tend to support the interpretation, and invariance would count against the interpretation.

The addition of a trait interpretation to a basic observable attribute increases the validation requirements substantially. In particular, because the latent trait that accounts for the observations is, by definition, not directly observable, it is necessary to investigate its role using a variety of indirect methods (Cronbach, 1971; Messick, 1989). As originally suggested by Cronbach and Meehl (1955), the validation of trait interpretations is likely to require a substantial program of research.

THE LIMITATIONS OF CONTENT-BASED
VALIDITY EVIDENCE

Content-related validity evidence has been criticized for being subjective and for having a confirmatory bias because the judgments about the appropriateness and representativeness of test content is usually made by the test developers, who have a natural tendency to find the content appropriate. These criticisms are accurate, but I think that they have been overstated. Some inferences in interpretive arguments (e.g., scoring) depend mainly on judgment, and many inferences (generalization, extrapolation, prediction) depend in part, on judgment. For example, all criterion-related validity studies require a criterion, which is usually justified on the basis of content-related evidence. Furthermore, given that content-based evidence is collected during the development phase, in which tests and procedures are being developed, it is not particularly surprising or objectionable that it has a confirmationist tendency.

A more serious objection to content-based validation strategies arises from their tendency to adopt a relatively simple content-based interpretation for purposes of validation, but to deploy a more ambitious interpretation in practice. In particular, validity arguments based mainly on content-based evidence tend to beg questions about extrapolation to target domains and about implicit trait interpretations. Messick (1989) suggested that content-related evidence had value in evaluating, "the domain relevance and representativeness of the test instrument" (p. 17), but he saw its role in validation as quite limited, because it doesn't provide direct evidence for the "inferences to be made from test scores" (p. 17). That is, content-based validity evidence can provide an adequate analysis of validity for observable attributes or operationally defined attributes, but is not adequate for trait measures or theoretical constructs, and is not generally adequate to justify particular test uses (Sireci, 1998).

Content-related validity evidence can be used to evaluate the relevance of test content and format, scoring rules and procedures. However, evaluations of test content and procedures may not provide strong support for extrapolation to target domains, and a content-based strategy is particularly problematic when it is used to justify interpretations that go beyond basic observable attributes (e.g., claims about traits, cognitive processes, or theoretical constructs). As Cronbach (1971) pointed out inferences about underlying traits or internal processes rely on hypotheses that require empirical studies for their evaluation while content-related validity studies focus on "the operational, externally observable side of testing" (p.452). That is, content-related validity evidence is essential for almost all interpretations, but it is, in itself, not enough for most interpretations, and particularly for those and make strong claims about explanations of performance.

CONCLUDING REMARKS

Validating proposed interpretations and uses is a difficult task, but it is not one that can be shirked, without potentially serious consequences. I don't know of anyone who has suggested that we draw inferences from test scores without good reason for believing that the inferences are justified, and I don't know of anyone who advocates using test scores to make high-stakes decisions without an evaluation of whether the decisions will generally lead to positive outcomes. However, it is possible to accept the obligation to investigate such assumptions, but to choose to not include these investigations under the heading of validity (Borsboom, 2006; Borsboom et al., 2004; Lissitz & Samuelson, 2007; Popham, 1997), but this approach runs counter to a long tradition in educational and psychological measurement, and without a strong commitment to educate all stakeholders about the changes, would invite confusion. Worse, it is likely to lead to some serious examples of the begging-the-question fallacy.

The kinds of evidence required for validation are contingent on the claims inherent in the interpretations and uses. If the interpretation is very limited, as it is for operationally defined attributes and for observable attributes, the requirements for validation are modest. If the claims are more ambitious, as they are for traits and constructs, more evidence and more kinds of evidence are required. In particular, if trait labels or descriptions suggest that test scores will be related to some other variables, an evaluation of the proposed interpretation would call for an examination of these claims. Similarly, if the trait label or description suggests that the test scores would be an appropriate basis for making certain decisions, these claims merit evaluation (Shepard, 1993).

Validating a broadly defined interpretation and a range of test-score uses can involve a substantial research effort, but this effort will generally be disturbed over a number of participants. Test developers necessarily play a large role in developing and evaluating the basic interpretations of test scores (Loevinger, 1957). The users of test scores have the primary responsibility for evaluating the decision that they adopt. For measures of constructs that are central to some area of study, all of the participants in that area play a role in defining, developing, and evaluating these constructs.

The professional organizations involve in educational and psychological measurement have recognized a need for standards for the use of measurement procedures and have adopted the *Standards* (1999) for this purpose. In developing these standards, these organizations have put the requirements for the evaluation of proposed interpretations and uses under the heading of validity. We can change that and put some or all of these issues under some other heading (Borsboom, 2006; Borsboom et al., 2004; Lissitz & Samuelson, 2007), but if we do so, we will have to reformulate much of the standard advice provided to test developers and users.

REFERENCES

American Educational Research Association, American Psychological Association, & National Council on Measurement in Education (1999). *Standards for educational and psychological testing.* Washington, DC: American Psychological Association.

Borsboom, D. (2006). The attack of the psychometricians. *Psychometrika, 71*(3), 425–440.

Borsboom, D., Mellenbergh, G. J., & van Heerden, J. (2004). The concept of validity. *Psychological Review, 111,* 1061–1071.

Brennan, R. (2001a). *Generalizability theory.* New York: Springer-Verlag.

Brennan, R. (2001b). An essay on the history and future of reliability from the perspective of replications. *Journal of Educational Measurement, 38*(4), 285–317.

Bridgeman, P. (1927). *The logic of modern physics.* New York: Macmillan.

Chapelle, C., Enright, M., & Jamieson, J. (2008). *Building a validity argument for the test of English as a foreign language.* New York: Routledge.

Clauser, B. (2000). Recurrent issues and recent advances in scoring performance assessments. *Applied Psychological Measurement, 24,* 310–324.

Cronbach, L. J. (1971). Test validation. In R. L. Thorndike (Ed.), *Educational measurement* (2nd ed., pp. 443–507). Washington, DC: American Council on Education.

Cronbach, L. J., & Meehl, P. E. (1955). Construct validity in psychological tests. *Psychological Bulletin, 52*, 281–302.

Crooks, T. J. (1988). The impact of classroom evaluation practices on students. *Review of Educational Research, 58*, 438–481.

Crooks, T., Kane, M., & Cohen, A. (1996). Threats to the valid use of assessments. *Assessment in Education, 3*, 265–285.

Cureton, E. E. (1951). Validity. In E. F. Lindquist (Ed.), *Educational measurement.* Washington, DC: American Council on Education.

Dwyer, C. A., Gallagher, A., Levin, J., & Morley, M. E. (2003). *What is quantitative reasoning? Defining the construct for assessment purposes.* Research Report 03-30. Princeton, NJ: Educational Testing Service.

Embretson, S. (1983). Construct validity: Construct representation versus nomothetic span. *Psychological Bulletin, 93*, 179–197.

Feldt, L. S. & Brennan, R. L. (1989). Reliability. In R. L. Linn (Ed.), *Educational measurement* (3rd ed., pp. 105-146). New York: American Council on Education and Macmillan Publishing Company.

Guion, R. M. (1980). On trinitarian conceptions of validity. *Professional Psychology, 11*, 385–398.

Gulliksen, H. (1950). *Theory of mental tests.* New York: Wiley.

Haertel, E. (2006). Reliability. In R. Brennan (Ed.), Educational measurement (4th ed., pp. 65–110), Westport, CT: American Council on Education and Praeger.

Kane, M. (2001). Current concerns in validity theory. *Journal of Educational Measurement, 38*, 319–342.

Kane, M. (2004). Certification testing as an illustration of argument-based approach validation. *Measurement: Interdisciplinary Research and Perspectives, 2*(3), 135–170.

Kane, M. (2006). Validation. In R. Brennan (Ed.), Educational measurement (4th ed., pp. 17–64). Westport, CT: American Council on Education and Praeger.

Lissitz, R. W., & Samuelsen, K. (2007). A suggested change in terminology and emphasis regarding validity and education. *Educational Researcher, 36*, 437–448.

Loevinger, J. (1957). Objective tests as instruments of psychological theory. *Psychological Reports, Monograph Supplement, 3*, 635–694.

Messick, S. (1989). Validity. In R. L. Linn (Ed.), *Educational measurement* (3rd ed., pp. 13–103). New York: American Council on Education/Macmillan.

Messick, S. (1994). The interplay of evidence and consequences in the validation of performance assessments. *Educational Researcher, 23*(2), 13–23.

Mislevy, R. (1996). Test theory reconceived. *Journal of Educational Measurement, 33*, 379–416.

Mislevy, R. (2008, October 9–10). *Validity from the perspective of model-based reasoning.* Paper presented at the conference on the concept of validity at the University of Maryland, College Park, MD.

Mislevy, R., Steinberg, L., & Almond, R. (2003). On the structure of educational assessments. *Measurement: Interdisciplinary Research and Perspectives, 1,* 3–62.

Popham, W. J. (1997) Consequential validity: Right concern—wrong concept. *Educational Measurement: Issues and Practice, 16*(2), 9–13.

Shepard, L. A. (1993). Evaluating test validity. In L. Darling-Hammond (Ed.), *Review of research in education* (Vol. 19, pp. 405–450). Washington, DC: American Educational Research Association.

Sireci, S. (1998). The construct of content validity. *Social Indicators Research, 45,* 83–117.

Sireci, S. (2008, October 9-10). *Packing and unpacking sources of validity evidence: History repeats itself again.* Paper presented at the conference on the concept of at the University of Maryland, College Park, MD.

Toulmin, S. E. (1958). *The uses of argument.* Cambridge: Cambridge University Press.

CHAPTER 4

VALIDITY AS CONTEXTUALIZED AND PRAGMATIC EXPLANATION, AND ITS IMPLICATIONS FOR VALIDATION PRACTICE

Bruno D. Zumbo

ABSTRACT

This chapter has two aims: provide an overview of what I consider to be the concept of validity and then discuss its implications for the process of validation. I articulate an explanation focused view of validity that centers on a contextualized and pragmatic view of explanation—in essence, a contextualized and pragmatic view of validity. In the closing section of the chapter I describe the methodological implications of this view in terms of not assuming homogeneity of populations (from the Draper-Lindley-de Finetti framework) and allowing for multilevel construct validation, as well as the overlap between test validity and program evaluation.

The Concept of Validity, pages 65–82

We are as sailors who are forced to rebuild their ship on the open sea, without ever being able to start fresh from the bottom up. Wherever a beam is taken away, immediately a new one must take its place, and while this is done, the rest of the ship is used as support. In this way, the ship may be completely rebuilt like new with the help of the old beams and driftwood—but only through gradual rebuilding. Otto Neurath (1921, pp. 75–76)

The philosopher Neurath's now famous nautical image in the quotation above is an important place to begin our voyage. There has been much discussion in the philosophy of science literature about the interpretations and implications of Neurath's analogy of scientific verification as the construction of a ship which is already at sea, but it certainly does highlight for us that over the nearly century of measurement work we, as a discipline, have built, rebuilt, re-visioned and otherwise restored and restocked the good ship *Validity* at sea. In this light, *The Maryland Validity Conference*, as it has now come to be called among many with whom I collaborate and correspond, and the proceedings for which this chapter is written, is a high mark in the nearly century-old history of *Validity*'s journey.

I have also chosen to open with Neurath's (1921) nautical quotation because I believe its message of ongoing building and rebuilding while at sea is one of the defining (and most complexifying) features of not just the concept of validity but of measurement validation. In short, it has been long recognized that activities of measurement validation are inextricably tied to theory building and theory testing so that one needs measures to help develop and test theory, but one cannot wait for the establishment of validity before one can get to the business of developing and testing theories. Likewise, almost by definition, measurement and testing are used ultimately for means such as the assessment of individuals for the ultimate aim of intervention or feedback, for decision-making, or for research and policy purposes. It is rare that anyone measures for the sheer delight one experiences from the act itself. Instead, all measurement is, in essence, something you do so that you can use the outcomes, and hence one cannot wait for validation to be completed before one gets to the matter of the use of the test and measurement outcomes. In short, the measurement enterprise is as close to Neurath's ship as one can imagine. That is, at the heart of validity and of validation is the matter of scientifically constructing, verifying, and appraising test score meaning as an on-the-fly activity that is conducted while the system is in operation.

I will consider the concept of "validity" for any kind of test or measure in social, behavioral, educational or health research, testing, or assessment settings. I believe that there is much more in common, than unique, among the various uses of tests and measures, that there is much to be gained by exploring this commonality, and that I wish to be a countervailing force to the creation of the various new disciplinary measurement sub-fields which act as silos. This general objective has me focusing on a meta-theory of validity rather than a tailored context for only, for example, cognitive, educational, language, health, policy, or behavioral measures. My aim is to think broadly so as to embrace and show the relations among many of the prominent views of validity, with an eye toward an articulation of a novel framework.

With this broad objective in mind, the terms "item" and "task" will be used interchangeably. Furthermore, the terms "test," "measure," "scale," and "assessment" will be used interchangeably, even though "tests" are, in common language, used to imply some educational achievement or knowledge test with correct and incorrect responses or partial credit scoring, and "assessment" typically implies some decisions, actions, or recommendations from the test and measurement results and implies a more integrative process involving multiple sources of information. Finally, in the parlance of day-to-day social and behavioral researchers, clinicians, and policy specialists, tests may be referred to as valid or invalid, but it is widely recognized that such references are, at best, a shorthand for a more complex statement about the validity of inferences made about test scores with a particular sample in a particular context and, more often, are inappropriate and potentially misleading.

The purpose of this chapter is to provide an overview of what I consider to be the concept of validity and then discuss its implications for the process of validation. Due to space limitations relative to the breadth and scope of the task at hand, for some issues I will provide details whereas for others more general integrative remarks.

AN EXPLANATORY-FOCUSED VIEW OF VALIDITY

To continue Neurath's analogy, when one is at sea one always keeps an eye on where one is going, and from where one has come. Even a cursory glance of the research literature (see, e.g., Hubley & Zumbo, 1996; Kane, 2006; Zumbo & Rupp, 2004; Zumbo, 1998) will reveal that validity theory and practices have changed over the last century. In brief, the early- to mid-1900s were dominated by the criterion-based model of validity, with some focus on content-based validity models (Sireci, 1998). This view is perhaps best seen in Anastasi's (1950) characterization in her highly influential paper in the leading measurement journal at the time: "It is only as a measure of a specifically defined criterion that a test can be objectively validated at all.... To claim that a test measures anything over and above its criterion is pure speculation" (Anastasi, 1950, p. 67).

The early 1950s saw the introduction of, and move toward, the construct model with its emphasis on construct validity with a seminal piece by Cronbach and Meehl (1955). Likewise, in another seminal paper, Loevinger

(1957) highlighted the important point that every test underrepresents its construct to some degree and contains sources of irrelevant variance, if for no other reason than it is a test and not a criterion performance. Clearly then, the early- to mid-1900s in the history of validity reflected Psychology's focus on observed behavior and theories of learning, as well as its relatively recent break from psychoanalytic and introspective methods. In the 1960s, the precursors to what we now call the cognitive revolution of the 1970s could be clearly seen. The period post Cronbach and Meehl, mostly the 1970s to the present, saw the construct validity model take root and saw the measurement community delve into a moral and consequential foundation to validity and testing by expanding to include the consequences of test use and interpretation (Messick, 1975, 1980, 1988, 1989, 1995, 1998).

It is worth noting that a subtle, but important, shift occurred with Cronbach and Meehl's (1955) publication wherein the dominant view of measures changed from being "predictive devices" to being "signs." Not all psychological phenomenon allow for a criterion; that is, some psychological phenomenon are abstract and do not necessarily have a "prediction." Suddenly, by the 1950s to early 1960s, it was safe and respectable, again, to talk in the language of unobservables (e.g., constructs) and hence the nature of tests and measures changed implicitly. In light of this, I believe that the operationalism that rests at the core of the predictive model (prior to the 1950s) was de-emphasized by Cronbach and Meehl in favor of the nomological network as supporting meaningfulness—i.e., the meaningfulness of the scores produced by tests/measures as reflective of an unobserved phenomenon, the construct. It is important to note that validity continues to be deeply rooted in the notion of "individual differences" or disposition theory, as dispositional theory has evolved over the decades.

Although it has been controversial, one of the current themes in validity theory is that construct validity is the totality of validity theory and that its demonstration is comprehensive, integrative, and evidence-based. What becomes evident is that the meaning of "construct validity" itself has changed over the years and is being used in a variety of ways in the current literature. Arguably in its most common current use, construct validity refers to the degree to which inferences can be made legitimately from the observed scores to the theoretical constructs about which these observations are supposed to contain information. In short, construct validity involves generalizing from our behavioral or social observations to the *conceptualization* of our behavioral or social observations in the form of the construct. The practice of validation aims to ascertain the extent to which an interpretation of a test is *conceptually* and *empirically* warranted and should be aimed at making explicit any ethical and social values that overtly or inadvertently influence that process (Messick, 1995).

The term "construct validity" has therefore evolved to be shorthand for the expression "an articulated argument in support of the inferences made from scores." I will argue later in this section that construct validity has, from its introduction, been focused on providing an explanation for test scores; that is, the argument in support of the inferences is a form of an explanation. As we all know, there are strong and weak forms of construct validity (Kane, 2001). The weak form is characterized by any correlation of the test score with another variable being welcomed as evidence for another "validity" of the test. That is, in the weak form, a test has as many "validities" and potential uses as it has correlations with other criterion (or convergent) variables. In contrast to the weak form of construct validity, the strong form is based on a well-articulated theory and well-planned empirical tests of that theory. In short, the strong form is theory-driven whereas the weak form implies that a correlation with some criterion (or convergent measure) is sufficient evidence to use the test as a measure of that criterion.

In my view (e.g., Zumbo, 2005, 2007a), the strong form of construct validity should provide an *explanation* for the test scores, in the sense of the theory having explanatory power for the observed variation in test scores. I share the view with other validity theorists that validity is a matter of inference and the weighing of evidence; however, in my view, explanatory considerations guide our inferences. Explanation acts as a regulative ideal; validity is the explanation for the test score variation, and validation is the process of developing and testing the explanation.

In essence, I see validation as a higher order integrative cognitive process involving every day (and highly technically evolved) notions like concept formation and the detection, identification, and generalization of regularities in data whether they are numerical or textual. From this, after a balance of possible competing views and contrastive data, comes understanding and explanation. What I am suggesting is a more technical and more data-driven elaboration of what we do on a day to day basis in an open (scientific) society; we are constantly asking why the things are the way we find them to be, answer our own questions by constructing explanatory stories, and thus come to believe some of these stories based on how good are the explanations they provide. This is, in its essence, a form of inference to the best explanation.

Figure 4.1 depicts the four core elements of the integrative cognitive judgment of validity and the process of validation: validity, psychometrics, social consequences, and matters of utility—all of which are tightly packed in the figure close to each other and hence influence, and shape, each other. We can see that validity is separate from utility, social consequences, and the psychometrics, but validity is shaped by these. Furthermore, the inferences are justified by the psychometric, social consequences, and utility but validity is something more because it requires the explanation.

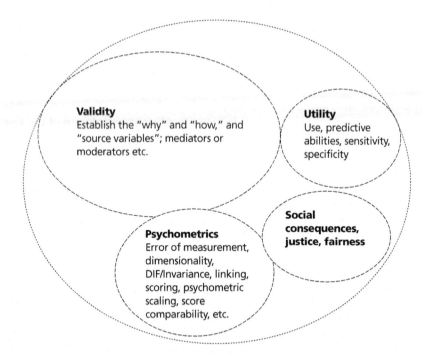

Figure 4.1 A depiction of the integrative cognitive judgment in the contextualized and pragmatic explanation view of validity and validation.

In short, Figure 4.1 shows that explanation is the defining feature of validity and hence supports the inferences we make from test scores. In terms of the process of validation, we can see in Figure 4.1 that the process of validation is distinct but is, itself, shaped by the concept of validity. The process of validation involves consideration of the statistical methods, as well as the psychological and more qualitative methods of psychometrics, to establish and support the inference to the explanation—i.e., validity itself; so that validity is the explanation, whereas the process of validation involves the myriad methods of psychometrics to establish and support that explanation. The process of validation also includes the utility and evidence from test use such as sensitivity and specificity of the decisions (e.g., pass/fail, presence/absence of disease) made from test scores and predictive capacity (e.g., predictive regression equations), as well as the fourth element of social consequences. This latter element in the cognitive process depicted in Figure 4.1 has me clearly aligned with Messick (e.g., Messick, 1998) in that empirical consequences of test use and interpretation constitutes validity evidence in the validation process.

The basic idea underlying my explanatory approach is that, if one could understand why an individual responded a certain way to an item or scored a particular value on a scale, then that would go a long way toward bridging the inferential gap between test scores (or even latent variable scores) and constructs. According to this view, validity per se, is not established until one has an explanatory model of the variation in item responses and/or scale scores and the variables mediating, moderating, and otherwise affecting the response outcome. This is a tall hurdle indeed. However, I believe that the spirit of Cronbach and Meehl's (1955) work was to require explanation in a strong form of construct validity. Overlooking the importance of explanation in validity we have, as a discipline, focused overly heavily on the validation process and as a result we have lost our way. This is not to suggest that the activities of the process of validation, such as correlations with a criterion or a convergent measure, dimensionality assessment, item response modeling, or differential item or test functioning, are irrelevant or should be stopped. Quite to the contrary, the activities of the process of validation must serve the definition of validity. My aim is to refocus our attention on why we are conducting all of these psychometric analyses: that is, to support our claim of the validity of our inferences from a given measure. For example, as Zumbo (2007b) highlighted conducting test and item bias is not just about protecting a test developer or test user against lawsuits; it is also a statistical methodology that ferrets out invalidity that distorts the meaning of test results for some groups of examinees and thus establishes the inferential limits of the test. One of the limitations of traditional quantitative test validation practices (e.g., factor-analytic methods, validity coefficients, and multitrait-multimethod approaches) is that they are descriptive rather than explanatory. The aim of my explanatory approach is to lay the groundwork to expand the evidential basis for test validation by providing a richer explanation of the processes of responding to tests and variation in tests or items scores and hence promoting a richer psychometric theory-building.

Rereading Foundational Papers on Validity from the Explanatory-Focused View

Placing explanation as the driving element of validity is an interesting meta-theoretical place from which to reread some classic papers in validity with an eye to further explicating my view of validity as contextualized and pragmatic explanation.

From my point of view, Cronbach and Meehl (1955) were also focused on providing explanation; however, reflecting the individual differences psychological focus of the time period, the construct and the nomological network was the explanation. Not only were Cronbach and Meehl focusing on explanation but, as suggested by Cronbach himself, they were presenting a variant on the then relatively recently introduced "covering law model," also called the deductive-nomological (DN), approach to explanation. It is should be noted that Cronbach and Meehl did not wholly adopt a strict DN form of explanation; however, its DN essence and purpose are very clear. Cronbach (1971, p. 481) acknowledged the influences of the (logical positivist) DN approach and stated that, in particular, Hempel's work in the 1950s and 1960s, was the clearest description of the philosophical bases of construct validation, as articulated in Cronbach and Meehl. Cronbach (1971, p. 481) went on to state that Ernst Nagel's characterization of theoretical entities, what Cronbach and Meehl called 'constructs', as instrumental tools (rather than descriptive or realist) is essentially the position taken by Cronbach and Meehl in advocating construct validation of tests.

From its earliest form, the DN approach (Hempel & Oppenheim, 1948) is an idea that has lingered from the logical positivist tradition and has been shown to be problematic—see for example, Suppe (1977) as well as work by Scriven (1962), and many others. Borsboom et al. (2004) provided an excellent description of this point. The nomological network was essential to Cronbach and Meehl's (1955) view and provided a variation on the so-called covering laws needed for the DN approach to be useful.

It is noteworthy that the "hypothetical construct" position that is at the root of Cronbach and Meehl (1955) importantly also offers an alternative to operational definitions, or other such correspondence rules. Therefore, Cronbach and Meehl's nomological network can be thought of as a sidestep around operational definitions in the so-called "problem of theoretical terms" in philosophy. In essence, however, a significant weakness of Cronbach and Meehl's DN variant is that the common use of nomological networks in empirical social sciences is more in line with a concept-map than a system of laws relating the theoretical terms to each other and to observations. So, even if one were to accept Cronbach and Meehl's variant on the covering law view of explanation, the "nomological networks" of typical social science do not suffice to meet the necessary conditions for the explanation.

Furthermore, and most importantly from my point of view, the fundamental problem with Cronbach and Meehl's nomological network approach is that it attempts, like its DN forefather, to characterize explanation as context free. From my own perspective, the core of meaning-making of empirical data, and hence measurement validity, is the explanation of the observed score variation. My view is clearly in line with the essence of Cronbach and Meehl (1955), but I focus on the importance that the context provides in the explanation.

As one might imagine, in philosophy there have been competing ideas about what is and qualifies as an explanation. As an alternative to covering law views, explanation has also been associated with causation; an explanation is a description of the various causes of the phenomenon, hence to explain is to give information about the causal history that led to the phenomenon. Salmon (1984, 1990, 1998) did a wonderful job of discussing and describing various views of scientific explanation. I will not attempt to go into the details of the various views, but suffice it to say that alternatives have been offered to the DN approach.

In this context of causation as explanation, it is important to acknowledge the seminal paper by Borsboom, Mellenbergh, and Van Heerden (2004). Although, in its core concepts, Borsboom and his colleagues' views share a lot in common with the view of validity I have espoused, I differ from their view on several important philosophical and methodological features. For example, Borsboom and his colleagues argue that a test is valid for measuring an attribute if, and only if, the attribute exists and variations in the attribute causally produce variations in the outcomes of the measurement procedure. Philosophically, this is, as the authors themselves acknowledge, a very tidy and simple idea that has a currency among researchers because it may well be implicit in the thinking of many practicing researchers. From my explanatory-focused view, relying on causality is natural and plausible and provides a clear distinction between understanding why a phenomenon occurs and merely knowing that it does—given that it is possible to know that a phenomenon occurs without knowing what caused it. Moreover, their view draws this distinction in a way that makes understanding the variation in observed item and test scores, and hence validity, unmysterious and objective. Validity is not some sort of super-knowledge of the phenomenon one wishes to measure, such as that embodied in the meta-theoretical views of Messick, Cronbach and Meehl, and myself, but simply more knowledge: knowledge of causes.

I am not fond of the exclusive reliance on "causal" models of explanation of the sort that Borsboom and his colleagues suggest. Their causal notions give us a restricted view of measurement because of the well-known objections to the causal model of explanation—briefly, that we do not have a fully adequate analysis of causation, there are non-causal explanations, that it is too weak or permissive, and that it undermines our explanatory practices. Also, like the covering law approaches, causal notions of explanation are typically aimed at context free explanations, which I do not accept as adequate for measurement purposes.

In addition to covering laws and causal views of explanation, there is a third broadly defined view of explanation that is often called the pragmatic approach and whose major proponents are, for example, Scriven and van Fraassen. According to Scriven (1962), in terms of context, all questions (and particularly all "why" questions) make presuppositions about what is known, and it is these presuppositions that supply the context of the answer. Therefore, an explanation is a body of information that implies that the phenomenon is more likely than its alternatives, where the information is of the sort deemed "relevant" in that context, and the class of alternatives to the phenomenon are also fixed by the context. This approach highlights the importance of context to explanation.

Both Scriven and van Fraasen (1980) agree that scientific explanations are just specific kinds of explanations. Scriven offers criteria for a good explanation: they must be accurate/correct (i.e., are true), complete/adequate (e.g., give the appropriate causal connection), and relevant/appropriate/proper (i.e., cite the appropriate context). Van Fraasen's explanatory view makes explanation out to be what I refer to above, surrounding my description of Figure 4.1, as the overall cognitive evaluation, and what Scriven might refer to as unified communication. I also agree with Scriven and van Fraasen that scientific explanations (in our case, explanations as measurement validity) are just explanations wherein context is just as important in the science of measurement as it is in ordinary, day-to-day situations. As has been shown by several counterexamples in the philosophical literature (e.g., Scriven's explanation of the stain in a carpet is nothing more than "I knocked over the ink bottle," or van Fraasen's tower shadow), explanation is not merely a matter of logic, and nor, by extension, can it be simply a matter of causal explanation, but that it is a matter of pragmatics. Pragmatics refers to the aspects of language that reflect the practical circumstances in which we put it to use and, hence, the conditions or contexts that make some statements appropriate or meaningful.

These distinctions among the various views of explanation may appear subtle, but are important differences that play themselves out in both what is considered validity and the process of validation wherein certain methods, approaches and strategies are more naturally affiliated to one view than the other. For example, Cronbach and Meehl (1955) with their construct as covering law focus are closely aligned to multitrait-multimethod whereas Borsboom and colleagues are well suited with cognitive approaches, whereas I emphasize "why" questions and am more ecological, sociological and contextual in orientation. Also, because I do not rely so heavily on "constructs" and "dispositions" but also focus on situational and contextual elements, my approach more easily and naturally focuses on the multi-level notions in the next section of this chapter.

Therefore, the strength of Cronbach and Meehl's (1955) work is that they conceptualized validity as explanation rather than the prediction/correlation approach that dominated the first half of the 1900s. This is important because, in its essence, statistical prediction on its own does not necessarily impart understanding. Our ability to give explanations precedes any scientific knowledge. However, over and above the concern for the "nomological network" notion as really often being seen as simply a concept map, the major limitation of Cronbach and Meehl's contribution is that, like its covering model explanatory parents, it treats explanations as context free. In so doing, it makes validity just about impossible to use because all measurement and testing are context bound. Instead, in the model I describe above in Figure 4.1, I wish to offer a context-bound sense of explanation and, hence, a context-bound view of validity.

As a side note, going back to the opening quotation from Neurath, one may ask: When can we start using a measure? Or do we need to establish the "validity" (i.e., the explanation for the test and item response variation) before we can use the measure to make inferences and research conclusions? The answer to this question is the same as the one for all the approaches to validity as explanation (e.g., it applies also to Cronbach and Meehl); that is, explanation is a regulative ideal therefore one can start (cautiously) using the measure as one gains a deeper understanding and explanation, but that the stakes for the measurement use should guide this judgment. What I am suggesting is that psycho-social, policy, and health studies research use the framework I describe surrounding Figure 4.1 to take on a robust and integrative research agenda in which the bounds and limitations of the inferences we can make from scores becomes a core task of the research agenda with an aim to providing a contextualized and pragmatic explanation of the test and/or item score variation.

IMPLICATIONS OF THE VALIDITY AS CONTEXTUALIZED AND PRAGMATIC EXPLANATION FOR VALIDATION PRACTICE

It is not sufficient, I believe, to just offer a new conceptualization of validity. Rather, one needs to explore the implications for day-to-day practice. In this final section, I aim to draw out the implications of my view of validity for the processes of validation. Note that my view of validity as contextualized and pragmatic explanation allows for all the methods currently used in validation research and also brings to the forefront, and out of the shadows, several interesting validation approaches that I wish to highlight. Due to space limitations, I will only be able to say a few words about each of these validation approaches, the Draper-Lindley-de Finetti framework and how it shines a light on modeling sample heterogeneity, a multi-level view of measurement, and the overlap between program evaluation and validation. See Zumbo (2007a) for a description of other statistical methods appropriate for the explanatory view of validation, and particularly the Pratt indices and variable ordering as tools in explanatory statistical modeling.

The Draper-Lindley-de Finetti Framework

As Sawatzky, Ratner, Johnson, Kopec, and Zumbo (in press) state, the Draper-Lindley-de Finetti (DLD) framework of measurement validity (Zumbo 2007a) provides a useful overview of the assumptions that must be tested to validate the use of a psychometric tool. According to Zumbo's DLD framework, measurement problems and sampling problems must both be examined when assessing measurement validity. Measurement problems include those problems pertaining to the exchangeability of the observed and unobserved items (the items you have versus the items you wish you had) whereas sampling problems refer to the degree to which the measurement structure is appropriate for all respondents (i.e., equivalent across different sampling units in the target population). As Sawatzky et al. go on to note, although measurement problems can be examined by testing the extent to which a particular factor analysis or IRT solution fits the data of a sample as a whole, an examination of sampling problems involves determining the extent to which the factor analysis or IRT solution is appropriate for all respondents. Zumbo (2007a) referred to this as "the exchangeability of sampled and unsampled units (i.e., respondents) in the target population" (p. 59). This aspect of measurement validation relates to the degree to which individuals interpret and respond to items in a consistent and comparable manner. The exchangeability of sampling units is a necessary condition for the generalizability of inferences made about the measurement structure of a particular instrument.

The DLD framework brings the matter of sample homogeneity to the forefront. This is an important issue for all model-based measurement (and particularly item response theory). In essence DLD highlights that model driven applications, like item response theory and, perhaps, computer adaptive testing, require that the sample is homogeneous with respect to the measurement model. Therefore, for model-based measurement practices, the model assumptions (such as unidimensionality and sample homogeneity) are part of the validity concerns.

As Zumbo (2007a) highlighted, contemporary measurement theory based on latent variable models hold central the notion of invariance. Invariance implies that the model fit in all corners of the data (see Rupp & Zumbo, 2003, 2004, 2006). Invariance, therefore, is a guiding principle of, and an ideal for, much of contemporary model-based measurement theory. Invariance, in essence, carries with it the covering law, logical positivist, notion of context free measurement. However, from my contextualized and pragmatic view of validity, the aim should be to always take the context into account in measurement rather than to wash it away.

From a statistical point of view, this implies, then, that psychometric modeling should explore and allow for latent class and mixture models. My view of validity can be seen as a foundation and focus for Muthen's program of research which since at least the mid 1980s has been developing a class of methods to model population heterogeneity. Muthen and his colleagues have created statistical theory and software (MPlus) to address the "why" question of validity highlighted in the description surrounding Figure 4.1, above (e.g., Muthen, 1985, 1988, 1989; Muthen & Lehman, 1985; Muthen, Kao, & Burstein, 1991). This class of approaches, which exploits, among other things, the multiple-indicators multiple causes structural equation model, and how this model relates to item response theory. As Zumbo (2007b) noted, one way of conceptualizing Muthen's work is that it is a merging of modeling item responses via contingency tables and/or regression models and item response theory frameworks. An essential feature of the Muthen approach, and one that is central to my view of validity, is that Muthen's approach explicitly and relatively easily allows the validity researcher to focus on sociological, structural community and contextual variables as explanatory sources of measurement invalidity (Zumbo & Gelin, 2005). Sawatzky, Ratner, Johnson, Kopec, and Zumbo (in press) provide a detailed example of using factor mixture models in validiation research from an explanatory point of view. In short, in my view of validity, measurement is not just the purview of psychology but must expand its view to be, as a start, more sociological and ecological in its orientation.

Multi-Level View of Measurement

As Zumbo and Forer (in press) noted, there are a growing number of testing and assessment programs in which one gathers individual person measures but, by design, makes inferences or decisions not about individual people but rather for an aggregate, such as a school district, neighborhood, or state. We called such measurement practices "multilevel measurement." In striking contrast to multilevel measurement, however, our widely-used measurement and testing models (including our psychometric and validation models) are, by historical precedent, geared to individual differences, as are our constructs and construct validation work.

The National Assessment of Educational Progress (NAEP) is an example of a multi-level measurement system. Educational testing and assessment in the domains of science and mathematics, for example, are focused on assessment *of* learning (i.e., summative) or even assessment *for* learning (i.e., formative) but, in both cases, the student's individual learning or knowledge is the focus. Contrary to our conventional individual differences use of such tests, however, NAEP is neither designed for, nor provides any, feedback to individual students or examinees, nor to paraprofessionals to provide feedback or planning for individual students. That is, NAEP is not used for individual decision-making but rather is used to inform policy and perhaps assess the impact of community-scale interventions and changes in the educational and social support system.

Instead of individual differences constructs, NAEP involves what Zumbo and Forer (in press) called "multilevel constructs" that have emerged at the confluence of multilevel thinking (and ecological perspectives) with psychology, health, and social policy. A multilevel construct can be defined as a phenomenon that is potentially meaningful both at the level of individuals and at one or more levels of aggregation, but the construct is interpreted and used only at the aggregate level. While all constructs reside in at least one level, an organizational setting like formal education is inherently multilevel, given the natural nesting of students within classes within schools within school districts. Having to deal with multilevel issues should be assumed when studying phenomena in these multilevel settings (e.g., Klein, Dansereau, & Hall, 1994; Morgeson & Hofmann, 1999).

The essential feature is that these multilevel measures are not conventional educational achievement or psychological measures because they have been designed to only provide aggregate level information, such as tracking how a state is performing on a mathematics or science assessment. This aggregate level information is in contrast to the typical use of educational and psychological measures that are used for assessment of individual differences. This essential feature is easily accommodated in my view of validity as contextualized and pragmatic explanation.

From my explanation focused point of view, the central messages and their implications, are that multilevel constructs are different in purpose and scope than individual differences constructs, although they still carry high stakes for the individual test taker. Likewise, multilevel constructs necessitate multilevel measures. Implied in my view is that solely applying traditional individual differences psychometric methods (e.g., correlation with another math score at the child level) and/or most cognitive assessment approaches is insufficient evidence for the support of multilevel validation inferences. In fact, as Zumbo and Forer (in press) noted, these individual differences methods are susceptible to cross-level inferential fallacies such as the ecological fallacy or atomistic fallacy.

Multilevel measurement and testing arise when one has a multilevel construct; an individual level measure (or assessment) and aggregating it to make inferences at a higher level. Historically, multilevel constructs have not been a widespread issue in measurement and validation because testing and measurement have been immersed in, and emerged from, an individual differences psychological school of thought. Given the move to the increased policy usage of assessment results, and the shift in educational and psychological theorizing toward ecological and sociological views of our phenomenon, I fully expect to see more multilevel constructs in the coming years.

The Overlap between Test Validity and Program Evaluation

I will only briefly explore using validity as a way of looking at program evaluation. Other theorists have approached validity from an evaluation point of view, but Ruhe and Zumbo (2009) modified Messick's (1989) view of validity and approached evaluation from that framework in what they called the Unfolding Model. The term "program," in program evaluation, has been defined as a set of resources and activities directed toward one or more common goals. By this definition, a test or measure is a program. Therefore, measurement validity and program evaluation share a common conceptual core, which involves determining the worth and merit of goal-oriented activities. Ruhe and Zumbo showed that Messick's framework is an omnibus model for program evaluation. In fact, Messick treats tests as if they were programs, and the categories of his model overlap with categories commonly used for evaluating programs (e.g., cost-benefit, relevance, values and unintended consequences).

In adapting Messick's (1989) framework into an evaluation model, are Ruhe and Zumbo (2009) implying that test validity and program evaluation are the same thing? Not exactly. Fifty years ago, when the fields of program evaluation and assessment were based on (quasi) experimental methodologies, there was substantial overlap between them. However, with the adoption of qualitative methodologies and the proliferation of new approaches to program evaluation, assessment and program evaluation later emerged as distinct fields. Even so, these two fields share a common conceptual core, which is determining the worth and merit of educational and/or social policy activities. Therefore, Messick's framework can be used to evaluate both standardized tests and educational programs. Because Ruhe and Zumbo's Unfolding Model is based on Messick's framework, it is a program evaluation model grounded in the science of test assessment and educational measurement. The key to the unfolding model, like Messick's validity model and the contextualized and pragmatic view of validity I describe above, is that it brings into the forefront several features (e.g., the role of values, or of sample heterogeneity) that are largely ignored.

CLOSING REMARKS

I began this chapter by reminding the reader of Neurath's (1921) analogy of scientific verification with the construction of a ship that is already at sea. Validity was rebuilt, yet again, as Neurath highlights, one plank at a time. Wholesale changes at sea are impossible. In light of this, this chapter had two aims, to provide an overview of what I consider to be validity as contextualized and pragmatic explanation and then discuss its implications for the process of validation. By building on the iconic works of Cronbach and Meehl (1955) and Messick (1989) and contrasting my view of validity as contextualized and pragmatic explanation, I was able to better explicate the subtleties of my own view. In the closing section of the chapter I described the implications of this view in terms of not assuming homogeneity of populations (from the point of view of the Draper-Lindley-de Finetti framework) and allowing for multilevel construct validation, as well as the overlap between test validity and program evaluation.

ACKNOWLEDGMENT

I would like to thank Professor Anita M. Hubley for feedback and for allowing for such a rich on-going discussion on validity and validation.

REFERENCES

Anastasi, A. (1950). The concept of validity in the interpretation of test scores. *Educational and Psychological Measurement, 10*, 67–78.

Borsboom, D., Mellenbergh, G. J., & Van Heerden, J. (2004). The concept of validity. *Psychological Review, 111,* 1061–1071.

Cronbach, L. J., & Meehl, P. (1955). Construct validity in psychological tests. *Psychological Bulletin, 52*(4), 281–302.

Cronbach, L. J. (1971). Test validation. In R. Thorndike (Ed.), *Educational measurement* (2nd ed., pp. 443–507). Washington, DC: American Council on Education.

Hempel, C., & Oppenheim, P. (1948). Studies in the logic of explanation. *Philosophy of Science, 15*, 135–175.

Hubley, A. M., & Zumbo, B. D. (1996). A dialectic on validity: where we have been and where we are going. *The Journal of General Psychology, 123*, 207–215.

Kane, M. T. (2001). Current concerns in validity theory. *Journal of Educational Measurement, 38,* 319–342.

Kane, M. (2006). Validation. In R. Brennan (Ed.), *Educational measurement* (4th ed., pp. 17–64). Washington, DC: American Council on Education and National Council on Measurement in Education.

Klein, K. J., Dansereau, F., & Hall, R. J. (1994). Levels issues in theory development, data collection, and analysis. *Academy of Management Review, 19*, 195–229.

Loevinger, J. (1957). Objective tests as instruments of psychological theory. *Psychological Reports, 3*, 635–694 (Monograph Supp. 9).

Messick, S. (1975). The standard problem: meaning and values in measurement and evaluation. *American Psychologist, 30*, 955–966.

Messick, S. (1980). Test validity and the ethics of assessment. *American Psychologist, 35*, 1012–1027.

Messick, S. (1988). The once and future issues of validity: assessing the meaning and consequences of measurement. In H. Wainer & H. I. Braun (Eds.), *Test validity* (pp. 33–45). Hillsdale, NJ: Lawrence Erlbaum Associates.

Messick, S. (1989). Validity. In R. L. Linn (Ed.), *Educational measurement* (3rd ed., pp. 13–103). New York: Macmillan.

Messick, S. (1995). Validity of psychological assessment: validation of inferences from persons' responses and performances as scientific inquiry into score meaning. *American Psychologist, 50,* 741–749.

Messick, S. (1998). Test validity: A matter of consequence. In B. D. Zumbo (Ed.), *Validity theory and the methods used in validation: Perspectives from the social and behavioral sciences* (pp. 35–44). Amsterdam: Kluwer Academic Press.

Morgeson, F. P., & Hofmann, D. A. (1999). The structure and function of collective constructs: Implications for multilevel research and theory development. *Academy of Management Review, 24,* 249–265.

Muthen, B. O. (1985). A method for studying the homogeneity of test items with respect to other relevant variables. *Journal of Educational Statistics, 10,* 121–132.

Muthen, B. O. (1988). Some uses of structural equation modeling in validity studies: Extending IRT to external variables. In H. Wainer & H. Braun (Eds.), *Test validity* (pp. 213–238). Hillsdale, NJ: Lawrence Erlbaum.

Muthen, B. O. (1989). Latent variable modeling in heterogeneous populations. *Psychometrika, 54,* 551–585.

Muthen, B. O., Kao, C., & Burstein, L. (1991). Instructionally sensitive psychometrics: An application of a new IRT-based detection technique to mathematics achievement test items. *Journal of Educational Measurement, 28,* 1–22.

Muthen, B. O., & Lehman, J. (1985). Multiple group IRT modeling: Applications to item bias analysis. *Journal of Educational Statistics, 10,* 133–142.

Neurath, O. (1921). *Antispengler* (T. Parzen, Trans.). Munich: Callwey.

Ruhe, V., & Zumbo, B. D. (2009). *Evaluation in distance education and e-learning: The unfolding model.* New York: Guilford Press.

Rupp, A. A., & Zumbo, B. D. (2003). Which model is best? Robustness properties to justify model choice among unidimensional IRT models under item parameter drift. [Theme issue in honor of Ross Traub] *Alberta Journal of Educational Research, 49,* 264–276.

Rupp, A. A., & Zumbo, B. D. (2004). A note on how to quantify and report whether invariance holds for IRT models: When Pearson correlations are not enough. *Educational and Psychological Measurement, 64,* 588–599. [Errata, (2004) *Educational and Psychological Measurement, 64,* 991]

Rupp, A. A., & Zumbo, B. D. (2006). Understanding parameter invariance in unidimensional IRT models. *Educational and Psychological Measurement, 66,* 63–84.

Salmon, W. (1984). *Scientific explanation and the causal structure of the world.* Princeton, NJ: Princeton University Press.

Salmon, W. (1990) *Four decades of scientific explanation.* Minneapolis: University of Minnesota Press.

Salmon, W. (1998). *Causality and explanation.* New York: Oxford University Press.

Sawatzky, R. G., Ratner, P.A., Johnson, J. L., Kopec, J., & Zumbo B.D. (in press). Sample heterogeneity and the measurement structure of the Multidimensional Students' Life Satisfaction Scale. *Social Indicators Research: International Interdisciplinary Journal for Quality of Life Measurement.*

Scriven, M. (1962). Explanations, predictions, and laws. In H. Feigl & G. Maxwell (Eds.), *Minnesota Studies in the Philosophy of Science* (Vol. 3, pp. 170–230). Minneapolis: University of Minnesota Press.

Sireci, S. G. (1998). The construct of content validity. In B. D. Zumbo (Ed.), *Validity theory and the methods used in validation: Perspectives from the social and behavioral sciences* (pp. 83–117). Amsterdam: Kluwer Academic Press.

Suppe, F. (1977). *The structure of scientific theories.* Chicago: University of Illinois Press.

van Fraassen, Bas C. (1980) *The scientific image.* Oxford: Clarendon Press.

Zumbo, B. D. (Ed.) (1998). Validity theory and the methods used in validation: perspectives from the social and behavioral sciences. Special issue of the journal *Social Indicators Research: An International and Interdisciplinary Journal for Quality-of-Life Measurement, 45*(1–3), 1–359. Amsterdam: Kluwer Academic Press.

Zumbo, B. D. (2005). *Reflections on validity at the intersection of psychometrics, scaling, philosophy of inquiry, and language testing* (July 22, 2005). Samuel J. Messick Memorial Award Lecture, LTRC 27th Language Testing Research Colloquium, Ottawa, Canada.

Zumbo, B.D. (2007a). Validity: Foundational issues and statistical methodology. In C.R. Rao & S. Sinharay (Eds.), *Handbook of statistics, Vol. 26: Psychometrics* (pp. 45–79). Amsterdam: Elsevier Science B.V.

Zumbo, B.D. (2007b). Three generations of differential item functioning (DIF) analyses: Considering where it has been, where it is now, and where it is going. *Language Assessment Quarterly, 4,* 223–233.

Zumbo, B. D., & Forer, B. (in press). Testing and measurement from a multilevel view: Psychometrics and validation. In J. Bovaird, K. Geisinger, & C. Buckendahl (Eds.), *High stakes testing in education—Science and practice in K-12 settings [Festschrift to Barbara Plake].* Washington, DC: American Psychological Association Press.

Zumbo, B. D., & Gelin, M.N. (2005). A matter of test bias in educational policy research: Bringing the context into picture by investigating sociological/community moderated (or mediated) test and item bias. *Journal of Educational Research and Policy Studies, 5,* 1–23.

Zumbo, B. D., & Rupp, A. A. (2004). Responsible modeling of measurement data for appropriate inferences: important advances in reliability and validity theory. In D. Kaplan (Ed.), *The SAGE handbook of quantitative methodology for the social sciences* (pp. 73–92). Thousand Oaks, CA: Sage Press.

CHAPTER 5

VALIDITY FROM THE PERSPECTIVE OF MODEL-BASED REASONING

Robert J. Mislevy

ABSTRACT

From a contemporary perspective on cognition, the between-persons variables in trait-based arguments in educational assessment are absurd oversimplifications. Yet, for a wide range of applications, they work. Rather than seeing such variables as independently existing characteristics of people, we can view them as summaries of patterns in situated behaviors that could be understood at the finer grainsize of sociocognitive analyses. When done well, inference through coarser educational and psychological measurement models suits decisions and actions routinely encountered in school and work, yet is consistent with what we are learning about how people learn, act, and interact. An essential element of test validity is whether, in a given application, using a given model provides a sound basis for organizing observations and guiding actions in the situations for which it is intended. This presentation discusses the use of educational measurement models such as those of item response theory and cognitive diagnosis from the perspective of model-based reasoning, with a focus on validity.

The Concept of Validity, pages 83–108
Copyright © 2009 by Information Age Publishing

83

*A test is valid for measuring an attribute if and only if (a) the attribute exists
and (b) variations in the attribute causally produce variations in the outcomes
of the measurement procedure.*

—Borsboom, Mellenbergh, and van Heerden (2004, p. 1)

*Validity is an integrated evaluative judgment of the degree to which empirical evidence
and theoretical rationales support the adequacy and appropriateness of inferences and
actions based on test scores or other modes of assessment.*

—Messick (1989, p. 13)

*All models are wrong; the practical question is how wrong do they have to be
to not be useful.*

—Box and Draper (1987, p. 74)

INTRODUCTION

The concept of validity in educational assessment extends back more than a century (Sireci, 2008). The term was initially associated with the accuracy of predictions based on test scores. Concern with test content and with the meaning of scores gained attention in the middle of the century, with Cronbach and Meehl's (1955) "Construct validity in psychological tests" a watershed publication. More recent developments are the argument-based perspective noted in Messick's (1989) chapter in the third edition of *Educational Measurement* (Linn, 1989) and developed more fully by Kane (1992), and the use of cognitive theory to guide task design (Embretson, 1983). The present chapter contributes to these latter two lines of work, drawing on recent developments in cognitive psychology. In particular:

- A sociocognitive perspective on the nature of human knowledge provides insight into just what we are trying to assess.
- Research on the role of metaphors in cognition helps us understand the psychological, in conjunction with the formal, foundations of tools in the psychometric armamentarium.
- Studies of model-based reasoning in science provide a basis for understanding the activity of psychometric modeling.

Together, these lines of research are seen to support a constructivist-realist view of validity.

PRELIMINARIES

Snow and Lohman's Assertion

In the 3rd edition of *Educational Measurement* (Linn, 1989), Messick (1989) defines a trait as "a relatively stable characteristic of a person—an attribute, enduring process, or disposition—which is consistently manifested to some degree when relevant, despite considerable variation in the range of settings and circumstances" (p. 15). This is a common interpretation of the variables in the models of educational and psychological measurement. Snow and Lohman's chapter on cognitive psychology in the same volume proposes an alternative:

> Summary test scores, and factors based on them, have often been though of as "signs" indicating the presence of underlying, latent traits. . . . An alternative interpretation of test scores as samples of cognitive processes and contents, and of correlations as indicating the similarity or overlap of this sampling, is equally justifiable and could be theoretically more useful. The evidence from cognitive psychology suggests that test performances comprise complex assemblies of component information-processing actions that are adapted to task requirements during performance.

> The implication is that sign-trait interpretations of test scores and their intercorrelations are superficial summaries at best. At worst, they have misled scientists, and the public, into thinking of fundamental, fixed entities, measured in amounts. (Snow & Lohman, 1989, p. 317)

This claim would seem to call into question the validity of inferences made through a conventional interpretation of test scores through educational and psychological measurement models.

Mixed-Number Subtraction

To illustrate ideas throughout the discussion, we will use an example drawn from the work of Kikumi Tatsuoka (e.g., Tatsuoka, 1983) on mixed number subtraction. Mixed-number subtraction problems require students to solve tasks such as $5\frac{1}{2} - 3\frac{3}{4}$, $7\frac{2}{3} - \frac{1}{3}$, and $\frac{11}{8} - \frac{7}{8}$. A Rasch item response theory (IRT) model (Rasch, 1960/1980) often provides a reasonable fit to the right/wrong item responses of a group of middle-school students on a test of, say, twenty such tasks in open-ended format. The probability that Student i will respond correctly to Item j, or P_{ij}, is given as follows:

$$P_{ij} = P(X_{ij} = 1 | \theta_i, \beta_j) = \frac{\exp(\theta_i - \beta_j)}{1 + \exp(\theta_i - \beta_j)} \tag{5.1}$$

where X_{ij} is the response of Student i to Item j, 1 if right and 0 if wrong; θ_i is a parameter for the proficiency of Student i; and β_j is a parameter for the difficulty of Item j. The less common multiplicative form of the model, an analogue of Newton's second law that we will discuss in a later section, is for the odds of a correct response:

$$\frac{P_{ij}}{1 - P_{ij}} = \xi_i / \delta_j \tag{5.2}$$

where $\xi_i = \exp(\theta_i)$ and $\delta_i = \exp(\beta_i)$ from Equation (5.1). IRT character-izations of students and items such as this are clearly simplifications, and they say nothing about the processes by which students answer items. They prove useful nevertheless for such purposes as tracking or comparing students' proficiency in this domain of tasks and quality-checking items.

In a series of publications in the 1980s, Tatsuoka and her colleagues developed a methodology for analyzing test item responses according to the rules—some correct, some incorrect—that students appeared to use to solve them (Birenbaum & K. Tatsuoka, 1983; Klein et al., 1981; Tatsuoka, 1983, 1987, 1990; Tatsuoka & M. Tatsuoka, 1987). Extending earlier work by Brown and Burton (1978) to a statistical classification technique she called Rule Space, Tatsuoka characterized students in terms of the subset of rules that best seemed to explain their responses. Similarly, a binary skills latent class model (Haertel, 1989; Maris, 1999) provides an expression for the probability that Student i will answer Item j correctly, now in terms of which of K skills Item requires and which of these skills Student i can apply. Let $q_j = (q_{j1}, \ldots, q_{jK})$ be a vector of 0's and 1's for the skills Item j requires and $\eta_i = (\eta_{i1}, \ldots, \eta_{iK})$ be a vector of 0's and 1's for the skills Student i can apply. Then the expression:

$$P_{ij} = P(X_{ij} = 1 | \eta_i, q_j) = \begin{cases} \pi_j & \text{if } \prod_k \eta_{ik}^{q_{jk}} = 1 \\ c_j & \text{if } \prod_k \eta_{ik}^{q_{jk}} = 0 \end{cases} \tag{5.3}$$

says that if Student i has all the skills Item j requires, the probability of getting it right is π_j, the true positive probability parameter for Item j, and if she lacks one or more of these skills, the probability is c_j, the false positive probability parameter for Item j. This is an example of what are now commonly called cognitively diagnostic models (CDMs; Leighton & Gierl, 2007; Nichols, Chipman, & Brennan, 1995).

While based on cognitive analyses of actual solutions, these models are also oversimplifications of students and solution processes. However, as Tatsuoka and her colleagues showed (also see VanLehn, 1990), they are useful for determining which concepts or procedures are useful for students to work on to improve their performance in the domain.

QUESTIONS

Snow and Lohman's assertion and the gainful use of different models for the same data raise philosophical questions about the nature of the parameters and probabilities in educational/psychological measurement models, the probabilities they entail, and of validity itself.

What is the nature of person parameters such as θ and η in latent variables models? Where do they reside?

What is the interpretation of the probabilities that arise from IRT and CDM models, and latent variable models in education and psychology more generally?

What are the implications of these observations for validity of models, assessments, and uses of them?

SOME RELEVANT RESULTS FROM COGNITIVE SCIENCE

Norman (1993) distinguishes between *experiential* and *reflective* cognition: "The experiential mode leads to a state in which we perceive and react to the events around us, efficiently and effortlessly.... The reflective mode is that of comparison and contrast, of thought, of decision making. Both modes are essential to human performance" (Norman, 1993, pp. 15, 20). Both modes of cognition are involved in assessment. From a sociocognitive perspective, the first of three subsections that follow focuses on experiential cognition. It sheds light on the processes that Snow and Lohman suggested we consider underlying test performances. The second discusses the roles of metaphor in cognition, and pertains to both experiential and reflective aspects. We see how metaphors ground the use of models in science, including in particular models such as those of IRT and CDM. The third describes model-based reasoning in greater detail, to set the stage for the discussion of IRT and CDMs from this perspective.

The Sociocognitive Perspective

Snow and Lohman's chapter is grounded in the cognitive revolution of the 1960s and 1970s, in which researchers such as Newell and Simon (1972) studied the nature of knowledge and how people might acquire, store, and retrieve it. The so-called first generation cognitive science drew on the metaphor of analytic computation, in the form of rules, production systems, task decompositions, and means–ends analyses. Contemporary work employs a connectionist metaphor to bring together results from psychology on learning, perception, and memory *within* individuals (e.g., Hawkins & Blakeslee, 2004) and fields such as linguistics and anthropology on the shared patterns of meaning and interaction *between* people (e.g., Gee, 1992; Strauss & Quinn, 1998). Linguist Dwight Atkinson (2002) calls this a sociocognitive perspective, to emphasize the interplay between the external patterns in the physical and the social world to which we become attuned, and the patterns we develop and employ internally to understand and act accordingly.

One particular area in which these processes have been studied is reading comprehension. We can summarize the key ideas of Kintsch's (1998) construction-integration (CI) model for comprehension, and like Kintsch, take it as paradigmatic of comprehension more generally. Kintsch distinguishes three levels involved in text comprehension, namely the *surface structure* of a text, the *text model*, and the *situation model*. The *surface structure* of a text concerns the specific words, sentences, paragraphs, and so on that constitute the text. The *text model* is the collection of interconnected propositions that the surface structures convey, and corresponds roughly to what might be called the literal meaning of a text. The *situation model* is a synthesized understanding that integrates the text model with the knowledge a reader brings to the encounter (also shaped by goals, affect, context, etc.), and constitutes that reader's comprehension of the text. Readers with different knowledge, affect, or purposes produce situation models that differ to varying degrees, and are unique due to each reader's history of experiences.

The construction (C) phase is initiated by features of stimuli in the environment and activates associations from long-term memory (LTM), whether they are relevant to the current circumstances or not. The associations include patterns of many kinds, from the forms of letters and grammatical constructions, to word meanings and discourse structures, to experiences with the subject matter at issue, such as the patterns and procedures in schemas for mixed number subtraction. The probability of activation of an element from LTM depends in large part on the strength of similarity of stimulus features and aspects of the elements of the schema. In the integration (I) phase, only the aspects of activated knowledge—both from contextual input and LTM—that are mutually associated are carried forward. The result, the *situation model*, is the reader's understanding of the text.

In assessment, the surface structure corresponds to the stimulus materials and conditions a task presents to the student. The text model is the intended meaning of that situation, within which the student is presumed to act. Situation models vary, often markedly, among students. A student may activate elements that are irrelevant from an expert's point of view, and in unsystematic ways from one task to another, depending on idiosyncratic features of tasks and how they match up with the student's prior experiences (Redish, 2003). Kintsch and Greeno (1985), for example, studied how students solved, or failed to solve, arithmetic word problems using schemas from arithmetic, structures of the English language, and conventions for task design. This is the level of analysis that Snow and Lohman call attention to, and there are no θs or ηs in these processes within persons.

Despite the uniqueness of the processes within individuals, patterns of similarities do emerge. Individuals build up experiences that share similar features when they participate in instruction that uses common representational forms and terminology, when they work on similar problems using similar procedures, when they talk with one another or read books based on the same concepts. As people acquire expertise in a domain, their knowledge becomes increasingly organized around key principles, and their perceptions and actions embody these shared ways of thinking. Although their experiences are unique, shared patterns in learning make for similarities in what students do in assessment situations. In the domain of mixed number subtraction, some students tend to solve more problems than others, and some items are harder than others as a result of the number and types of procedures they typically require. This observation motivates the idea of using of an IRT model to capture, express, and use these patterns for educative purposes. Patterns in what makes tasks hard and where students succeed and fail, appear in relation to procedures and strategies. This motivates the use of a cognitive diagnosis model to guide instruction. Both models are wrong, to paraphrase the statistician George Box, but either might be useful in the right circumstances.

Metaphors in Human Cognition

Individual cognition is a unique blend of particular circumstances and more general patterns that are partly personal, due to our unique experiences, but partly shared with others, because they tap shared cultural models and because they build up as extensions of universal human experiences. With regard to the last point, one line of research in "embodied cognition" studies the roles of metaphor in cognition (Lakoff & Johnson,

1980, 1999). Lakoff asserts that our conceptual system, in terms of which we both think and act, is fundamentally metaphorical in nature, building up from universal experiences such as putting things into containers and making objects move by bodily action. Our cognitive machinery builds from capabilities for interacting with the real physical and social world. We extend and creatively recombine basic patterns and relationships to think about everything from everyday things (a close examination of language shows it is rife with metaphor, much of which we do not even recognize as such) to extremely complicated and abstract social, technical, conceptual, and philosophical realms. The following sections consider four examples of metaphorical frames that are central to the use of models of educational and psychological measurement: containers, measurement, cause and effect, and probability. The section that follows this overview will show how these metaphors work together in measurement models in assessment.

Containers

The most fundamental metaphors are based on physical and spatial relationships in the world as humans, from birth, experience it. Examples are front and back ("We've fallen behind schedule"), moving along a path ("I'll start with a joke, move to my main points, and end with a moral"), up and down (with "up" as "good"), and the cause-and-effect metaphor discussed below. Containership is a basic physical and spatial relationship, where a container has an inside and an outside and is capable of holding something else. Dogs, apes, and parrots reason literally about containers, and employ them to achieve their ends. People reason metaphorically through the same structural relationships, continually and implicitly through the forms and the concepts based on containership relationships that are ubiquitous in all human languages, and formally and explicitly as the foundation of set theory and the classical definition of categories in philosophy (Lakoff & Johnson, 1999). As we noted earlier and will return to in a following section, latent class models build on the container metaphor.

Measurement

Measurement builds up from the physical experience of comparing objects in terms of their length or height. We experience "longer," "shorter," or "the same." Formalization from these simple foundations leads to more abstract concepts of catenation and measuring devices for physical properties, then derived properties such as acceleration, axiomatization of measurement relationships, and the even more abstract relationships in the extension to conjoint measurement in social sciences (Michell, 1999). In abstract applications, the measurement metaphor posits variables that can be used to characterize all objects in a collection, each object is represented by a number, and the numbers can be used in further quantitative structures to characterize other events or relationships that involve the objects. The following paragraphs illustrate the role of measurement in quantitative structures within the cause-and-effect metaphor, specifically physical measurement in Newtonian mechanics and social-science measurement with the Rasch IRT model.

Cause and Effect

Cause-and-effect reasoning is central to human reasoning in everyday life as well as in the disciplines. A dictionary definition is straightforward: One event, the cause, brings about another event, the effect, through some mechanism. Lakoff (1987, pp. 54ff) proposes that reasoning about causation extends from a direct-manipulation prototype that is basic to human experience, pushing a ball, for example, as shown in Figure 5.1a. He characterizes an idealized cognitive model for causation in terms of the following cluster of interactional properties:

1. *There is an agent that does something.*
2. *There is a patient that undergoes a change to a new state.*
3. *Properties 1 and 2 constitute a single event; they overlap in time and space; the agent comes in contact with the patient.*
4. *Part of what the agent does (either the motion or the exercise of will) precedes the change in the patient.*

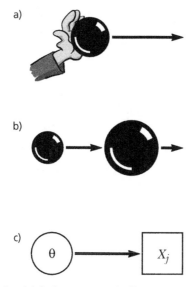

Figure 5.1 Situations in which the cause and effect metaphor is employed: (a) Foundational experience; (b) Newtonian mechanics; (c) IRT model.

5. *The agent is the energy source; the patient is the energy goal; there is a transfer of energy from the agent to patient.*
6. *There is a single definite agent and a single definite patient.*
7. *The agent is human.*
8. *(a) The agent wills the action. (b) The agent is in control of his action. (c) The agent bears primary responsibility for both his actions and the change.*
9. *The agent uses his hands, body, or some instrument.*
10. *The agent is looking at the patient, the change in the patient is perceptible, and the agent perceives the change* (pp. 54–55).

Lakoff claims that the most representative examples of causation have all of these properties (e.g., Max broke the window). Less prototypical instances that we still consider causation lack some of the properties, indirect causation lacks Property 3, and billiard-ball interactions that characterize much reasoning in the physical sciences just have properties 1–6 (Figure 5.1b). Newtonian mechanics extends the cause-and-effect frame with sophisticated concepts such as mass, acceleration, and decomposition of forces, and adds a layer of quantitative relationships. Given a collection of springs and a collection of balls, for example, Newton's Second Law tells us how much acceleration results when each spring is used to propel each ball in terms of the spring's force, F_i and the ball's mass, M_j:

$$A_{ij} = F_i / M_j \qquad\qquad 5.4$$

Latent variable models in educational and psychological measurement abstracting the cause-and-effect metaphor even further (Figure 5.1c). It is no coincidence that the multiplicative form of the Rasch model in Equation (5.2) mirrors Newton's Second Law in Equation (5.4). In his 1960 book *Probabilistic models for some intelligence and attainment tests*, Rasch explicitly lays out the analogy between ability and force, mass and item difficulty, and acceleration and probability of correct response. The measurement metaphor is intentional; how accurately and broadly it describes observations in given arenas of people and situations in a given application is to be determined. The latent class CDM model also draws on the causation metaphor, but with a different metaphor for the relationship between people and tasks, namely the container metaphor, and a correspondingly different quantitative layer.

Probability

Formal development of probability models began with systematic observations of games of chance. Shafer (1976) argues that these tangible, replicable situations ground reasoning about probability more generally. Kolmogorov's set theoretic basis of probability uses both the container metaphor and the measurement metaphor to describe what we see in repeated trials, and is an abstract foundation for a frequentist view of probability. This interpretation of the metaphor considers probabilities to be a property of the world, induced by distributions of entities, mechanisms, or procedures. The same axioms ground reasoning using the same formal structure in further abstracted situations, as embodied in the personalistic or subjectivist Bayesian framework for probability (de Finetti, 1974; Savage, 1954). In this interpretation, probabilities are tools of the user, for reasoning about situations through a model, that is, an aspect of the formal, abstracted, specified, and situated applications of metaphors we discuss below as model-based reasoning. Either way, the use of the formal structures of probability models allow for reasoning about evidence and uncertainty in far more subtle and complex situations than unaided intuition can reckon with (Pearl, 1988; Schum, 1994).

The practical question in any application is whether the quantitative structure afforded by the probability framework, as particularized in terms of particular variables, models, and relationships, proves suitable for structuring reasoning in situations of interest. As we will see, the probability framework comes with some techniques that help one make this determination.

Model-Based Reasoning

A model is a simplified representation focused on certain aspects of a system (Ingham & Gilbert, 1991; cited in Gobert & Buckley, 2000). The entities, relationships, and processes of a model constitute its fundamental structure. They provide a framework for reasoning about patterns across any number of unique real-world situations, in each case abstracting salient aspects of those situations and going beyond them in terms of mechanisms, causal relationships, or implications at different scales or time points that are not apparent on the surface. To think about a particular situation for a particular purpose, scientists reason from principles in the domain to formulate a model that represents salient aspects of the situation, elaborate its implications, apprehend both anomalies and points of correspondence, and as necessary revise the model, the situation, or their theories in cycles of inquiry (Clement, 1989). Table 5.1 is based on Stewart and Hafner's (1994) and Gobert and Buckley's (2000) parsing of aspects of model-based reasoning.

Figure 5.2, based on Greeno (1983), suggests central properties of a model. The lower left plane shows phenomena in a particular real-world situation. A mapping is established between this situation and, in the center, structures expressed in terms of the entities, relationships, and properties of the model. Reasoning is carried out in these terms. This process

TABLE 5.1   Aspects of Model-Based Reasoning in Science

Model formation	Establishing a correspondence between some real-world phenomenon and a model, or abstracted structure, in terms of entities, relationships, processes, behaviors, etc. Includes scope and grain-size to model, and determining which aspects of the situation(s) to address and which to leave out.
Model elaboration	Combining, extending, adding detail to a model, establishing correspondences across overlapping models. Often done by assembling smaller models into larger assemblages, or fleshing out more general models with more detailed models.
Model use	Reasoning through the structure of a model to make explanations, predictions, conjectures, etc.
Model evaluation	Assessing the correspondence between the model components and their real-world counterparts, with emphasis on anomalies and important features not accounted for in the model.
Model revision	Modifying or elaborating a model for a phenomenon in order to establish a better correspondence. Often initiated by model evaluation procedures.
Model-based inquiry	Working interactively between phenomena and models, using all of the aspects above. Emphasis on monitoring and taking actions with regard to model-based inferences vis-à-vis real-world feedback.

constitutes an understanding of the situation, which can lead, through the machinery of the representation, to explanations, predictions, or plans for action. Above the plane of entities and relationships in the models are two symbol systems that further support reasoning in the model space, such as the matrix algebra and path diagram representations used in structural equation modeling. Note that they are connected to the real-world situation through the model.

The real-world situation is depicted in Figure 5.2 as fuzzy, whereas the model is crisp and well defined. This suggests that the correspondence between the real-world entities and the idealizations in the model are never exact. Not all aspects of the real-world situation are represented in the model. The model conveys concepts and relationships that the real-world situation does not. The reconceived situation shows a less-than-perfect match to the model, but is overlaid with a framework for reasoning that the situation itself does not possess in and of itself. These "surrogative inferences" (Swoyer, 1991) are precisely the cognitive value of a model (Suárez, 2004). A given model may, for example, support reasoning about missing data elements or future states of a situation.

It is particularly important that not everything in a real-world situation is represented in a model for that situation. Models address different aspects of phenomena, and can be cast at different levels. Different models address

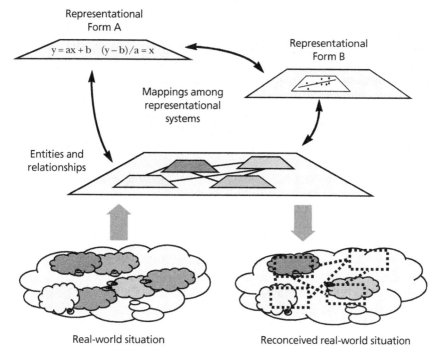

Figure 5.2 Reconceiving a real-world situation through a model.

to different aspects of phenomena, and as such are tuned to reasoning about different problems. This observation underscores the user's active role in model choice and construction, and the purpose for which the model is thought to be instrumental. One can examine aspects of transmission genetics with models at the level of species, individuals, cells, or molecules. One might model water as molecular to study Brownian motion but as continuous to study flow through pipes (Giere, 2004). Newtonian mechanics has been superseded by relativity and quantum theory, but it works fine for designing bridges. The constructivist-realist view holds that models are human constructions, but successful ones discern and embody patterns that characterize aspects of more complex real-world phenomena. Model-based reasoning is not just a dyadic relationship between a model and system, but a four-way relationship among a model, a situation, a user, and a purpose (Giere, 2004). In applied work, the issue is not a simple question of truth or falsity of a model, but of aptness for a given purpose.

The middle layer in Figure 5.2 is semantic, the narrative space of entities and relationships that are particularized to build stories to understand particular real-world situations. Metaphors play their roles here, as when we reason through the measurement metaphor when we use IRT and through the container metaphor when we use CDMs. In models that include quantitative layers, mathematical structures indicate forms of relationships, associations, and properties, and values of parameters in those models indicates the extent, strength, or variation within those forms as they might be used to approximate a given situation. These layers vary in their prominence across modeling enterprises and domains. Some models are strictly qualitative, and gain their power from the structures of entities, relationships, and processes they provide to reason through. Others, such as those in advanced physics, gain their power mainly through the mathematical relationships, and their users consider the narrative representations seriously inadequate on their own. Galileo famously said "Mathematics is the language with which God has written the universe."

Models can additionally include probability components in two ways. The first is as a substantive component of the model, when some of the relationships within a quantitative or qualitative layer are expressed in terms of probabilistic relationships. Item and person parameters in IRT models imply probabilities of responses, and variance components indicate relationships among and ranges of data values or parameter values; these are inherently probabilistic relationships that obtain even if all data and parameters were known with certainty. The second is an overlay of the substantive model with a probabilistic layer that models the user's knowledge and uncertainty about parameters and the structures within the substantive model, and the degree to which real-world observations accord with the patterns the model can express. Modern psychometric models are probabilistic in both senses (Lewis, 1986).

The expression of a model's fit to data gives rise to an armamentarium of tools for exploring not only how well, but in what areas and in what ways the reconceived situation departs from the actual situation. A user can examine both the immediate model-data relationship and the quality of predications outside the immediate data such as predictions and appropriateness for new data. When the model is meant to serve a given purpose, it is of interest especially to see how well that purpose is subsequently served. This is the basis of predictive and consequential lines of validity argumentation in educational and psychological measurement.

PSYCHOMETRICS AS MODEL-BASED REASONING

A current active and productive line of research in educational assessment is developing a view of assessment as evidentiary argument (e.g., Bachman, 2003; Kane, 1992, 2006; Mislevy, 2003, 2006). This work adapts tools and concepts from evidentiary reasoning (e.g., Schum, 1994; Toulmin, 1958; Wigmore, 1937) to help construct, critique, and validate assessments as instruments for reasoning from limited observations of students in particular situations to what they know or can do more broadly. The metaphorical and quantitative components of measurement models such as IRT and CDM serve as warrants in such applications.

An evidentiary argument is a series of logically connected claims or propositions that are supported by data by means of warrants (Toulmin, 1958). The claims in assessment arguments concern aspects of students' proficiency (Figure 5.3). Data consist of aspects of their performances in task situations and the salient features of those tasks. Warrants posit how responses in situations with the noted features depend on proficiency. Some conception of knowledge is the source of warrants, and shapes the nature of the claims a particular assessment is meant to support and the tasks and data needed to ground them (Mislevy, 2003, 2006). Alternative explanations weaken inference, and in arguments that rely on models this includes ways that the model ignores or misrepresents aspects of the situation that would in fact be relevant to the targeted inferences.

An assessment based on the Rasch IRT model, for example, takes its IRT framework as its warrant. This includes both the metaphorical frame that characterizes persons and items by ability and difficulty parameters and the

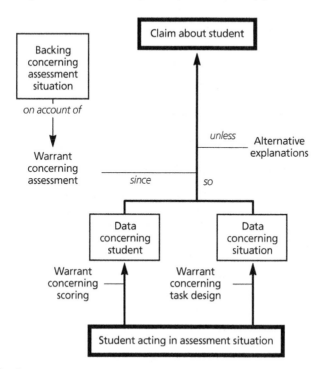

Figure 5.3 Assessment argument.

mathematical frame that gives probabilities of item response conditional on parameter values. Inferring the ability of a given student conditional on her observed responses (and good estimates of item parameters) requires reasoning back through the IRT model by means by Bayes theorem. An assessment based on the CDM takes the container metaphor as its narrative frame (you are in the container determined by your unobservable ηs) and conditional probabilities for item response given ηs; inferring a student's mastery of skills again requires reasoning back through the model via Bayes theorem to obtain posterior probabilities for ηs, i.e., container membership.

Note again the metaphor drives not only the nature of the claim, but the aspects of the students' performances and the task situations that are deemed relevant. Figure 5.3 represents these determinations as embedded arguments, supported by warrants that justify the use of the IRT model in the context at hand. In mixed number subtraction, we might attend to different aspects of solutions in accordance with different psychological perspectives: correctness only from a trait perspective; specific answer, right or wrong, from an information-processing perspective in order to infer production rules; or adaptation of solution given hints when needed under a sociocultural perspective. Anticipation of what is important to observe similarly drives task construction, so the performance situation will be able to evoke the observations that are needed under the form of the warrant (Messick, 1994).

Alternative explanations in Toulmin's scheme condition an argument, and address ways that the data could be observed as it was, yet the claim not be correct. There are exception conditions to the warrant, for example, or misfit of the model in important respects. But how can one know what respects are important? This is where the purpose, or intended use, of the assessment comes into play. Bachman (2003) calls the extension of the scheme to prediction, selection, instructional intervention, or program evaluation assessment the argument use argument (Figure 5.4). The claim emanating from the assessment argument is data for the assessment use argument. An inference about the student in the form of an IRT θ estimate or the most likely η vector in a CDM, is a summary of selected aspects of performance as it can be expressed through the model—both as to its semantic content, in terms of the metaphorical frame, and its quantitative content, in terms of the mathematical structure associated with the model. This is the encoding of the information about the student as it will be employed in the use argument, which may, but need not, share the same view of the proficiency. Alternative explanations in the assessment use argument thus concern ways that the model-based inference from the assessment argument proper may be inadequate or misleading for the purpose at hand. In

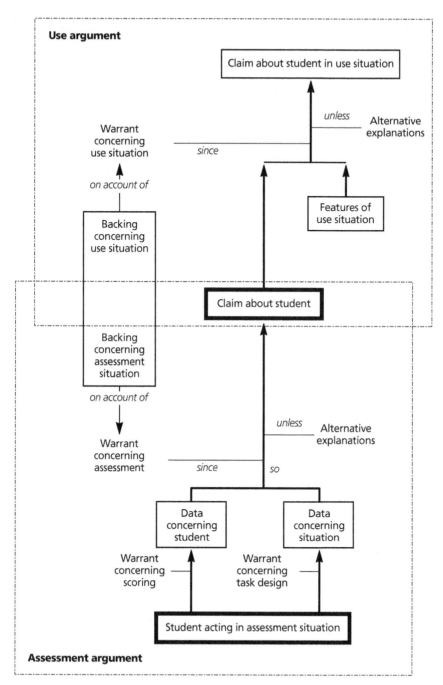

Figure 5.4 Assessment argument followed by assessment use argument.

particular, neither the IRT nor the CDM model are faithful representations of the processes that produced responses, as viewed from the perspective of sociocognitive research.

IMPLICATIONS FOR VALIDITY

We are now in a position to consider validity in educational assessment from the perspective of model-based reasoning. The discussion does so in relation to the quotations from Borsboom and Messick that appear at the beginning of this presentation.

Borsboom's Definition

Borsboom's definition of validity requires that the attribute an assessment is meant to measure *exists*, and that it *causes* variation in observations. We consider these points in turn.

Existence

Psychological research reinforces Snow and Lohman's doubts that trait interpretations are faithful representations of the cognition that produces test performances. In the learning sciences, both research and experience call attention to the situativity of cognition, as predictable from work like Kintsch's on reading comprehension. Examples include the context-dependent nature of reasoning in physics (e.g., Redish, 2003), language use (e.g., Chalhoub-Deville, 2003), and mathematics (Saxe, 1988). As a result, differences in contexts, formats, and degrees of familiarity affect the performance and consequent meaning of test scores both within and across examinees. This phenomenon is well known to practitioners of educational and psychological measurement, in terms of method factors. What it suggests, however, is that attributes such as mixed-number subtraction ability are, as Snow and Lohman suggest, higher-level manifestations of more variegated processes rather than well-defined independently-existing properties of students.

Nevertheless, given specifications of conditions, task domains, and targeted testing populations, it may indeed be the case that students' propensities for actions in those tasks situations *can* be said to exist, and lead them to exhibit patterns that can be approximated to some degree by models such as IRT and CDM. This is the constructivist realist position as it applies to practical educational and psychological measurement. Despite its inadequacy as a foundational explanation, the degree to which a given modeled representation suffices can be quite suitable for a given application. Snow and Lohman properly warn us against over-interpreting the model. An awareness of the finer-grained sociocognitive genesis of test performances continually suggests alternative explanations. Design principles and attention to context and use help us avoid inferential errors, and techniques including model-fit analyses such as manifest and latent differential item functioning (Cohen & Bolt, 2005) and richer data such as talk-aloud solutions help us investigate them after the fact.

The first implication of a model-based reasoning perspective for Borsboom's definition of validity, then, is a softened view of an attribute's existence—one that brings in the four-way relationship among the model, the system, the user, and the purpose, and the adequacy of what the model does capture and the extent to which it does so, for the purpose at hand. Person parameters such as θ and η in psychometric models reside in the mind of the analyst rather than the mind of the subject, although their value depends on a resonance with discernable patterns in the real world associated with the subject.

Wiley (1991), like Borsboom, objected to Messick's inference-bound definition of validity. He argued that a test designer cannot be held responsible for validating all possible uses of a test, even though prior research and experience could ground the construction of a test that could be said to measure some attribute. I would hold that such circumstances do occur, but they hide assumptions about conditions, target populations, and purposes. As experience with certain kinds of tasks and accompanying models accumulates and exhibits broader usefulness (they are said to be "fecund"), we gain confidence that the patterns they capture do reflect robustness that could be modeled in sociocognitive terms. However, I would hold also that we would be better served by viewing them as contingent outcomes of dissimilar processes at a finer grainsize, with uses therefore best confined to circumstances and purposes we should investigate and make ever more explicit. As discussed in the next section, the activities needed to do so comport nicely with the evolving tradition of test validation (Kane, 2006).

Causation

If θ and η in psychometric models reside in the mind of the analyst rather than the mind of the subject, how can they possibly be said to cause item responses x? The answer is straightforward from the perspective of model-based reasoning: when we have ascertained that the rationale and the evidence are sufficient to justify the use of an IRT or CDM model in a given application, the cause-and-effect metaphor is an appropriate structure to guide reasoning from observed responses to the targeted predictions, decisions, instructional feedback, and so on. This is so even though the IRT or CDM model is not a satisfactory explanation of responses, and even though the same structure applied to the same data could be misleading for different target inferences.

Messick's Definition

Messick (1989) defines validity as "an integrated evaluative judgment of the degree to which empirical evidence and theoretical rationales support the adequacy and appropriateness of inferences and actions based on test scores or other modes of assessment" (p. 20). From the perspective of model-based reasoning, the attention to "adequacy and appropriateness of inferences and uses" is spot on. So is the criterion of "the degree to which empirical evidence and theoretical rationales" support this reasoning. I would disagree with Messick, however, and in so doing agree with Borsboom, Mellenbergh, and van Heerden (2004), that "Validity is not a judgment at all. It is the property being judged." From a model-based reasoning perspective, however, the property being judged must address the four-way relationship rather than the model-system dyad. Either way, assessing it does indeed require an integrated evaluated judgment.[1]

And this is just what test validation has evolved to become in the special case of educational and psychological measurement (Kane, 2006). Figure 5.5 shows that well-established lines of validation argumentation can be parsed in terms of model-based reasoning:

1. Theory and experience supporting the narrative/scientific layer of the model. Although all models are wrong, we are more likely to have sound inference with models that are consistent with cognitive research and have proven practically useful in applications similar to the one at hand. As in physics, it is not that a model must be a faithful representation of a system, but that it captures the important patterns in ways that suit the intended inferences. Indeed, our uses of models like IRT and CDM are more likely to be successful if we *don't* believe the model is correct; we are more apt to be aware of alternative explanations, be diligent in model criticism, and stay within justifiable ranges of contexts, inferences, and testing populations.
2. Theoretical and empirical grounding of task design. Not only is model formation a matter of construction and choice, so too is the design of the situations in which performance will be observed. What does the theory of knowledge and performance in a domain tell us about the features of tasks that are needed to prompt the targeted cognition? How do the features of the task situations align with features of future situations about which inference is intended? Embretson (1983) calls this the construct representation line of validity

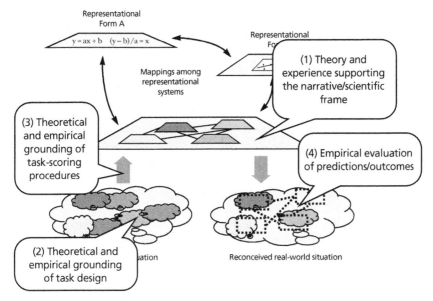

Figure 5.5 Lines of validity argumentation from the perspective of model-based reasoning.

argumentation. Consistent with the spirit of model-based reasoning, design efforts can be based on finer-grained, higher-fidelity, or more encompassing psychological models than the simplified model that is used to synthesize data. Examples that use IRT or classical test theory include Embretson's (1998) cognitive-processing model for an analytic reasoning test, Bachman and Palmer's (1996) framework for tests that encompasses sociocultural aspects of language use, and Katz's (1994) use of information-processing theory to ground task design in assessing proficiency in architectural design.

3. Theoretical and empirical grounding of task-scoring procedures. We saw that an assessment argument also embeds an argument from students' performances to values of the observable variables that enter psychometric models. Another active line of research in educational and psychological measurement is increased attention to exactly what to identify and evaluate in performances, as motivated by more cognitively detailed understandings of the nature of proficiency and performance. The economically-motivated move to automated scoring of complex performances has spurred this development, because doing a practically better job has been found to require doing a scientifically better job (Williamson, Mislevy, & Bejar, 2006).

4. Empirical evaluation of internal fit, predictions, and outcomes. A model's structure supports reasoning both about and beyond the

data at hand. In models such as IRT and CDM with a quantitative, probabilistic layer as well as a semantic, metaphorical layer, we can ask how well the model's representation accords with the observed data. How good is the correspondence, where does it fail, and does it fail in ways that might be predicted by alternative explanations (e.g., differential item functioning)? These internal investigations must be supplemented by external investigations, such as correlations with other data and predictions of criterion performance that more directly address the quality of inferences obtained through the model.

ANSWERS

We conclude with answers from the perspective of model-based reasoning to the questions posed earlier in the presentation about the nature of parameters, models, inferences, and validity.

What is the nature of person parameters such as θ and η in latent variables models? Where do they reside?

Person parameters in latent variables models are characterizations of patterns we observe in real-world situations (situations that we in part design for target uses), through the structure of a simplified model we are (provisionally) using to think about those situations and the use situations. They are in the heads of us, the users, but they aren't worth much unless they reflect patterns in examinees' propensities to action in the world. They are more likely to do so as (1) they accord with research and experience about the underlying nature of those propensities and actions, and (2) we design task situations and conditions of use in light of this emerging knowledge in such ways that will likely be robust with respect to the inevitable simplifications in the models. This view can be described as constructivist-realist.

What is the interpretation of the probabilities that arise from IRT and CDM models, and latent variable models in education and psychology more generally?

Probabilities are characterizations of patterns we observe in situations and our degree of knowledge about them, again through the structure of a simplified model we are (provisionally) using to think about those situations. The facts that (1) probabilities address the model space directly and only directly the real world though surrogative inference, and (2) different users and different purposes entail different models means that different probabilities can arise from different models. In addition to guiding inference through the model, the probabilistic layer of a quantitative model provides tools for seeing where the model may be misleading or inadequate.

What are the implications of these observations for validity of models, assessments, and uses of them?

A model-based reasoning perspective on the use of educational and psychological measurement is consistent with the currently dominant view of validity, which addresses "the degree to which empirical evidence and theoretical rationales support the adequacy and appropriateness of inferences and actions based on test scores or other modes of assessment" (Messick, 1989, p. 13). This is because model-based reasoning is concerned with the four-way relationship among a model, a system, a user, and a purpose (Giere, 2004). Sources of validity evidence and lines of validity argumentation that have developed in the educational and psychological literature are nicely compatible with justifications of model-based reasoning in the scientific literature more generally.

ACKNOWLEDGMENT

The work was supported by a grant from the Spencer Foundation.

NOTE

1. Knowing the care with which Messick wrote, I have to believe he called validity the "judgment" rather than "the degree" intentionally. Was this a step from a constructivist-realist position toward a more radical constructivist position?

REFERENCES

Atkinson, D. (2002). Toward a sociocognitive approach to second language acquisition. *The Modern Language Journal, 86,* 525–545.

Bachman, L.F. (2003). Building and supporting a case for test use. *Language Assessment Quarterly, 2,* 1–34.

Bachman, L. F., & Palmer, A. S. (1996). *Language testing in practice: Designing and developing useful language tests.* Oxford: Oxford University Press.

Birenbaum, M., & Tatsuoka, K. K. (1983). The effect of a scoring system based on the algorithm underlying the students' response patterns on the dimensionality of achievement test data of the problem solving type. *Journal of Educational Measurement, 20,* 17–26.

Borsboom, D., Mellenbergh, G. J., & van Heerden, J. (2004). The concept of validity. *Psychological Review, 111,* 1061–1071.

Box, G., & Draper, N. (1987). *Empirical model building and response surfaces.* New York: Wiley.

Brown, J. S., & Burton, R. (1978). Diagnostic models for procedural bugs in basic mathematical skills. *Cognitive Science, 2,* 155–192.

Chalhoub-Deville, M. (2003) Second language interaction: Current perspectives and future trends. *Language Testing, 20,* 369–383.

Clement, J. (1989) Learning via model construction and criticism: Protocol evidence on sources of creativity in science. In J. A. Glover, R. R. Ronning, & C. R. Reynolds (Eds), *Handbook of creativity: Assessment, theory and research* (pp. 341–381). New York: Plenum Press.

Cohen, A. S., & Bolt, D. M. (2005). A mixture model analysis of differential item functioning. *Journal of Educational Measurement, 42,* 133–148.

Cronbach, L. J., & Meehl, P. E. (1955). Construct validity and psychological tests. *Psychological Bulletin, 52,* 281–302.

de Finetti, B. (1974). *Theory of probability* (Vol. 1). London: Wiley.

Embretson, S. (1983). Construct validity: Construct representation versus nomothetic span. *Psychological Bulletin, 93,* 179–197.

Embretson, S. E. (1998). A cognitive design system approach to generating valid tests: Application to abstract reasoning. *Psychological Methods, 3,* 380–396.

Gee, J. P. (1992). *The social mind: Language, ideology, and social practice.* New York: Bergin & Garvey.

Giere, R. (2004). How models are used to represent reality. *Philosophy of Science, 71,* Supplement, S742–752.

Gobert, J. (2000). A typology of models for plate tectonics: Inferential power and barriers to understanding. *International Journal of Science Education, 22,* 937–977.

Gobert, J., & Buckley, B. (2000). Special issue editorial: Introduction to model-based teaching and learning. *International Journal of Science Education, 22,* 891–894.

Greeno, J. G. (1983). Conceptual entities. In D. Gentner & A. L. Stevens (Eds.), *Mental models* (pp. 227–252). Hillsdale, NJ: Lawrence Erlbaum Associates.

Haertel, E. H. (1989). Using restricted latent class models to map the skill structure of achievement test items. *Journal of Educational Measurement, 26,* 301–321.

Hawkins, J., & Blakeslee, S. (2004). *On intelligence.* New York: Times Books.

Ingham, A. M., & Gilbert, J. K. (1991). The use of analogue models by students of chemistry at higher education level. *International Journal of Science Education, 13,* 193–202.

Kane, M. (1992). An argument-based approach to validation. *Psychological Bulletin, 112,* 527–535.

Kane, M. (2006). Validation. In R. J. Brennan (Ed.), *Educational measurement* (4th ed., pp. 18-64). Westport, CT: Praeger.

Katz, I. R. (1994). Coping with the complexity of design: Avoiding conflicts and prioritizing constraints. In A. Ram, N. Nersessian, & M. Recker (Eds.), *Proceedings of the Sixteenth Annual Meeting of the Cognitive Science Society* (pp. 485–489). Mahwah, NJ: Erlbaum.

Kintsch, W. (1998). *Comprehension: A paradigm for cognition.* New York: Cambridge University Press.

Kintsch, W., & Greeno, J.G. (1985). Understanding and solving word arithmetic problems. *Psychological Review, 92,* 109–129.

Klein, M. F., Birenbaum, M., Standiford, S. N., & Tatsuoka, K. K. (1981). *Logical error analysis and construction of tests to diagnose student "bugs" in addition and subtraction of fractions.* Research Report 81-6. Urbana: Computer-based Education Research Laboratory, University of Illinois.

Lakoff, G. (1987). *Women, fire, and dangerous things: What categories reveal about the mind*. Chicago: University of Chicago Press.

Lakoff, G. P., & Johnson, M. (1980). *Metaphors we live by*. Chicago: University of Chicago Press.

Lakoff, G., & Johnson, M. (1999). *Philosophy in the flesh: The embodied mind and its challenge to western thought*. New York: Basic Books.

Leighton, J. P., & Gierl, M. J. (Eds.). (2007). *Cognitive diagnostic assessment: Theories and applications*. Cambridge: Cambridge University Press.

Lewis, C. (1986). Test theory and *Psychometrika*: The past twenty-five years. *Psychometrika, 51*, 11–22.

Linn, R. L. (Ed.). (1989). *Educational measurement* (3rd ed.) New York: American Council on Education/Macmillan.

Maris, E. (1999). Estimating multiple classification latent class models. *Psychometrika, 64*, 187–212.

Messick, S. (1989). Validity. In R. L. Linn (Ed.), *Educational measurement* (3rd ed., pp. 13–103). New York: American Council on Education/Macmillan.

Messick, S. (1994). The interplay of evidence and consequences in the validation of performance assessments. *Educational Researcher, 23*(2), 13–23.

Michell, J. (1999). *Measurement in psychology: A critical history of a methodological concept*. New York: Cambridge University Press.

Mislevy, R. J. (2003). Substance and structure in assessment arguments. *Law, Probability, and Risk, 2*, 237–258.

Mislevy, R. J. (2006). Cognitive psychology and educational assessment. In R. L. Brennan (Ed.), *Educational measurement* (4th ed., pp. 257–305). Westport, CT: American Council on Education/Praeger Publishers.

Newell, A., & Simon, H. A. (1972). *Human problem solving*. Englewood Cliffs, NJ: Prentice-Hall.

Nichols, P. D., Chipman, S. F., & Brennan, R. L. (Eds.). (1995). *Cognitively diagnostic assessment*. Hillsdale, NJ: Erlbaum.

Norman, D. A. (1993). *Things that make us smart*. Boston: Addison-Wesley.

Pearl, J. (1988). *Probabilistic reasoning in intelligent systems: Networks of plausible inference*. San Mateo, CA: Kaufmann.

Rasch, G. (1960/1980). *Probabilistic models for some intelligence and attainment tests*. Copenhagen: Danish Institute for Educational Research/Chicago: University of Chicago Press (reprint).

Redish, E. F. (2003). *Teaching physics with the physics suite*. New York: John Wiley & Sons, Inc.

Savage, L. J. (1954). *The foundations of statistics*. New York: John Wiley &. Sons, Inc.

Saxe, G. B. (1988). Candy selling and math learning. *Educational Researcher, 17*, 14–21.

Schum, D. A. (1994). *The evidential foundations of probabilistic reasoning*. New York: Wiley.

Shafer, G. (1976). *A mathematical theory of evidence*. Princeton, NJ: Princeton University Press.

Sireci, S. (2008, October 9–10). *Packing and unpacking sources of validity evidence: History repeats itself again*. Paper presented at the conference "The Concept of Validity: Revisions, New Directions and Applications," University of Maryland, College Park, MD.

Snow, R. E., & Lohman, D. F. (1989). Implications of cognitive psychology for educational measurement. In R. L. Linn (Ed.), *Educational measurement* (3rd ed., pp. 263–331). New York: American Council on Education/Macmillan.

Stewart, J., & Hafner, R. (1994). Research on problem solving: Genetics. In D. Gabel (Ed.), *Handbook of research on science teaching and learning* (pp 284–300). New York: Macmillan.

Strauss, C., & Quinn, N. (1998). *A cognitive theory of cultural meaning.* New York: Cambridge University Press.

Suárez, M. (2004). An inferential conception of scientific representation. *Philosophy of Science, 71,* Supplement, S767–779.

Swoyer, C. (1991). Structural representation and surrogative reasoning. *Synthese, 87,* 449–508.

Tatsuoka, K. K. (1983). Rule space: An approach for dealing with misconceptions based on item response theory. *Journal of Educational Measurement, 20,* 345–354.

Tatsuoka, K. K. (1987). Validation of cognitive sensitivity for item response curves. *Journal of Educational Measurement, 24,* 233–245.

Tatsuoka, K. K. (1990). Toward an integration of item response theory and cognitive error diagnosis. In N. Frederiksen, R. Glaser, A. Lesgold, & M. G. Shafto, (Eds.), *Diagnostic monitoring of skill and knowledge acquisition* (pp. 453–488). Hillsdale, NJ: Erlbaum.

Tatsuoka, K. K., & Tatsuoka, M. M. (1987). Bug distribution and statistical pattern classification. *Psychometrika, 52,* 193–206.

Toulmin, S. E. (1958). *The uses of argument.* Cambridge: Cambridge University Press.

VanLehn, K. (1990). *Mind bugs: The origins of procedural misconceptions.* Cambridge, MA: MIT. Press.

Wigmore, J.H. (1937). *The science of judicial proof* (3rd ed.). Boston: Little, Brown, & Co.

Wiley, D. E. (1991). Test validity and invalidity reconsidered. In R. Snow & D. E. Wiley (Eds.), *Improving inquiry in social science* (pp. 75–107). Hillsdale, NJ: Lawrence Erlbaum.

Williamson, D. M., Mislevy, R. J., & Bejar, I. I. (Eds.). (2006). *Automated Scoring of complex performances in computer based testing.* Mahwah, NJ: Erlbaum.

PART II

RELATIVELY DIVERGENT

CHAPTER 6

INVALIDITY IN VALIDITY

Joel Michell

ABSTRACT

The concept of test validity was proposed in 1921. It helped allay doubts about whether tests really measure anything. To say that the issue of a test's validity is that of *whether it measures what it is supposed to measure* already presumes, first, that *the test measures something* and, second, that *whatever it is supposed to assess can be measured*. An attribute is measurable if and only if it possesses both ordinal and additive structure. Since there is no hard evidence that the attributes that testers aspire to measure are additively structured, the presumptions underlying the concept of validity are invalidly endorsed. As directly experienced, these attributes are ordinal and non-quantitative. The invalidity in validity is that of feigning knowledge where ignorance obtains.

SOME HISTORY: VALIDITY AND THE MYTH OF MENTAL MEASUREMENT

Over the past half-century, I have not only been involved in many facets of the theory and practice of testing but, also, I have been interested in understanding measurement as a scientific method.[1] Measurement has always been an aspiration of testers,[2] however, it has long been an achievement of physical scientists and, so, I reasoned, any attempt to understand it must

The Concept of Validity, pages 111–133

begin with measurement as understood in physics. As a result, I came to see that the way in which tests and testing are discussed (the *discourse of testing*) is not squarely based upon what is known about tests and testing (the *science of testing*). The discourse of testing, in particular presenting testing as if it were a form of measurement, outstrips the science upon which testing is based. There is no evidence either that tests *measure* anything or that the attributes that testers aspire to measure are *measurable*, so presenting tests as if they were instruments of measurement is presenting a myth,[3] the myth of mental measurement, as if it were a known fact. Furthermore, because the concept of validity is integral to this myth, if there is some dissatisfaction with this concept (Lissitz & Samuelsen, 2007), it is not within a mainstream still in thrall of this myth. Only when this myth is jettisoned will the discourse of testing, including talk of validity find a basis in reality. Since this myth is held in place by enduring social factors extrinsic to the science of testing, this is not likely to happen in the short term. We can get some idea of what these factors are by looking at the history of the concept of validity.

Rogers (1995) describes *validity*'s arrival in the mainstream testing movement:

> The year 1921 emerges as pivotal in the emergence of validity as part of the institutional proceedings of the testing field. This is when the idea gained clear acceptance. The Standardization Committee of the National Association of Directors of Educational Research[4] polled its members about the desirability of publishing an official list of terms and procedures. The results of this survey were announced in Courtis[5] (1921). Of particular note is this statement: "Two of the most important types of problems in measurement are those connected with the *determination of what a test measures* [italics added], and of how consistently it measures. The first should be called the problem of *validity* [italics added], the second, the problem of reliability" (p. 80). This is the first institutional definition of validity. (p. 246)

There were powerful pressures at work in education and psychology[6] bringing the burgeoning testing industry under the control of the profession and crafting the concept of *validity* was part of this process. As Courtis' ink was drying, Buckingham[7] (1921) reiterated, "By validity I mean the extent to which they [i.e., tests] measure what they purport to measure" (p.274). *Validity* was soon in the title of journal articles (e.g., Davis, 1922) and the concept was broadcast via McCall's[8] (1922) textbook, *How to Measure in Education*. Kelley's[9] (1927) text, *Interpretation of Educational Measurement*, reaffirmed that "The problem of validity is that of whether a test really measures what it purports to measure" (p.14) and by then this understanding was entrenched in the discourse of testing. It is there in the most recent of texts, such as Furr and Bacharach (2008, p.168), whose "basic definition" of validity, echoes Ebel's[10] earlier "basic notion" that "validity is the degree to which a test measures what it is supposed to measure" (1961, p. 642). Borsboom, Mellenbergh and van Heerden (2004) correctly note that this is *validity*'s core meaning.

By 1921, testers had developed a culture in which tests were marketed as instruments of measurement and test scores called "measures" as a matter of course and the concept of validity was integral to this culture, for to say that validity is the issue of *whether a test measures what it is supposed to measure*, already presumes, first, *that the test measures something* and, second, *that what it is supposed to assess is measurable*. In 1921, neither presupposition was scientifically defensible and testers, in feigning knowledge where none yet existed invoked the myth of mental measurement, the idea that mental traits are quantitative attributes.

However, this myth had its detractors.[11] For instance, in 1920, the *American Journal of Psychology* published a paper by Edwin G. Boring,[12] *The logic of the normal law of error in mental measurement*, arguing that psychological tests deliver only ordinal assessments. It was directed at the "mental test as a newcomer" (p. 1) to quantitative psychology and criticized the fact that testers inferred units of measurement by imposing a distributional form upon observed scores. He noted that distributional forms can only be discovered after units are determined and "The great difficulty is ... to find anything that we may properly call a psychological unit" (p. 31). He concluded, "We are left then with rank-orders ... and it is with these rank-orders that we must deal. We are not yet ready for much psychological measurement in the strict sense" (p. 32).

This was decades before Stevens[13] introduced his definition of measurement and its associated theory of scales. In distinguishing rank-orders from "measurement in the strict sense," Boring was saying that testers were not able to *measure* in the same sense of *measure* as used in physical science. It was an unpalatable indictment, for testers marketed tests as measurement devices and thought that assessment via tests was "in general the same as measurement in the physical sciences" (McCall, 1922, p. 5). In an address given at the annual meeting of the National Vocational Guidance Association in Atlantic City in 1921, Morris Viteles[14] premised his call for tests to be used in industry as extensively as in education upon the assumption that "Tests are the devices by which mental abilities can be measured" (1921, p. 57). This view was typical and all testers would have understood the tension between it and Boring's reality check.

However, the myth had its champion: Truman Lee Kelley. Described by Boring (1929) as "Thorndike's pupil and Stanford University's copy of Karl Pearson, perhaps now America's leading psychologist-statistician" (p. 528), Kelley (1923) adopted an unashamedly pragmatic view and argued that Boring's agonies over units were unnecessary because "starting with units however defined, if we can establish important relationships between phenomena measured in these units, we have proceeded scientifically. The choice of unit is purely a question of utility" (p. 418). This was smoke and mirrors. While the fact that test scores relate to important criteria needs explaining, the assumption that they do this *only* because they *measure* something presumes that the relevant attributes are quantitative. Units presume quantity and in science the hypothesis that attributes are quantitative, like any empirical hypothesis, is not made true by wishing.

Despite Kelley's question begging or, actually, because of it, the testing community embraced his stance. While lone voices still asked whether tests deliver measurements (e.g., Adams, 1931; Brown, 1934; Johnson, 1936; Smith, 1938), doubt withered within the mainstream and the issue hibernated. The presuppositions behind the concept of validity were endorsed to advance the reception of tests as instruments of measurement. The process whereby the rhetoric of measurement became entrenched within the testing community was facilitated from the 1930s by the adoption of operationalism.[15] The basic tenet of this philosophy is that within science, the meaning of any concept is synonymous with the corresponding set of operations used to measure it. This was taken to imply that the concepts that testers aspire to measure should be identified with the testing operations involved. Unfortunately, operationalism is based upon the confusion of *what* is measured with *how* it is measured (i.e., the confusion of a concept with how that concept is known (Michell, 1990)) and, so, any attempt to use it to save the myth of mental measurement must be logically defective, no matter how popular it proved to be historically.

The rhetoric of measurement was further reinforced when Stevens' (1946) operational definition of measurement[16] was adopted as part of an emerging, post-Second World War methodological consensus in psychology. This definition appeared to justify the kind of loosening of the term *measurement* from its scientific moorings that had occurred in psychology over the preceding decades: any rule for assigning numerals to things could now be called "measurement" it seemed.[17]

Part of this consensus, as well, was the new concept of *construct validity* (Cronbach & Meehl, 1955). While these authors attempted to correct the confusion involved in operationalism by distinguishing testing operations from the relevant concepts (or *constructs*) that testers aspire to measure, they committed a fallacy of the same kind in confusing the validity of a test with the process of validating it (i.e., they thought of the validity as qualifying an inference from relevant data to the claim that the test measures a nominated construct). As Borsboom et al. (2004) argue, if the concept of validity is to make any sense, it must be understood as a property of tests (i.e., a test, T, may have the relational property of measuring attribute, A)

and not as a property of the process of showing that test T measures A (i.e., the means by which T's validity is known).

This new concept did little to resolve the tension between myth and reality. While it raised the issue of whether a test actually measures a nominated construct, and did this in a way that recognized it as an empirical issue, highlighting the inferential gap between what a test *actually* assesses and what it is *intended* to assess, and recognizing that this gap could be bridged by discovery of lawful relationships (Meehl's *nomological networks*), the two presuppositions, *that tests measure something* and *that psychological constructs are measurable* remained securely locked in place. In fact, construct validity's official imprimatur[18] served to further protect these myths and those who attempted to make it the standard concept of validity (e.g., Messick, 1989) were wont to call test scores "measures" as indiscriminately as testers had done half a century before. *Construct validity*, along with other validity concepts (e.g., *predictive*, *concurrent*, and *content*) was understood by the mainstream as just another variation upon the theme of Courtis's core concept.

To summarize to this point: the concept of validity entered the testing profession at a time when the idea that testing was a form of measurement was still questioned within the mainstream; the concept quickly became an important component of testing discourse and its specific function was to reassure testers that even though they might not yet know *what* tests measured, they could sleep easy because their "mental tests measure something" (Kelley, 1929, p. 86); and, so, it was still safe to promote tests as instruments of measurement.

Objectively speaking, the presuppositions upon which the concept of validity is based remain as questionable now as in 1921. Testers are deeply confused about the concept of measurement.[19] They incant Stevens' definition when pressed for a form of words, but when it comes to theorizing, they necessarily, but usually unwittingly presume that the attributes they aspire to assess are quantitative (i.e., they presume that "*To be measurable an attribute must fit the specifications of a quantitative variable*" (Jones,[20] 1971, p.336, italics in original)). However, because they rarely consider these specifications in detail, testers just as rarely come face to face with the extent of their confusion. When these specifications are faced, it is clear that the issue of whether psychological attributes are measurable remains an open question.

SOME PHILOSOPHY: QUANTITATIVE STRUCTURE AND MEASUREMENT

Here is not the place for a detailed description of quantitative structure.[21] Instead, I will briefly indicate the kind of structure necessary for interval scale[22] measurement, this being the form usually presumed in testing. Our paradigm of quantitative structure is the real number line, which is why we resort to geometric diagrams when theorizing about quantitative attributes. Just as the number line consists of an ordered series of points, so any quantitative attribute consists of an ordered series of *magnitudes*.[23] Order presumes the *mutual homogeneity*[24] of the magnitudes or *degrees*[25] involved. For example, if one degree of an attribute is greater than another, they must be degrees *of the same attribute*, for to be *greater than* is always to be *greater than in some respect*. But order is just one component of quantity.

Quantitative structure also requires that *differences between magnitudes* be mutually homogeneous, for it is necessary that these differences also be ordered. Furthermore, given any two such differences, if the attribute is quantitative, then there always exists a third difference that makes up the deficit between them. For the attribute to be quantitative, this relation of composition must satisfy the *commutative* and *associative* laws of addition.[26] In short, with quantitative attributes, differences between magnitudes are mutually homogeneous and *additively* structured.

Quantitative structure then consists of ordinal structure and additive structure: the class of magnitudes of the attribute and the class of differences between magnitudes are each mutually homogeneous and the differences are composed additively. To complete the picture, it is also usually required that first, there be no least difference, second, no greatest difference, and third, that the ordered sequence of differences contain no gaps (i.e., that the attribute be continuous).

The virtue of this concept of continuous quantity is that it entails that ratios between differences are positive real numbers. The importance of this cannot be stressed too much: it is a door by which real numbers enter science. If any one difference is designated as the unit of measurement, each other difference between magnitudes already possesses a measure, this being the ratio it stands in to the unit. Measurement, in the scientific sense of the term is *the estimation of these ratios*.[27]

Of course, the word "measurement" has a further range of colloquial meanings, a fact Stevens exploited in selling his definition.[28] Only the above meaning matters in science and there is no legitimate role for Stevens' definition. Once that is recognized, it is clear that Boring was right to say, "We are not yet ready for much psychological measurement in the strict sense" (1920, p. 32), for as far as we know, the attributes testers aspire to measure are only ordinal structures.

SOME LOGIC: THEORY OF ORDINAL, NON-QUANTITATIVE STRUCTURES AND AN EXAMPLE

Characterizing quantitative structure indicates the locus of the distinction between quantitative and merely ordinal attributes.[29] This distinction lies in two possible sources. First, a merely ordinal attribute might be such that *the differences between its degrees are not intrinsically greater than, equal to or less than one another.* Even though the degrees of such an attribute are ordered, *the differences between those degrees* might only be the same or different in relation to one another. Then the differences between degrees show *qualitative difference,* but imply no *quantitative distance.*[30] Johannes von Kries (1882)[31] was the first to signal this possibility to psychologists and John Maynard Keynes (1921), through his work on the concept of probability made it more widely known.[32]

Second, even if the differences between its degrees are intrinsically ordered, it does not automatically follow that the attribute involved must be quantitative. For such an attribute to be quantitative, *the compositional relations between differences must be additive* and that possibility does not follow simply from the fact that the differences are ordered. It is an issue that can only be addressed by gaining access, either direct or indirect, to the specific ordinal relations between these differences. The theory of difference structures[33] indicates which relations upon differences entail quantity and which do not. In the philosophy of measurement, Hölder (1901) seems to have been the first to attend to this issue.[34]

Quantitative psychology is notorious for neglecting these two possibilities.[35] From Fechner onwards, the mainstream accepted the "constantly recurring argument" that any ordinal attribute is measurable "because we can speak, intelligently and intelligibly, of 'more' and 'less' of it" (Titchener, 1905, p. lxiii).[36] That is, they believed, erroneously, that mere order entails quantity[37] and ignored the fact that the attributes they aspired to measure might be merely ordinal. This was an egregious oversight because *prima facie* we have more reason to think of mental attributes as merely ordinal than as quantitative.

Differences between merely ordinal and quantitative attributes are significant because they mark a boundary between quantitative and non-quantitative science. A feature that gives quantitative science (e.g., physics) explanatory power is the range of quantitative relationships holding between measured attributes. In his review of the recent book by Cliff and Keats (2003) on ordinal analysis, Luce[38] recommended that our "goal really should be ratio scale measures, and we should not remain content with ordinal scales" because without ratio scales "no strong formal theories relating attributes are possible" (2004, p. 785). That is, without quantitative attributes, quantitative laws cannot exist. Nonetheless, non-quantitative science is possible and, indeed, persists in psychology, even if as a poor cousin (Marchel & Owens, 2007).[39] However, non-quantitative (i.e., qualitative) research should not be downgraded because our primary goal in science is not to *presume* answers to questions, but to *discover* the real structure of attributes. If the real structure of attributes that testers aspire to measure is merely ordinal, we must live with that situation, as Boring (1920) recognized and not pretend otherwise.

As an example of a non-quantitative, ordinal attribute, consider the scale Embretson (2006) calls the "Functional Independence Measure." It is a series of items assessing how independently the elderly are able to function physically in their daily lives. Each item specifies an activity, such as climbing stairs, transferring to a bathtub, or bathing.[40] It appears that elderly people generally lose the ability to climb stairs unaided before losing the ability to transfer unaided to a bathtub and that ability, in turn, is generally lost before the ability to bathe independently, and so on. These sorts of facts order the items. A person's pattern of physical capabilities, as assessed via this scale indicates a specific degree of functional independence.[41] The idea is that a person able to complete all of the activities that another person can plus at least one further activity on the list is the more independent of the two. Different degrees of functional independence are, consequently, mutually homogeneous.

However, *differences between degrees* seem to be mutually heterogeneous. For example, the difference between being able, on the one hand, and being unable, on the other, to climb stairs, and the difference between being able and being unable to transfer to a tub are differences of qualitatively diverse kinds, and each of these in turn is of another kind to that between being able and being unable to bathe independently, and so on for the other differences between degrees of this attribute. Because of this, it is not obvious that *the differences between degrees* of functional independence stand in intrinsic relations of *greater than, less than* or *equality* to one another.

If we try to think of such differences as thoroughly homogeneous, we face the question, what could a decrease in functional independence be other than an inability to do some kind of specific daily activity that one was previously able to do independently? As far as I can see, there is no homogeneous stuff, *independence,* adhering in various amounts to each person; there is only the set of distinct capacities to do the range of different daily activities constituting total functional independence from others, which, in being lost one by one, mark decreasing degrees of that attribute. Before it would be safe to conclude that *differences between degrees* of functional independence are ordered, evidence of non-arbitrary order relations between such differences would be required. Otherwise, the safest conclusion would be that functional independence is a merely ordinal attribute.

If functional independence is merely ordinal, it cannot stand in quantitative relationships to other attributes. This is not to say that we could not identify ordinal relationships, such as, *in old age, functional independence is likely to decrease as age increases*. However, it would mean that there could be no quantitative relationship between attributes, like age, and functional independence itself, such as *degree of functional independence is inversely proportional to the logarithm of age*. With quantitative attributes, like age or length, an increase of any given specific amount, such as of one year or one meter, can occur anywhere along the attribute's range. However, with functional independence, a person, at, say, the top of the scale, who loses the capacity to climb stairs unaided, and thereby suffers a decrease in independence, cannot suffer that same decrease again from a degree lower down the scale. Any further decrease must be in functions of other kinds and is, therefore, a decrease of a different qualitative kind and, so, one that is not necessarily equal to, greater than, or less than any other difference between degrees of this attribute.

What this means is that in charting the relationship between ordinal attributes, as opposed to quantitative ones, quite different causal laws may apply at different degrees of the attribute. This, I think, is one reason why Luce says that without ratio scales "no *strong* formal theories relating attributes are possible" (2004, p. 785; my emphasis). While formal theories always remain possible with merely ordinal attributes, they would lack the sweeping scope possible with quantitative attributes because of the heterogeneity of the differences between degrees. Therefore, with ordinal, non-quantitative attributes, theorizing about them qualitatively, not quantitatively would be the only way to make scientific progress. Attempting to fit quantitative models to such attributes would be to seek a level of mathematical structure not present in the situation modeled and would be an instance of sterile overmathematization.

Embretson (2006) notes that the Rasch model fits Functional Independence scale data "reasonably well" (p. 52). Is this not evidence that functional independence is a quantitative attribute? It is said that because item response models "are routinely tested against empirical data," the hypothesis that the relevant attributes are quantitative is thereby also tested (Borsboom & Mellenbergh, 2004, p.106). However, whatever the value of these models, the question of order versus quantity is not an issue easily settled by fitting IRT models, for it has also been said that "a given data set that is fit by an IRT model can be fit equally well by another model for which the form of the response curves is a monotonic increasing function of the form specified in the first model" (Jones & Appelbaum, 1989, pp. 25–26). If so, then such tests are only indicative of ordinal structure because it is order, not additive structure that is the invariant with monotonically interrelated models. Embretson (2006) nailed it when she concluded, "Model-based measurement, which includes IRT, does not provide a universal metric with zero points and interval widths," noting, "How such metrics could be obtained is difficult to envision for most psychological constructs" (p. 53). Evaluating test data against IRT models, by itself may provide no good reason to think the relevant attributes are quantitative.[42]

A more sensitive approach would be through identifying experimental outcomes specifically diagnostic of additive structure. The theory of conjoint measurement (Krantz et al., 1971) provides an avenue for this.[43] If abilities (for instance) are quantitative attributes, then given any pair of test items assessing the same ability, the difference between them in degree of difficulty will be equal to, greater than or less than the difference in degree of difficulty between any other such pair of items. Furthermore, any such ordinal relationship between differences in degrees of difficulty would not exist without a basis in the items themselves. That is, it would be due to identifiable features of the items involved. If such features exist, it would, in principle, be possible to engineer pairs of items for which it is known in advance that one difference between degrees of difficulty exceeds another. If such item engineering can be achieved, then conjoint measurement theory, with its hierarchy of cancellation conditions (Michell, 1990) could be applied to response data to test whether abilities are quantitative. However, despite the valuable research of Embretson and others[44] into item features, we are still a long way from identifying features systematically linked to the presumed additive structure of abilities and this is because if abilities possess additive structure, we do not yet know enough about this structure or the features of test items related to it. We cannot know whether abilities are quantitative until we have good theories connecting the hypothesized additive structure of abilities to features of test items.

Standard test theories, such as IRT models are less suited to coming to grips with the distinction between quantitative and merely ordinal attributes because they represent an approach in which theories are tailored to fit existing instruments (viz., mental tests) on the assumption that relevant attributes are already known to be quantitative and instruments, already known to be capable of measuring. On these assumptions, theories exist chiefly to justify instruments. Such an approach puts the instrumental cart before the scientific horse. What is really required are instruments tailored to true theories about the psychological processes involved in the attributes we wish to assess. In the absence of such theories we cannot determine whether our attributes are quantitative, no matter how well data fit our models.

The attributes that testers aspire to measure are experienced *only* as ordinal and, furthermore, in so far as we experience differences between degrees of such attributes, we seem to experience them as heterogeneous, not as differences in amounts of some homogeneous stuff.[45] For example, it seems that a person of high mathematical ability, say, does not differ from a person of merely moderate ability by possessing the same kind of knowledge, skills and strategies that distinguish the moderately able from persons of low ability. Instead such a person has a high degree of ability precisely because of the qualitatively different, superior mathematical knowledge, skills and strategies possessed. If such attributes are quantitative, then not only is their quantitative structure yet to be discovered, but also their character as different amounts of some homogeneous quantity is yet to be specified.

SOME IMPLICATIONS: THE SCIENTIFIC
AND INSTRUMENTAL TASKS OF ASSESSMENT

In Michell (1997) I distinguished the *scientific* and *instrumental tasks* of measurement. The *scientific task* is to investigate whether the relevant attribute is quantitative; if it is, then the *instrumental task* is to devise measurement instruments by locating standardized operations the outcomes of which are sensitive to the relevant attribute's quantitative structure. While the scientific task is *logically prior* to the instrumental, in practice the two tasks may be undertaken jointly. In relation to the present discussion, the distinction between these two tasks can be extended from the domain of measurement to the more general one of assessment.

So extended, the *scientific task of assessment* would be to investigate the structure of the relevant attribute. Attributes possess their own natural structure and they should not be presumed to only possess structures that we consider desirable, such as quantitative structure. Nor should it be presumed, as is customary in psychology, that all attributes possess one of just two kinds of structure, quantitative and classificatory structures (e.g., Meehl, 1992). Between merely classificatory attributes (like *nationality* or the various diagnostic categories for mental disorders) and quantitative attributes (like *length* and *mass*), there is an array of possible ordinal structures, like the various kinds of partial orders, weak orders and simple orders (Michell, 1990). Since most of the attributes that testers aspire to measure seem at first sight to be in some sense ordinal and since there is no evidence that these attributes are quantitative, it is this array of intermediate, ordinal structures that are most relevant to testing. However, here testers are let down by their education (Michell, 2001), for an introduction to these intermediate structures is not generally included in the testing curriculum. While there seems little point in calling for revision of relevant university course syllabuses,[46] it is obvious that a necessary condition for thinking in terms of a specific set of concepts is that of first being made aware of their existence.

An attribute is ordinal if for at least some pairs of its degrees, one degree is greater than another (in the relevant sense), where this *greater than* relation is transitive and asymmetric. Identification of the kind of ordinal structure involved in particular cases requires not only defining the relevant attribute explicitly, but also identifying the relevant *greater than* relation. The difficulties involved in doing this will vary from context to context. In the case of achievement testing, where the tester is attempting to assess the level of a person's knowledge in some circumscribed domain, it will be much easier than in, say, the case of ability assessment, where characterizing the relevant ability requires framing hypotheses about cognitive processes and, so, must build upon discoveries in cognitive psychology. However, the scientific task of discovering the attribute's structure cannot be accomplished until testers are able to define the attribute to be assessed and identify the *greater than* relationship for that attribute. Where this has not been done for any attribute, claims to measure it are vacuous because they are made not only in ignorance of what *measurement* means, but also in ignorance of the character of the attribute involved.

The *instrumental task of assessment* is to construct tests, performance upon which reflects aspects of the structure of the relevant attribute. If this task seems like test validation, only by another name, then the distinction needs to be clarified for, while superficially similar, the instrumental task of assessment is different to test validation. In the first place, test validation focuses first on the particular *test* under investigation, while the instrumental task focuses first on the *attribute* to be assessed. Second, given a specific test, validation attempts to discover the *attribute or attributes* underlying test performance, while given a specific attribute, the instrumental task attempts to discover the *features of test items* sensitive to structural properties of that attribute. Third, as already noted in this paper, test validation presumes that something is *measured*, while the instrumental task aspires to *assessment* (a much wider concept than measurement).

If tests are useful for the assessment of certain attributes, then this must be because of the features of the items involved. The instrumental task of assessment is primarily concerned with discovering, for some nominated and explicitly defined attribute (relative to which the *greater than* relation is identifiable), the features of test items that cause individual differences in performance to be sensitive to the ordinal (or possibly, quantitative) properties of the relevant attribute. Only when such item-features are identified and understood will it be possible to engineer tests whose capacity to assess the relevant attribute is known in advance. In this way, the testers' knowledge of the relevant attribute and relevant item-features would make the concept of test validation entirely redundant.

CONCLUSION: INVALIDITY IN VALIDITY

It is the hiatus between what is *known* about psychological attributes (viz., that they are ordinal) and the *myth* (viz., that they are known to be quantitative) that explains certain features of the concept of validity. It explains the presumptions underlying the concept, viz., that psychological attributes are quantitative and tests, instruments of measurement. It explains why the concept emerged when it did. It emerged in time to deflect attention away from the two issues that it presumed answers to. Boring's critique was published in 1920 and the next year the problem of test validity was first announced to the testing profession. And it explains the concept's durability. In the past century, many things have changed in testing, but not the core understanding of validity, as Borsboom et al. (2004) point out. This is because the concept is still useful in disguising the gap between what testers know and the myth of mental measurement. The invalidity in validity is that the concept feigns knowledge where such does not yet exist.

But does not this invalidity hide a genuine problem, if not that of what tests *measure*, then the problem of what they *assess* and, so, might not the concept of validity be rehabilitated in these terms? Can we not ask of any test, *what attributes does that test enable us to assess?* Of course we can, but it is an odd situation to first have constructed an instrument of assessment and then to ask what it assesses. Such a situation would not arise if the character of the target attribute was investigated in advance and when understood sufficiently well, a test aimed at that target then constructed through knowledge of relevant item features. There is no analogue of the problem of test validity in physical measurement.[47] There, instruments are engineered using knowledge of laws relating features of the instrument to the structure of the relevant attribute. In this respect, test theory is an anomalous enterprise:[48] a body of theory constructed for the assessment of we know not what, on the basis of laws yet unproven. Boring (1920) closed his paper with a still relevant admonition:

> But, if in psychology we must deal—and it seems we must—with abilities, capacities, dispositions and tendencies, the nature of which we cannot accurately define, then it is senseless to seek in the logical process of mathematical elaboration a psychologically significant precision that was not present in the psychological setting of the problem. Just as ignorance will not breed knowledge, so inaccuracy of definition will never yield precision of result. (p. 33)

That is, focus upon the attributes to be assessed; investigate their structure and their lawful connections to features of test items. Few testers realize that knowledge of the structure of attributes is necessary to provide a scientific base for testing practice.[49] Sadly, testing became a profession prior to developing a scientific base and for nearly a century the concept of validity has obscured this lack. In accepting this concept, testers embraced the "the seeming truth which cunning times put on to entrap the wisest."[50]

APPENDIX 1: THE AXIOMS OF QUANTITY AND THE CONCEPT OF MEASUREMENT

Measurable quantitative attributes have a distinctive structure. It is useful to think in terms of an example, such as length. Quantitative structure is the same in length as in other attributes, only more evident. We experience length via specific lengths, say the length of a pen or a cricket pitch. These specific lengths are *magnitudes* of length. What makes length quantitative is the way in which its magnitudes interrelate. These interrelations may be stated in seven propositions, sometimes called "axioms of quantity" (e.g., Hölder, 190151). The first four state what it is for length to be additive. The remaining three ensure that all lengths are included. Let a, b, c, be any magnitudes of length, then length is additive because:

1. For every pair of magnitudes, a and b, one and only one of the following is true:
   (i) a is the same as b (ie, $a = b$);
   (ii) there exists a magnitude, c, such that $a = b + c$;
   (iii) there exists a magnitude, c, such that $b = a + c$.
2. For any magnitudes, a and b, $a + b > a$.
3. For any magnitudes, a and b, $a + b = b + a$.
4. For any magnitudes, a, b, and c, $a + (b + c) = (a + b) + c$.

Axiom 1 says that any two lengths are either identical or different and if different, there is another length equaling the difference; Axiom 2 says that if a length is entirely composed of two discrete parts, then it exceeds each; Axiom 3 that if a length is entirely composed of two discrete parts, the order of composition is irrelevant; Axiom 4 that where a length is entirely composed of three discrete parts, it is always the composition of *any* one with the remaining two.

The following three axioms ensure the completeness of this characterization:

5. For any length a, there is another b, such that $b < a$.
6. For any two lengths a and b there is another c such that $c = a + b$.
7. For every non-empty class of lengths having an upper bound, there is a least upper bound.

Axiom 5 means that there is no smallest length; Axiom 6 that there is no greatest; and Axiom 7 says that there are no gaps in the ordered sequence of lengths, that is, length is continuous.

These axioms entail that the ratio of any one magnitude of length to any other is a positive real number.[52] For example, one length might be twice another or three and a half times another or the square root of two times another. The *measure* of one length, c, relative to another, d, is the ratio of c to d. In practice, ratios are rarely specified precisely because measurement procedures possess only finite resolution. *Measurement* is the estimation of the ratio of one magnitude of a quantity to another magnitude (the unit) of the same quantity.

When we claim to be able to measure psychological attributes, such as abilities using tests, we are claiming that these attributes have this kind of structure[53] and that tests are sensitive to this kind of structure. Of course, generally, psychologists do not claim to be able to measure on ratio scales. Typically, they want to claim measurement on interval scales. This makes little difference to the issues under discussion. On an interval scale, measures of intervals are on a ratio scale. Hence, what psychologists are claiming is that *differences* between levels of ability possess quantitative structure (i.e., satisfy Axioms 1–7) and that tests are sensitive to this structure upon differences.

APPENDIX 2: THE FUNCTIONAL INDEPENDENCE SCALE

The series of activities comprising the so-called "functional independence measure" as ordered from most to least difficult (Embretson, 2006) is as follows:

1. Climbing stairs;
2. Transferring to bathtub;
3. Bathing;
4. Walking;
5. Dressing upper body;
6. Independent toileting;
7. Transferring to bed;
8. Dressing lower body;
9. Mobility without a wheelchair;
10. Bladder control;
11. Performing personal grooming; and
12. Bowel control.

ACKNOWLEDGMENT

I am grateful to members of the Models & Measurement Seminar, School of Psychology, University of Sydney for comments upon an earlier version.

NOTES

1. My thoughts on this are given in Michell (2005).
2. I use the term "testers" to refer to psychologists, educationalists, and social scientists involved in the construction and use of tests and in the development of associated theories and methods.
3. In this context, by a *myth* I mean a theory or hypothesis believed because it eases our minds.
4. The National Association of Directors of Educational Research (NADER) was the American Educational Research Association (AERA) in embryo.
5. Stuart A. Courtis, a founding member of NADER who "printed tests and sold them to school districts across the country" (Mershon & Schlossman, 2008, pp. 315–316), later became disillusioned with tests as measurement instruments (Courtis, 1928).
6. See Mershon and Schlossman (2008) and von Mayrhauser (1992).
7. Burdette R. Buckingham, also a founder of NADER was then editor of the *Journal of Educational Research* and Director of the University of Illinois' Bureau of Educational Research (Mershon & Schlossman, 2008).
8. William Anderson McCall (1891–1982) had been Thorndike's student and became professor of educational measurement at Columbia University.
9. Truman Lee Kelley (1884–1961) also Thorndike's student, taught at Stanford University from 1920 and was professor of education at Harvard Graduate School of Education from 1931 to 1950 and president of the Psychometric Society in 1938–39 (Stout, 1999).
10. Robert L. Ebel's (Vice President at ETS (1957–1963) and Professor of Education and Psychology at Michigan State University (1963–1982) espoused controversial views on validity (Cizek et al., 2006).
11. While early on, Binet (1905) recognized that his scale "does not permit the measure of intelligence, because intellectual qualities are not superposable" (p.151), doubts about mental measurement had long been voiced in the adjacent field of psychophysics. However, by 1905 most psychologists accepted psychophysical measurement (Titchener, 1905), but doubts persisted (e.g., Brown, 1913).
12. Edwin G. Boring (1886–1968) was then professor of experimental psychology at Clark University. During World War I he had served in the US Army's mental testing program. From 1922, he taught at Harvard, becoming its first professor of psychology in 1934. He is remembered best for writings on the history of psychology (Reed, 1999).

13. Stevens (1946). Stevens was Boring's student (and, incidentally, at one time, Kelley's). His definition and theory of scales shaped the post-war understanding of measurement in psychology (Michell, 1997, 1999).

14. Morris Viteles (1898–1996) was a pioneer of industrial psychology in the United States and authored influential books in the field (Thompson, 1998).

15. Operationalism was a philosophy of science proposed by the Nobel prize-winning physicist, Percy W. Bridgman (1927) and energetically promoted in psychology by Stevens (e.g., Stevens, 1935).

16. He defined measurement as the assignment of numerals to objects or events according to rule.

17. See Michell (1999).

18. The term "construct validity" was introduced in 1954 in the *Technical Recommendations for Psychological Tests and Diagnostic Techniques* published by the American Psychological Association. Paul Meehl was a member of the subcommittee recommending it. The concept reflects the logical empiricist philosophy of science then dominant in the United States. However, the concept was not universally accepted and some influential testers dissented (see, e.g., Ebel, 1961; Horst, 1966).

19. See, for example, Michell (1997, 1999).

20. Lyle V. Jones is one of the few members of the testing community to candidly note this.

21. However, see Appendix 1.

22. Stevens' (1946) distinguished *nominal, ordinal, interval* and *ratio* scales. Only the latter two depend upon the relevant attribute being quantitative in structure.

23. Following time-honored usage, the term *magnitude* refers to any specific level of a quantitative attribute.

24. Euclid noted this as long ago as the fourth century BC in Book V of his *Elements* (Heath, 1908).

25. The term *degree* refers to any specific level of an ordinal or quantitative attribute without any implied commitment to quantity. Hence, all magnitudes are degrees but not all degrees are magnitudes.

26. These correspond to Axioms 3 and 4 of Appendix 1.

27. For example: "Any measured quantity may thus be expressed by a number (the magnitude ratio) and the name of the unit" (Wildhack, 2005, p. 487).

28. As noted, most testers lean towards Stevens' definition. However, in so far as testers believe that the attributes that they aspire to measure are quantitative attributes (and this is what they are committed to in their theories), Stevens' definition amounts to a form of false consciousness and in accepting that definition testers misunderstand what they are about.

29. The concept of an ordinal attribute is wide, ranging from simple orders to partial orders (Michell, 1990). Here, for convenience, I consider mainly strict simple orders (i.e., attributes, the degrees of which are ordered by a transitive, asymmetric and connected relation).

30. As David Hume (1888) noted, "any great *difference* in the degrees of any quality is called a *distance* by a common metaphor... The ideas of distance and difference are, therefore, connected together. Connected ideas are readily

taken for each other" (p. 393). This tendency is a cause of the cognitive illusion I call the psychometricians' fallacy (Michell, 2006, 2009).

31. Johannes von Kries (1853–1928) was a sensory physiologist and critic of psychophysical measurement, proposing the so-called *quantity objection* (Titchener, 1905). Niall (1995) gives an English translation.

32. John Maynard Keynes (1883–1946) wrote his dissertation on the concept of probability. He followed von Kries in thinking that probabilities are only quantitative in very special cases. In most cases, he thought, they are at best ordinal and non-quantitative. Later, this observation influenced his economic thought (e.g., Keynes, 1936).

33. See Krantz et al. (1971).

34. Psychologists ignored Hölder until Krantz et al. (1971). See Michell and Ernst (1996, 1997).

35. However, some quantitative psychologists considered related possibilities. For example, Stevens (1957) distinguished *prothetic* and *metathetic* continua, the former being continuous attributes in which degrees differ according to *how much* and the latter, continuous attributes in which different values of the same attribute differ *in kind*.

36. Titchener was reviewing psychophysics, but similar arguments were used in testing. For example, McCall (1922), echoing Thorndike (1918), argued that "whatever exists at all exists in some amount" and "anything that exists in amount can be measured."

37. Psychologists were not alone in doing this: philosophers, mathematicians, and economists also committed this fallacy (e.g., see Michell, 2007). It was so ubiquitous in psychology that I have called it *the psychometricians' fallacy* (Michell, 2006, 2009). Typically, in psychology, ordinal scales are seen as obstacles to be overcome (e.g., Harwell & Gatti, 2001) rather than as intrinsically worthwhile structures.

38. Along with Patrick Suppes, R. D. Luce is the leading measurement theorist of recent time (e.g., see Luce, 2005).

39. The distinction between quantitative and qualitative methods resides in the character of the attributes investigated (i.e., whether they are quantitative or not) and the recent association of qualitative methods with non-realist philosophies of science is actually a red herring and not an intrinsic feature of such methods (Michell, 2003).

40. The full set is listed in Appendix 2.

41. I use this scale as an example because the attribute assessed is not mental, so it avoids a number of problems intrinsic to psychology but extrinsic to the issues considered here. Functional independence is a social attribute, which the scale indexes via a range of physical abilities, absence of any one of which contributes to a person's dependence upon helpers. Thus, the attribute assessed is actually a rather complex socio-physical one.

42. If the relevant attribute is merely ordinal, then there will always exist subsets of test items that could fit IRT models, such as the Rasch model. In a test construction context where items are successively culled to give a best-fitting set, therefore, the fit of data to such a model is a biased test of whether the relevant attribute is quantitative.

43. Most testers have resisted applying this theory. Cliff (1992) and Borsboom (2005) suggest reasons, but not the primary one, viz., testers presume that the attributes they aspire to measure are already known to be quantitative and, so, have no use for a theory enabling empirical tests of that presumption (Michell, 1999).

44. See, for example, Embretson and Gorin (2001).

45. In this respect, psychological attributes are similar in structure to the kinds of attributes that R. G. Collingwood (1933) called *scales of forms*. Putting Collingwood's metaphysical concerns to one side, it is notable that he explicitly recognised that attributes having this kind of structure cannot be measured. Collingwood's concept had little impact in psychology, although it has received attention in other disciplines (e.g., Allen, 2008).

46. Such calls have been made, vainly, for decades (e.g., Sutcliffe, 1976).

47. Borsboom (2005) notes this. There are, of course, issues of quality control with instruments of physical measurement, such as those of calibration. These are discussed in standard works on metrology (see, e.g., Laaneots & Mathiesen, (2006).

48. I would maintain that this situation exists because the concept of validity is an integral part of the discourse of a pathological science (see Michell, 2000, 2008).

49. One of the few to come close to recognising this was Loevinger (1957) in her emphasis upon trait structure. However, in the time-honoured tradition of psychometrics, she distinguished only two sorts of structure, *quantitative* and *classificatory*. This, of course, anticipated the more recent concern with the distinction between *categories* and *continua* (e.g., Meehl, 1992; De Boeck, Wilson & Acton, 2005). Loevinger showed little interest in characterising explicitly the sorts of structure involved and testers have followed her in this respect.

50. William Shakespeare, *Merchant of Venice III, ii, 100.*

51. The axioms given here are based on Hölder's (Michell, 1999), but are not identical to his. For an English translation of the relevant part of Hölder's classic paper see Michell and Ernst (1996).

52. The *ratio* of one length to another is the magnitude of the first relative to the second (Heath, 1908).

53. Which is not to say that at the same time we claim to know how to test such a proposition. Most of the attributes known to be quantitative are physical but even in physics evidence for quantitative structure is typically indirect, with the exception, of course, of *extensive quantities*, like length, time and weight. For more on this see Michell (1990, 1999, 2005).

REFERENCES

Adams, H. F. (1931). Measurement in psychology. *Journal of Applied Psychology, 15,* 545–554.

Allen, R. T. (2008). Art as scales of forms. *British Journal of Aesthetics, 48,* 395–409.

Binet, A. (1905). *L'Étude expérimentale de l'intelligence.* Paris: Schleicher.

Boring, E. G. (1920). The logic of the normal law of error in mental measurement. *American Journal of Psychology, 31,* 1–33.

Boring, E. G. (1929). *A history of experimental psychology.* New York: Appleton-Century-Crofts.

Borsboom, D. (2005). *Measuring the mind: Conceptual issues in contemporary psychometrics.* Cambridge: Cambridge University Press.

Borsboom, D., & Mellenbergh, G. J. (2004). Why psychometrics is not pathological: A comment on Michell. *Theory & Psychology, 14,* 105–120.

Borsboom, D., Mellenbergh, G. J., & van Heerden, J. (2004). The concept of validity. *Psychological Review, 111,* 1061–1071.

Bridgman, P. W. (1927). *The logic of modern physics.* New York: Macmillan.

Brown, J. F. (1934). A methodological consideration of the problem of psychometrics. *Erkenntnis, 4,* 46–61.

Brown, W. (1913). Are the intensity differences of sensation quantitative? IV. *British Journal of Psychology, 6,* 184–189.

Buckingham, B. R. (1921). Intelligence and its measurement: A symposium. XIV. *Journal of Educational Psychology, 12,* 271–275.

Cizak, G. J., Crocker, L., Frisbie, D. A., Mehrens, W. A., & Stiggins, R. J. (2006). A tribute to Robert L. Ebel: Scholar, teacher, mentor, and statesman. *Educational Measurement: Issues and Practice, 25,* 23–32.

Cliff, N. (1992). Abstract measurement theory and the revolution that never happened. *Psychological Science, 3,* 186–190.

Cliff, N., & Keats, J. A. (2003). *Ordinal measurement in the behavioural sciences.* Mahwah, NJ: Lawrence Erlbaum.

Collingwood, R. G. (1933). *An essay on philosophical method.* Oxford: Clarendon Press.

Courtis, S. A. (1921). Report of the standardization committee. *Journal of Educational Research, 4,* 78–80.

Courtis, S. A. (1928). Education: a pseudo-science. *Journal of Educational Research, 17,* 130–132.

Cronbach, L. J., & Meehl, P. E. (1955). Construct validity in psychological tests. *Psychological Bulletin, 52,* 281–302.

Davis, R. (1922). The validity of the Whipple Group Test in the fourth and fifth grades. *Journal of Educational Research, 5,* 239–244.

De Boeck, P., Wilson, M., & Acton, G. S. (2005). A conceptual and psychometric framework for distinguishing categories and dimensions. *Psychological Review, 112,* 129–158.

Ebel, R. L. (1961). Must all tests be valid? *American Psychologist, 16,* 640–647.

Embretson, S. E. (2006). The continued search for non-arbitrary metrics in psychology. *American Psychologist, 61,* 50–55.

Embretson, S., & Gorin, J. (2001). Improving construct validity with cognitive psychology principles. *Journal of Educational Measurement, 38,* 343–368.

Furr, R. M., & Bacharach, V. R. (2008). *Psychometrics: An introduction.* Los Angeles: Sage.

Harwell, M. R., & Gatti, G. G. (2001). Rescaling ordinal data to interval data in educational research. *Review of Educational Research, 71,* 105–131.

Heath, T. L. (1908). *The thirteen books of Euclid's elements, vol. 2.* Cambridge: Cambridge University Press.

Hölder, O. (1901). Die Axiome der Quantität und die Lehre vom Mass. *Berichte über die Verhandlungen der Königlich Sächsischen Gesellschaft der Wissenschaften zu Leipzig, Mathematisch-Physische Klasse, 53,* 1–46.

Horst, P. (1966). *Psychological measurement and prediction.* Belmont CA: Wadsworth.

Hume, D. (1888). *A treatise of human nature.* Oxford: Clarendon Press.

Johnson, H. M. (1936). Pseudo-mathematics in the social sciences. *American Journal of Psychology, 48,* 342–351.

Jones, L. V. (1971). The nature of measurement. In R. L. Thorndike (Ed.), *Educational measurement* (2nd ed., pp.335–355). Washington, DC: American Council on Education.

Jones, L. V. & Appelbaum, M. I. (1989). Psychometric methods. *Annual Review of Psychology, 40,* 23–43.

Kelley, T. L. (1923). The principles and techniques of mental measurement. *American Journal of Psychology, 34,* 408–432.

Kelley, T. L. (1927). *Interpretation of educational measurements.* New York: World Book Company.

Kelley, T. L. (1929). *Scientific method: its function in research and in education.* Columbus: Ohio State University Press.

Keynes, J. M. (1921). *A treatise on probability.* London: Macmillan.

Keynes, J. M. (1936). *The general theory of employment, interest and money.* London: Macmillan.

Krantz, D. H., Luce, R. D., Suppes, P., & Tversky, A. (1971). *Foundations of measurement, vol. 1.* New York: Academic Press.

Laaneots, R., & Mathiesen, O. (2006). *An introduction to metrology.* Estonia: TUT Press.

Lissitz, R. W., & Samuelsen, K. (2007). A suggested change in terminology and emphasis regarding validity and education. *Educational Researcher, 36,* 437–448.

Loevinger, J. (1957). Objective tests as instruments of psychological theory. *Psychological Reports, 3,* 635–694.

Luce, R. D. (2004). Ordinal attributes, ordinal analyses only. Review of Cliff and Keats (2003). *Contemporary Psychology, 49,* 783–785.

Luce, R. D. (2005). Measurement analogies: comparisons of behavioral and physical measures. *Psychometrika, 70,* 227–251.

McCall, W. A. (1922). *How to measure in education.* New York: Macmillan.

Marchel, C., & Owens, S. (2007). Qualitative research in psychology: Could William James get a job? *History of Psychology, 10,* 301–324.

Meehl, P. E. (1992). Factors and taxa, traits and types, differences of degree and differences of kind. *Journal of Personality, 60,* 117–174.

Mershon, S., & Schlossman, S. (2008). Education, science, and the politics of knowledge: The American Educational Research Association, 1915–1940. *American Journal of Education, 114,* 307–340.

Messick, S. (1989). Validity. In R. L. Linn (eds.), *Educational measurement* (3rd ed., pp.13–103). London: Collier Macmillan.

Michell, J. (1990). *An introduction to the logic of psychological measurement.* Hillsdale, NJ: Erlbaum.

Michell, J. (1997). Quantitative science and the definition of *measurement* in psychology. *British Journal of Psychology, 88,* 355–383.

Michell, J. (1999). *Measurement in psychology: a critical history of a methodological concept.* Cambridge: Cambridge University Press.

Michell, J. (2000). Normal science, pathological science and psychometrics. *Theory & Psychology, 10,* 639–667.

Michell, J. (2001). Teaching and misteaching measurement in psychology. *Australian Psychologist, 36,* 211–217.

Michell, J. (2003). The quantitative imperative: positivism, naïve realism and the place of qualitative methods in psychology. *Theory & Psychology, 13,* 5–31.

Michell, J. (2005). The logic of measurement: a realist overview. *Measurement, 38,* 285–294.

Michell, J. (2006). Psychophysics, intensive magnitudes, and the psychometricians' fallacy. *Studies in History and Philosophy of Biological and Biomedical Sciences, 17,* 414–432.

Michell, J. (2007). *Bergson's and Bradley's versions of the psychometricians' fallacy argument.* Paper presented at the First Joint Meeting of ESHHS and CHEIRON, University College Dublin, Ireland.

Michell, J. (2008). Is psychometrics pathological science? *Measurement: Interdisciplinary Research and Perspectives, 6,* 7–24.

Michell, J. (2009). The psychometricians' fallacy: too clever by half? *British Journal of Mathematical and Statistical Psychology, 62,* 41–55.

Michell, J. & Ernst, C. (1996). The axioms of quantity and the theory of measurement, Part I. [An English translation of Hölder (1901), Part I.] *Journal of Mathematical Psychology, 40,* 235–252.

Michell, J. & Ernst, C. (1997). The axioms of quantity and the theory of measurement, Part II. [An English translation of Hölder (1901), Part II.] *Journal of Mathematical Psychology, 41,* 345–356.

Niall, K. K. (1995). Conventions of measurement in psychophysics: von Kries on the so-called psychophysical law. *Spatial Vision, 9,* 275–305.

Reed, J. W. (1999). Boring, Edwin Garrigues. *American national biography* (Vol. 3, pp. 217–218). New York: Oxford University Press.

Rogers, T. B. (1995). *The psychological testing enterprise: An introduction.* Pacific Grove CA: Brooks/Cole.

Smith, B. O. (1938). *Logical aspects of educational measurement.* New York: Columbia University Press.

Stevens, S. S. (1935). The operational definition of psychological terms. *Psychological Review, 42,* 517–527.

Stevens, S. S. (1946). On the theory of scales of measurement. *Science, 103,* 677–680.

Stevens, S. S. (1957). On the psychophysical law. *Psychological Review, 64,* 153–181.

Stout, D. (1999). Kelley, Truman Lee. *American national biography* (Vol. 12, pp. 491–492). New York: Oxford University Press.

Sutcliffe, J. P. (1976). *Mathematics needed for particular social sciences.* Sydney: Academy of Social Sciences in Australia.

Thompson, A. S. (1998). Morris S. Viteles (1898–1996). *American Psychologist, 53,* 1153–1154.

Thorndike, E. L. (1918). The nature, purposes, and general methods of measurements of educational products. In G. M. Whipple (Ed.), *Seventeenth yearbook of the national society for the study of education* (Vol. 2, pp. 16–24). Bloomington IL: Public School Publishing.

Titchener, E. B. (1905b). *Experimental psychology: a manual of laboratory practice. Vol. II: Quantitative experiments. Part II: Instructor's manual.* London: Macmillan.

Viteles, M. (1921). Tests in industry. *Journal of Applied Psychology, 5*, 57–63.

von Kries, J. (1882). Über die Messung intensiver Grössen und über das sogenannte psychophysische Gesetz. *Vierteljahrsschrift für wissenschaftliche Philosophie, 6*, 257–294.

von Mayrhauser, R. T. (1992). The mental testing community and validity. *American Psychologist, 47*, 244–253.

Wildhack, W. A. (2005). Physical measurement. In M. D. Licker (Ed.), *McGraw-Hill concise encyclopedia of physics* (pp. 483–487). New York: McGraw-Hill.

CHAPTER 7

THE END OF CONSTRUCT VALIDITY

Denny Borsboom, Angélique O. J. Cramer, Rogier A. Kievit, Annemarie Zand Scholten, and Sanja Franić

ABSTRACT

Construct validity theory holds that (a) validity is a property of test score interpretations in terms of constructs that (b) reflects the strength of the evidence for these interpretations. In this paper, we argue that this view has absurd consequences. For instance, following construct validity theory, test score interpretations that deny that anything is measured by a test may themselves have a high degree of construct validity. In addition, construct validity theory implies that now defunct test score interpretations, like those attached to phlogiston measures in the 17th century, 'were valid' at the time but 'became invalid' when the theory of phlogiston was refuted. We propose an alternative view that holds that (a) validity is a property of measurement instruments that (b) codes whether these instruments are sensitive to variation in a targeted attribute. This theory avoids the absurdities of construct validity theory, and is broadly consistent with the view, commonly held by working researchers and textbook writers but not construct validity theorists, that a test is valid if it measures what it should measure. Finally, we discuss some pressing problems in psychological measurement that are salient within our conceptualization, and argue that the time has come to face them.

The Concept of Validity, pages 135–170

INTRODUCTION

Construct validity theory, as Cronbach and Meehl (1955) introduced it, holds that a test score interpretation in terms of a nomological network (a set of laws relating theoretical terms in that network to each other and to observational terms) is valid to the degree that the network itself is supported by the evidence. This idea leaned heavily on the philosophical framework provided by logical positivism, which used the same construction as a general account of the relation between theoretical terms and observations in scientific theory. For the positivists, the nomological network served to endow the terms in it with meaning through so-called implicit definitions (Carnap, 1950). Roughly, the idea was that the meaning of a theoretical term (like 'mass' or 'force') was given, implicitly, by the laws in which such terms play a role. A replica of the positivist idea of fixing the meaning of theoretical terms through the use of implicit definitions occurs in Cronbach and Meehl's (1955) theory of construct validity: the meaning of terms such as 'general intelligence' is to be fixed by pointing at the laws in which these terms play a role, and the validity of interpretations of test scores in terms of such networks is subsequently determined by the degree to which the networks are corroborated by evidence.

At the time—which, methodologically, was thoroughly dominated by behaviorism and operationalism—this move created some leeway for tests that were to be interpreted in theoretical terms (like 'general intelligence' or 'neuroticism') but that had no direct characterization in terms of test content, nor a satisfactory criterion that could function as a 'gold standard.' Unfortunately, the idea of construct validity did not actually work, because there were (and are) no nomological networks involving concepts like general intelligence. Although various models and mechanisms have been suggested for such psychological attributes, these do not resemble the kind of strict laws that could function to build up a nomological network in the positivist sense (e.g., see Suppe, 1974).

To see this, it is useful to shortly discuss what kind of networks the positivists had in mind, because the term 'nomological network' has been used in psychology to indicate everything from a theoretical hunch to a regression model, but rarely to anything that the positivists would have recognized as a nomological network. In the positivists' account of scientific theories, one first requires a division of one's vocabulary into observation sentences ("John sits at home with a book on Saturday night") and theoretical sentences ("John has property i"). Second, observation sentences are to be connected to theoretical sentences by correspondence rules ("a person has i if and only if that person sits at home with a book on Saturday nights"). Third, the terms mentioned in the theoretical sentences are to be connected by laws, for instance $i = f(e)$, where e is another theoretical term hooked up to the observations through its own correspondence rules (e.g., "a person has *e* if and only if that person is at a party at least once a week"). The properties *i*, *e*, and others (say, *c*, *a*, and *o*), together with the laws that relate them to each other and the correspondence rules that relate them to observation sentences, then make up a nomological network. The theoretical terms in this network are taken to be symbols that are implicitly defined by their role in the network (i.e., their relation to observation sentences through correspondence rules and to other theoretical terms through scientific laws). Good overviews of this program can be found in Carnap (1950) and especially Suppe (1974).

This analytical scheme has never been successfully applied to any real science, and psychology is no exception to that rule. The reasons for this are many. First, it is not clear that the division between observational and theoretical vocabularies is tenable, because scientific observation usually presupposes theory and almost always requires some theory in the description of observations (this is the so-called problem of theory-ladenness). Second, psychology, like most other sciences, has no unambiguous connections between 'theoretical sentences' and 'observation sentences' in the form of correspondence rules. The representational theory of measurement, as proposed in Krantz et al. (1971), could have served to fill this gap if it were successful (Borsboom, 2005; Stegmüller, 1979), but so far it has not been able to play such a role (an issue we will come back to later; see also Batitsky, 1998; Cliff, 1992; Domotor & Batitsky, 2008). Third, psychology has few to no laws to connect the theoretical terms to each other, thereby limiting the prospects for nomological networks that are actually *nomological*. It sometimes appears that, in construct validity theory, the idea is entertained that a set of correlations or regression functions or loose verbal associations is sufficient to serve as a nomological network, but it is unclear how this could work because loose associations do not uniquely fix the meaning of the theoretical terms (e.g., see Borsboom, Mellenbergh, & Van Heerden, 2004).

Cronbach and Meehl (1955) were clearly aware of the fact that there was something problematic going on here, but deflected the problem by stating that psychology's nomological networks are 'vague' (pp. 293–294). This was not true at the time, and it is not true now. Psychology simply had *no* nomological networks of the sort positivism required in 1955, neither vague nor clear ones, just as it has none today. For this reason, the idea of construct validity was born dead. Contrary to what is widely believed, construct validity as proposed by Cronbach and Meehl (1955) never saw any research action. In accordance, there are few traces of the nomological network idea in current validity theory (Kane, 2006; Messick, 1989). However, it is an interesting historical fact that even though the core of their theory was defective from the outset, several more peripheral aspects of their theory actually did survive, and in fact, are largely constitutive of the construct validity doctrine as it exists today. These residues of Cronbach and Meehl's vision of construct validity theory are (a) the idea that validity involves the interpretation of test scores; (b) the idea that, as a result, the property of validity is a property of propositions ('test score interpretations') rather than of tests; and (c) the idea that validity is a function of the evidence that can be brought to bear upon such propositions.

We will interpret current accounts of validity consistent with these tenets as instances of construct validity theory, because they have a common origin in Cronbach and Meehl's (1955) paper. Naturally, we recognize that there are significant differences between, say, the accounts of Messick (1989) and Kane (2006), and that not all of the relevant scholars hold the same view on, for instance, the necessity to invoke constructs in test interpretations (e.g., see Kane, 2006, who does not require this). However, in the present context these differences are best viewed as variations on a theme, especially when compared to the radically different view of validity that we propose (see also Borsboom et al., 2004).

The purpose of this chapter is to attack the central elements of the construct validity doctrine and, in doing so, the doctrine itself (for it consists of little more than the conjunction of the above ideas). In what follows, we argue that validity, as *normally understood*—that is, as it is understood by almost everybody except construct validity theorists—does patently *not* refer to a property of test score interpretations, but to a property of tests (namely, that these tests measure what they should measure). We will denote this property with the term *test validity* and take it to coincide with validity as defined and elaborated on in Borsboom et al. (2004). Second, we argue that test validity—in contradistinction to the notion of construct validity—is not a function of evidence, but a function of truth. Third, we argue that to assess test validity, one has to adopt a realist approach to measurement, because one needs to fill in the semantics of measurement for this purpose, and we know of no successful alternatives to realism in this respect.

In addition, we argue that the notion of a 'construct', as used in construct validity theory, functions in two ways that are mutually inconsistent; namely, it is used both to refer to the theoretical term used in a theory (i.e., a symbol), and to designate the (possible) referent of the term (i.e., the phenomenon that is targeted by a researcher who uses a measurement instrument). This double usage has created an enormous amount of confusion, but has become so entrenched in both construct validity theory and methodological language that it has by now become too late to change it; therefore, we propose to do away with the term 'construct' altogether. Instead, we propose to use 'theoretical term' to designate a theoretical term, and 'psychological attribute' to designate the psychological attribute, if there is any, that the theoretical term refers to. Also, we argue that the notion of validity, as normally understood, is both theoretically and practically superior to the notion of construct validity. Finally, we contend that the construct validity doctrine keeps researchers hidden behind smoke and mirrors, safe from some real problems of psychological measurement we should all deeply care about. Therefore, it fulfills a dubious function in current methodology, because it detracts from the research questions that should be pursued if we are to make any real progress in solving the problem of validity.

VALIDITY AND TEST SCORE INTERPRETATIONS

According to construct validity theory, one cannot obtain evidence for tests, only for propositions. If these propositions involve test scores that are to be interpreted as measures of a psychological attribute, and construct validity is considered to be a function of the evidence for a nomological network involving these test scores and attributes, then it follows immediately that construct validity is also a property of test score interpretations rather than of tests (Cronbach & Meehl, 1955; Messick, 1989). Thus, according to construct validity theory, validity does not refer to the question whether, say, IQ-tests really measure intelligence, but only to the question how well certain IQ-score interpretations are backed by the evidence.

Although this is an integral element of construct validity theory as set up by Cronbach and Meehl (1955) and followed up by writers such as Messick (1989) and Kane (2001, 2006), it clashes with both the ordinary meaning of test validity—whether a test measures what it purports to measure—and with common sense. The reason for this is that the notion of a test score interpretation is too general. It applies to every possible inference concerning test scores—even inferences that have nothing to do with measurement, or that in fact deny that anything is being measured at all.

For instance, suppose we administer the following test, which we will designate as Test X: throw a coin ten times and count how often it falls heads. We conceive of each of the individual trials as an item, and of the number of successes (heads) as the total test score on Test X. Imagine we administer Test X to a sample of people and record the resulting scores. Our interpretation of the test scores is as follows: 'The scores on Test X measure nothing at all'.

To evaluate the construct validity of this test score interpretation, we need to look at the evidence for it. The test score interpretation makes quite a strong, empirically informative claim. For instance, from the proposition considered, one easily derives the following hypotheses: 'Scores on Test X will not show substantive correlations with extraversion, intelligence, or attitude tests'; 'The distribution of scores on Test X do not vary across sex, age, or educational level'; 'Scores on Test X are not sensitive to experimental manipulations involving stereotype threat'; 'Scores on Test X do not suffer from social desirability effects', etc. Note that the list can be lengthened indefinitely; hence, the logical content of the test score interpretation, as for instance Popper (1959) would view it (i.e., the totality of empirical results that the interpretation rules out) is truly enormous, and the potential for falsification is equally impressive. One could venture to gather support for the aforementioned hypothesis, but obviously it is in everybody's interest to refrain from such an undertaking; for we may safely assume that the evidence for the proposed test score interpretation will be overwhelming.

Because construct validity is a function of the evidence for a test score interpretation, we are forced to conclude that the proposed test score interpretation 'scores on Test X measure nothing at all' has an extremely high degree of validity. We therefore establish the following result: *Construct validity applies to test score interpretations that deny that the test in question measures anything whatsoever just as easily as it does to test score interpretations that do claim that something is measured.*

Thus, it is entirely consistent to state that a proposition that *denies* validity as normally understood (i.e., as the claim that the test under consideration measures a psychological attribute) *itself* has high construct validity. This straightforward consequence of the way construct validity theory is set up establishes that construct validity does not cover test validity as normally understood; it is rather entirely orthogonal to it. For many involved in psychometric research, this may be an unanticipated consequence. At the very least, it shows that the question of whether a test measures what it should measure is not necessarily or specifically covered by construct validity theory. If we want a validity theory that addresses our ordinary conception of validity, and thus speaks to the question whether the test measures what it should measure, then validity should not be conceptualized as a property of test score interpretations generally; hence, construct validity theory has to be added to, specified in greater detail, or replaced by something.

EVIDENCE AND TRUTH

One very significant problem that is raised for construct validity theory by the previous example is this: If, as would appear plausible, we would want to limit the notion of validity to 'positive' test score interpretations (i.e., interpretations that *do* state that something is being measured) we are obliged to fill in *what would make such interpretations true.* And in answering this question, it is a serious mistake to answer: *the evidence does.* For propositions are not made true by the evidence that exists for them, but by their conformity to the state of affairs in the world, as is evident from the fact that one can have massive amounts of evidence for a false proposition (e.g., 'time and space are absolute' or 'energy is continuous' before the early 20th century) and lack any evidence for a true one (e.g., 'time and space are relative' or 'energy is discrete' before the early 20th century).

Construct validity theory, however, has tended to specifically define validity in terms of evidence (Cronbach & Meehl, 1955; Messick, 1989; Kane, 2001). One might therefore be inclined to simply add the requirement of truth to the requirement of evidence. However, if one wants to uphold that validity of the test score interpretation 'IQ-test scores are measures of general intelligence' depends on whether that proposition is true *and* that the validity of the interpretation is a function of the evidence, one encounters serious problems.

To elucidate how this happens, consider the example of phlogiston measurement, as it existed in the 17th and 18th centuries. The theory of phlogiston, proposed by Becher in 1667, held that substances contained a certain amount of phlogiston ('fire-stuff'), which they emitted when burned (Bowler & Morus, 2005). The amount of phlogiston a given material possessed was measured indirectly, by subtracting its weight after burning from its original weight. The phlogiston theory, in its day, was used to devise explanations of various phenomena, such as the fact that some materials burn better than others (they contain more phlogiston), and that burning naturally stops when the burning material is placed in a sealed container (the air in the container has only limited capacity to absorb the phlogiston emitted from the material).

Phlogiston measurement took place against the backdrop of a theory that, compared to most psychological theories currently in existence, was very well worked out. Phlogiston figured in explanatory systems that were at least as aptly described as 'nomological networks' as most current psychological theories, made successful predictions, and therefore were quite strongly supported by 'theoretical rationales' and 'empirical evidence'. (We think that the evidence for phlogiston theory was stronger than *any* evidence for *any* current psychological theory we know—but one need not agree on this to see the force of the point we are about to make.) Alas for phlogiston theory, some materials did not lose, or even gained weight when burned, which conflicted with the prediction of the theory. Although some attempted to save the theory by invoking negative amounts of phlogiston, the curtain fell in 1775, when Lavoisier presented evidence to the French Academy of Sciences to show that burning is a reaction with oxygen, and can be explained without making reference to phlogiston.

Now consider the current doctrine of construct validity theory, which says that the construct validity of a test score interpretation depends on the evidence and theory supporting that interpretation. Let us consider the interpretation 'the difference between the weight of a substance before and after burning is a measure of the amount of phlogiston it contains'. Surely, the evidence for this interpretation was quite strong before the late 18th century. Therefore, we must conclude that it had a high (in comparison to most cases of psychological measurement, overwhelmingly high) degree of construct validity at that time. In 1775, however, the construct validity of the interpretation sharply dropped when Lavoisier presented his results, and now, at the beginning of the 21st century, its degree of construct validity is zero (or, for those who think that validity is never an all-or-none issue, *close* to zero). Figure 7.1 provides a graphical display of the construct validity of the test score interpretation in terms of phlogiston.

Now, it seems to us (and we assume you will agree) that the weight measures referred to in the figure *never* measured phlogiston, neither in 1670 nor in 1830 nor today. We therefore feel a compelling urge, and we hope you do as well, to accept the conclusion that the test *never* had *any* validity for measuring phlogiston. In fact, it seems to us that, in the graph, the validity of the test score interpretation should be considered to be described by a flat line corresponding to the function f(validity|time) = 0. However, it is clear that current construct validity cannot agree with this conclusion without throwing one of its main tenets—construct validity reflects the strength of the evidence—out of the window.

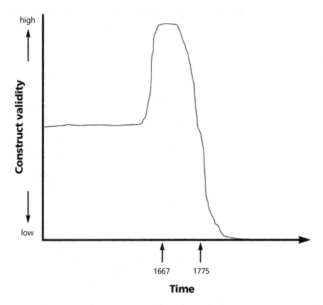

Figure 7.1 Construct validity of phlogiston measures as a function of time. As the figure shows, construct validity was initially undecided, there being no evidence for or against it. A marked increase is visible soon after 1667, when Becher first proposed the theory and evidence started to mount, but validity decreases to nearly zero after Lavoisier published his refutation of the phlogiston theory in 1775.

As a second example, consider the geocentric theory that held that Earth is at the center of the universe, and that the planets and the sun rotated around it, constrained by a system of perfect spheres (Barker & Goldstein, 1992). This theory, at its high time, could accommodate for the observed behavior of the planets. For instance, Gearhart (1985) showed that the predictions of the geocentric system fell within the margins of error of the available data. One of the reasons for this success was that, whenever the empirical discrepancies between observations and predictions became too great, an increasingly elaborate system of epicycles, deferents, equants and eccentrics was proposed to accommodate the anomalous behaviors of certain planets. These ad hoc adjustments were accurate enough that the Ptolemaic system remained widely accepted until well into the Middle Ages, when Copernicus proposed that the Sun might be the center of the universe. The transition was far from complete though; Copernicus still adhered to circles and epicycles, and more importantly, his view could still not outperform the geocentric view in terms of empirical accuracy (Gearhart, 1985). It was not until Johannes Kepler discarded all received notions and proposed elliptical orbits of the planets around the Sun that we saw the first contemporary model of the Solar System.

Now suppose that a geocentric scholar had used astronomical data to measure the time it takes for Mars to complete its epicycle, while a heliocentric scholar used the same data to measure the time it takes Mars to complete its orbit around the Sun. Each scholar interprets the data in terms of a theory; each scholar's interpretation therefore has a degree of validity. So, whose is higher? As in the case of phlogiston, the answer to this question appears to depend on the time at which it is evaluated—before, during, or after the revolution that Copernicus instigated. According to construct validity theory, one is bound to say that the construct validity of geocentric interpretations of the data was higher than these of heliocentric interpretations at least up to Copernicus, and possibly up to Kepler.

One may object to this that the geocentric theory was grossly overparameterized and therefore scored very badly on the criterion of parsimony at the outset. However, this introduces the delicate question of how to weigh parsimony and empirical adequacy in the evaluation of scientific theories. We do not know what construct validity theory has to say on such matters, but submit that instead of bailing one's way out through the invocation of methodological criteria like parsimony and empirical accuracy, there is a much easier way out of this problem—namely, by acknowledging that interpretations of the data in terms of geocentric theories were simply never valid, so that there was never a valid measure of the time it took Mars to complete its epicycle.

We take these examples to be a *reductio ad absurdum* of the dual thesis that construct validity *both* refers to the truth-value of a proposition, say, 'weight differences measure phlogiston' *and* is a function of the evidence. In our view, one of the two theses has to go. Thus, one must either accept that validity is not a function of evidence but of truth, *or* one must accept the thesis that the state of affairs in the world, insofar as it does not show up in the evidence, is *irrelevant to the determination of construct validity*. There is ample documentation supporting the claim that construct validity theorists explicitly favor an interpretation of validity in terms of evidence (e.g., Cronbach & Meehl, 1955; Kane, 2006 Messick, 1989), thus taking the latter route. This implies that they should take seriously the graph in Figure 7.1 and accept the conclusion that logically follows from it: *The interpretation of weight differences as measures of phlogiston had a high degree of construct validity between 1667 and 1775.*

REFERENCE AND REALITY

The above arguments aim to establish that (a) the idea that validity refers to interpretations of test scores is in need of qualification (namely, we need to consider certain *kinds* of interpretations, not just *any* interpretation is eligible) and (b) the idea that validity is a function of evidence is problematic, if one wants to be able to say such commonplace things as 'test score interpretations in terms of phlogiston never were valid, even though people thought they were'. Construct validity theory is thus underspecified (i.e., too general) and focuses on the wrong thing (i.e., evidence). Consequently it is unable to incorporate test validity as normally understood; the fact that there is evidence for some test score interpretation does not entail that the test in question actually measures the targeted attribute. Thus, the questions 'does the test measure what it should measure?' and 'how much evidence is there for this or that test score interpretation?' are different questions that are conflated in the construct validity literature.

We do not entirely see how this situation came about, but we suspect that it has something to do with the positivist heritage which, in its attempt to exorcise metaphysics from the scientific world view, tried to evade referential connections between theoretical terms ('general intelligence') and the structures that such terms refer to (a single linearly ordered property, if there is one, that causes individual differences on IQ-tests). The positivist program attempted to make sense of measurement without incorporating realist commitments (i.e., metaphysical ones) about the properties targeted by the measurement procedure. So, what the positivists tried to do is to make sense of statements like 'this test measures general intelligence' *without* engaging in the commitment that there actually is *something out there* to measure, i.e., without assuming that such a thing as general intelligence exists independently of the researcher's scaling activities. If successful, this would allow one to craft a validity concept that does not postulate, at the outset, that the existence and causal efficacy of X are required, if X is to be considered a property that can be measured. Such an approach, however, does not work.

Basically, the problem is that, to evade realism, one has to twist the natural interpretation of the word 'measurement' (which is that one has an instrument that is sensitive to differences between objects with respect to some property, in the sense that it gives different outcomes for different instances of the property) to such a degree that (a) the term no longer means what scientists routinely take it to mean, or (b) the assumptions required for the interpretation of measured properties as constructions are so strong as to imply that measurement is impossible. Two corresponding twists that have been worked out in detail are operationalism and representational measurement theory.

Operationalism famously holds that scientific concepts are synonymous with the procedures used to measure them (Bridgman, 1927), which does not necessarily imply that the properties measured do not exist, but is clearly compatible with that thesis. This doctrine is defective for two reasons. First, because it is incoherent (a linguistic concept such as 'general intelligence' cannot stand in a relation of synonymy to a set of actions, for instance a researcher administering an IQ-test). Second, because it implies that no two measurement procedures could measure the same thing (i.e., a mercury thermometer cannot measure the same property as an electronic thermometer because each defines its own concept), and therefore flies in the face of scientific practice. Thus operationalism twists the meaning of the word 'measurement' to be completely at odds with the way scientists work.

The other alternative, representationalism, holds that measurement consists of the assignments of numerals to objects or events in such a way that the numerical relations between these numerical assignments are isomorphic (i.e., structurally equivalent) to the empirical relations between the objects and events in question (Narens & Luce, 1986). This theory was developed in great detail in the three-volume work *Foundations of Measurement* (Krantz et al., 1971; Luce et al., 1990; Suppes et al., 1989). Representationalism essentially consists of two steps.

First, in the representational step, an empirical relational structure is established by determining the set of objects and the *empirical* relations between objects on some property of interest (e.g., the ordering of minerals according to their hardness). It is important that these relations are qualitative and need no reference to numbers. Also, the relations must be detectable in a straightforward manner by the researcher. If an empirical relational structure conforming to these requirements can be established, then it needs to be proven that a numerical relational structure exists, consisting of a set of numbers and *numerical* relations, that perfectly represents the empirical relational structure. In the aforementioned *Foundations of Measurement* such proof is provided in the form of axioms that are used to prove representation theorems for many different types of empirical relational structures.

The second step involves showing how the specific numerical scale that was chosen, relates to other possible instantiations (other scales) of the numerical relational structure. The functional relation that relates all possible numerical scales to each other is described in a uniqueness theorem and determines the level of measurement. For example, scales that are isomorphic representations of the hardness of minerals are unique up to monotonically increasing transformations; because minerals can only be ordered according to their hardness, any order-preserving transformation of a 'correct' numerical scale will do equally well in reflecting these empirical order relations.

Representationalism can be used, in principle, to evade realist metaphysics. The way in which this could be done is to establish qualitatively which relations hold between objects (in psychology, these are normally people or items, resulting in relations such as 'John is less intelligent than Jane'), to code these in a matrix, and to find a way to attach a number to each entry in the matrix so that all the empirical relations coded in it are preserved by the numerical relations (say, John's intelligence is represented by the number 95 and Jane's intelligence is represented by the number 120). If this is possible, one can go on to establish the uniqueness of the properties of the representation, and define the measurement level associated with the measurement procedure. One could then use the term 'general intelligence' to refer to the constructed scale, which, evidently, is a human-made construction that one need not necessarily assume exists independently of the researcher or is causally responsible for the observed relations between measured objects (Borsboom, 2005).

Of course representational measurement does not exclude the possibility that the measured property is causally responsible for the variation in measurement outcomes, but it certainly does not require it. Thus, it would seem to provide an excellent way to circumvent realist commitments. But even though the theoretical quality of this work is not in doubt, it is questionable whether realism can be evaded in practice (Batitsky, 1998; Borsboom, 2005; Domotor & Batitsky, 2008). The main problems with representationalism, if it should serve as a way of exorcizing metaphysics, are the following.

First, the empirical relations should be observed without inconsistency and second, the empirical relations between objects as coded in the matrix should be 'observable with the naked eye' (Batitsky, 1998; Domotor & Batitsky, 2008; Van Fraassen, 1980) or something similar. Unfortunately it remains unclear which exact types of observation satisfy this requirement of representational measurement theory and what types of observational aids would be allowed, if any. We have no choice therefore, but to take the requirement literally. Now the naked eye is an untrustworthy source of information, in the sense that it is unreliable in certain situations; specifically, it is easy to find a level of grain size on which the eye starts behaving erratically, sometimes saying that, for example, A is larger than B and sometimes that B is larger than A (or A is larger than B, B is larger than C, but C is larger than A). If one demands that no reference to the structure of the world is made except to what we can see with the unaided eye, then it directly follows that measurement in the representationalist sense is highly problematic, for what one will get are inconsistent systems of empirical relations that do not allow for the intended isomorphic representations in a numerical system. Hence, we are forced to conclude that measurement is impossible (see also Batitsky, 1998, for an excellent, and more extensive, exposition of such difficulties). This, obviously, flies in the face of scientific practice.

Even if observation is aided (e.g., by microscopes or amplifiers), the empirical relational structure will exhibit some degree of inconsistency. Normally, of course, the will-o-the-wisp behavior of the eye, aided or unaided, is not interpreted to mean that the relation of 'longer than' between A and B shifts randomly from one moment to the next (although, of course, it may in some contexts). Rather, such inconsistencies are routinely interpreted as measurement error. Thus, what one will do, for instance, is introduce the idea that relations between objects are *imperfectly* picked up by the measurement procedure (e.g., the use of the naked eye) and deal with these imperfections by using some statistical theory.

These statistical measurement models can be less or more elaborate in the explicitness, testability and type of measurement assumptions. Some models allow one to test measurement assumptions, be it indirectly; this is, for instance, the case for the Rasch (1960) model. This model is structurally similar to a subtype of representational measurement theory (additive conjoint measurement theory) and therefore it indirectly ensures that measurement assumptions are met, at least, if the model is true. Statistical theory can also be used to form probabilistic versions of representational measurement theory (Karabatsos, 2001). This results in models that capture measurement error but still allow for a relatively direct test of the axioms of representational measurement theory.

However, as soon as we employ any of these statistical measurement models, we immediately fail at our attempt to get rid of metaphysics. For it is exceedingly difficult to make sense of the idea that there is error in the measurements, if one is not allowed to make reference to a true value of these measurements (or true relations that exist between objects). Introducing true values means that one needs something that makes these values true independently of the researcher doing the measurement work. The prime candidate for being the truth maker here, naturally, is the property targeted by the measurement procedure, and it appears hard (at least, we have not seen successful attempts) to find a plausible alternative candidate for the job at hand. That is the reason why representationalism does not buy one a way out of metaphysics.

Hence, operationalism is inconsistent and representationalism is too strong. There are, as far as we know, no other reasonable candidates to take care of the semantics of measurement—except for realism. Realism, in the context of measurement, simply says that a measurement instrument for an attribute has the property that it is *sensitive* to differences in the attribute; that is, when the attribute differs over objects then the measurement procedure gives a different outcome. This implies that there must be a causal chain that describes the working of the measurement procedure, in which the measured attribute plays a role in determining what the outcomes of the measurement procedure are.

So, a pan balance measures weight because the weight difference between two objects, one placed in each of the pans, determines to which side the balance will tilt. (If gravity can be considered to be (roughly) constant, as on Earth, then the decisive factor would be mass, and we can say that the procedure measures differences in mass). This, it appears to us, is a sensible way to construct the idea of measurement. However, this is not a bargain, as the price paid for these semantics is that one has to make reference to the property measured as a causal force that steers the direction of the measurement outcomes. This is no small matter. It requires a very strong assumption about what the world is like, namely that it contains some property that exist independently of the researcher measuring it. This assumption may be much too strong for many psychological properties. It also obliges the researcher to explicate what the property's structure or underlying process is and how this structure or process influences the measurement instrument to result in variations in the measurement outcomes. This seems to be a very daunting task indeed for many psychological properties that researchers claim to measure.

How does a realist approach to measurement relate to the concept of validity? Well, usually one has the idea that there is some property that determines differences within or between individuals, and one attempts to create an instrument (e.g., an item, test, or observational procedure) that will do one thing if the targeted property has a certain value and will do another if it doesn't. Then one applies the instrument and gets data representing the different outcomes of the measurement procedure. Obviously, these differences have to come from somewhere, i.e., there is a causal antecedent process in which something makes a difference to the outcomes. The hypothesis involved in the question of test validity is that the term one uses to name the property in question (say 'general intelligence') *refers* to the property that causes the differences in measurement outcomes. Or, in an alternative formulation, the term 'general intelligence' *co-refers* with the description 'the property that causes differences in the measurement outcomes'. Thus, what is at stake in posing the question of validity is the empirical hypothesis that the description 'what is measured by the test' and the term 'general intelligence' designate the same property.

Construct validity theory does not address this type of measurement issue at all. It is, for instance, hard to find a definition of the word 'measurement' in papers on construct validity (for instance, try Messick, 1989, or Kane, 2006). This is remarkable since validity, at its base, is a characteristic of measurement, regardless of whether one views validity as a property of test score interpretations or as a property of tests. A clear definition of measurement would seem essential for any hope of a coherent theory of validity. In our view, a realist approach to measurement is the only tenable one. This poses problems for construct validity however, since it must restrict its scope considerably, in order to reconcile itself with this approach. Construct validity can only account for the realist measurement approach by limiting the allowable propositions to one very special test score interpretation, namely that the test scores can be interpreted as measures of the targeted attribute simply because the targeted attribute is causally relevant to the test scores.

Two things follow from this. First, for the proposition 'the test measures what it should measure' to have any truth conditions at all, one needs to fill in the notion of measurement as we have expounded above. Second, what makes the 'test score interpretation' above true is a *property of the test*, namely that it has what it takes to be used *as* a measurement instrument for the targeted attribute. We submit, therefore, that what really matters in validity is *how the test works*, and this is certainly *not* a property of test score interpretations, or even of test scores, but of *the measurement instrument itself* (i.e., of the concrete, physical thing that you can drop on your feet, rather than of a linguistic entity, set-theoretical object, or statistical construction). In fact, we think that all the talk about 'test score interpretations' has not led construct validity theory to a greater level of sophistication, as is commonly assumed, but in point of fact has served to detract the theory from the main issue in test validity and the proper objective of validation research, which is *showing that the test indeed has the relevant capacity to pick up variation in the targeted attribute and that it actually does so in the typical research settings in which the test is used.*

CONSTRUCTS?

So what about constructs? How should *they* be taken to serve the function of measurement? Are they made of the right stuff? Could they possibly determine the outcome of the measurement process? Or are they post hoc inventions, figments of the scientist's imagination? Can constructs, in fact, *be measured?*

We do not know the answer to these questions because we do not know what constructs are, that is, we have rarely come across a clear description of what something should be like in order to deserve the label 'construct'. Constructs, as far as we are concerned, are truly shrouded in mystery, and not in the good old scientific sense that we currently don't know what they are, but will know when we're finished doing the relevant research, but in the sense that we don't really know what we are talking about in the first place.

The main problem, as we take it, is this: Construct validity theorists have the habit of using one word for two things, without clearly indicating when they mean what. In particular, the term 'construct' is used to refer to (a) a theoretical term (i.e., the linguistic, conceptual, symbolic entity) that we use as a placeholder in our theories ('general intelligence', '*g*', 'theta', 'the factor at the apex of this hierarchical factor model', etc.), and (b) the property that we think plays a role in psychological reality and of which we would like to obtain measures (i.e., a linearly ordered property that causes the positive correlations between IQ-tests—assuming, of course, that there is such a property).

Now, one cannot measure constructs in sense (a) above. That will not work, no matter how good one's measurement instruments become or how much one learns about the research domain of interest. The reason for this is not that constructs, interpreted in this particular sense, are 'latent' or 'unobservable' or 'vague' or 'complex'. The reason is that trying to measure a construct in sense (a) is very much akin to trying to climb the word 'tree'. That is, one is mistaking a symbol for the thing it refers to (see also Maraun & Peters, 2005). Constructs in sense (a) are purely theoretical terms, symbols concocted by the researcher for the purpose of scientific communication; and these symbols are causally impotent in the measurement process.

One *can* measure constructs in sense (b), that is, the properties our words refer to, but obviously this will only work if these properties are capable of doing causal work. That is, there has to be some property (structure, attribute, entity, trait, process) that listens to its name (the theoretical term) and that actually *does* steer the measurement outcomes in one or the other direction because, whatever else one thinks symbols are good for, they are not up to that particular job.

Loevinger (1957) saw the importance of this issue clearly, when she addressed the semantics of the word 'construct':

> *construct* connotes construction and artifice; yet what is at issue is validity with respect to exactly what the psychologist does not construct: the validity of the test as a measure of traits which exist prior to and independently of the psy-

chologist's act of measuring. It is true that psychologists never know traits directly but only through the glass of their constructs, but the data to be judged are manifestations of *traits*, not manifestations of *constructs*. (Loevinger, 1957, p. 642, italics in original)

Now, if such a property ('trait' in Loevinger's terms) does not exist, then one cannot measure it, however hard one tries. Of course, one still has the theoretical term (all one has to do to bring that into existence is write it down) but one is misdirected if one tries to interpret test scores as measures of the symbolic entity that figures in scientific communication. (Unless, perhaps, if one comes up with a good answer to the question how one measures properties that do not exist, i.e., gives an empiricist interpretation of the measurement process that does not fly in the face of scientific practice or is so strong as to preclude the very possibility of measurement. This project is, to the best of our knowledge, still outstanding.)

Coming back to the issue of phlogiston measurement, we may plausibly conclude that phlogiston did very well as a construct in sense (a)—better, in fact, than most psychological constructs—but not at all in sense (b). The same holds for aether, elán vital, absolute space, and many other obsolete concepts that have been proposed in the history of science. We are currently in a state of ignorance regarding most of the attributes proposed in psychological theorizing, but suppose that one who hopes to measure such attributes surely does not want them to fall in this particular category of concepts.

Thus, what one needs in measuring a psychological attribute is not just a fitting statistical model, or a theory that offers an explanation of why that model should hold, or a corroborated nomological network; one needs a referential connection between one's construct in sense (a) and one's construct in sense (b). That is, it is important that one's theoretical term designates a property that is sufficiently structured to perform causal work in the measurement process. We think that much of the confusion surrounding the notion of a construct stems from the fact that the term 'construct' is used both to indicate a theoretical term and a property measured.

As long as one clearly recognizes which of the two meanings is intended, there is of course little to worry about. Polysemy is a natural feature of language, and we suppose that physicists have no problem deciding when they take, say, 'charm' to refer to a property of subatomic particles, or to the new secretary. However, in construct validity theory one sees properties that can be attributed to only one of the two types of constructs, being transported to the other one. So, people say that it is important to *find out* what the *meaning* of a construct or test score is. This is clearly confused; one can *find out* things about the property measured—i.e., the sense (b) construct—but it is hard to see why one should do empirical research to find out things about the symbol that purportedly designates that property—i.e., the sense (a) construct. In contrast, the utilized symbol—the sense (a) construct—clearly has *meaning*, and one could say sensible things about that; but the property referred to—the sense (b) construct—has no more meaning than the tree in your back yard. Similarly, one can *measure* the sense (b) construct, but not the sense (a) construct; one can *rule out alternative explanations* to the hypothesis that the sense (b) construct causes the correlations between observables, but not to the hypothesis that the sense (a) construct does so. One can look at causal effects of some variable on the sense (b) construct, but not on the sense (a) construct. The sense (a) construct may be 'implicitly defined' through a theory, but not the sense (b) construct, because that is a phenomenon in reality and not a theoretical term. And so on.

We hope that the reader is as confused by the use of the terminology of 'sense (a)' and 'sense (b)' constructs as we are. It is clearly a bad idea to utilize such terminology, and we would strongly advise against it. Moreover, the word 'construct' is so thoroughly infected with both meanings that we see no possibility to restrict is usage to indicate either sense (a) or sense (b). The only viable option, we think, is to dispose of talk about constructs altogether and explicitly refer to 'theoretical terms' for sense (a) constructs and 'psychological attributes' for sense (b) constructs. In essence, this means that the theory and vocabulary of construct validity is abandoned entirely.

INTERMEZZO

We could lengthen our critique of construct validity theory almost indefinitely by playing variations of the above themes. However, we prefer to lay the issue to rest here. Those who, at this point, remain unconvinced of the inadequacy of construct validity theory are unlikely to be swayed by further argumentation and are probably beyond salvation.

In the next section, we will therefore turn to some positive remarks regarding the possibilities and challenges provided by a notion of validity that has shaken off the blurry visions of construct validity. As an intermediate conclusion that serves to substantiate these, however, we suggest that the following theses are securely established by the above discussion:

1. Construct validity is about test score interpretations, not about tests. However, regardless of whether one thinks that we need a concept like construct validity to indicate the quality of the evidence for a given test score interpretation, there is a separate issue, important in its own right, that is not specifically covered by construct validity theory, namely whether a *test* is valid for *measuring* an attribute.

2. To say anything sensible about this property, one has to establish the semantics of the word *measurement*. In our view, the only viable candidate for such semantics is realism; that is, the notion of measurement presupposes that there exists some sort of structure that the test is sensitive to, in the sense that the test elicits processes that result in different measurement outcomes dependent on the position of the object or person, subjected to the measurement procedure, on the attribute in question.

3. The question of test validity involves the issue of whether a psychological attribute (e.g., 'general intelligence') exists and coincides with the attribute that the test in fact measures (assuming that there is one). In this case, for instance, the terms 'general intelligence' and 'the attribute measured by the test' co-refer to the same structure. Validating a test is just doing research to figure out whether this is true or not.

4. Whether a test actually has what it takes to serve as a measurement device for the attribute targeted by the researcher is independent of the evidence for test validity. Thus, we may have a valid test without knowing it, and we may have good evidence for validity even though the test in question does not measure the attribute for which it was designed. This is because validity is a function of facts, not of opinions, and our evaluations of the evidence may be mistaken.

5. As a result, construct validity may be high, whereas test validity (as we defined it) is absent, and vice versa. In general, the relation between construct validity and test validity is contingent on the substantive situation examined. Contrary to what is widely thought, one cannot expect construct validity to generally coincide with or imply test validity.

In our opinion, test validity is what researchers are primarily interested in when they talk about validity. Construct validity is relevant only insofar as it concerns the evidential backup of one particular test score interpretation, namely the one that corresponds to test validity: that the test scores can be interpreted as measures of the targeted attribute because the test is sensitive to differences in that attribute.

THE REAL PROBLEMS OF PSYCHOLOGICAL MEASUREMENT

The question of test validity, as conceptualized here, raises many interesting issues about the way tests work that, in our view, receive too little attention in scientific psychology. In this section, we outline some examples of important questions that are rarely addressed but, in our view, stand in need of investigation if we are to make serious progress in the realm of psychological measurement.

Reflective measurement models.   In the literature on test theory, almost all models that have been considered are variants of what has been called the reflective measurement model (Edwards & Bagozzi, 2000) or the effect indicators model (Bollen & Lennox, 1991). Such models assume that the indicators (item or test scores) depend on a (set of) latent variables through some functional relationship between parameters of the observed score distribution and the position of people and items in the latent space. In the majority of cases (Borsboom, 2008), these models are formally indistinguishable from common cause models; specifically, they require that the latent variable screens off correlations between the observables (Pearl, 2000), a requirement known as local independence in the psychometric literature. Thus, such models assume that there is an underlying variable that affects each of the observables, thereby explaining the correlations between them.

The idea that a set of items depends on an underlying variable appears to be the general motivation for treating the item or test scores as measurements in the first place. This is understandable, as it is hard to see how such scores could be sensibly interpreted as measurements if they did not depend on the same latent variable. Naturally, one can see a latent variable model as a purely heuristic device used to organize the data, or to scale the test scores in some pragmatically useful way, or to reason about one's data; but equally naturally, the fact that a latent variable model can be used in such a manner does not automatically imbue the item scores with the status of measurements; for one can *always* use models pragmatically, regardless of how the data arise. To sensibly interpret the item or test scores as *measurements,* and the instrument that yields them as a *measurement instrument,* the model should not just be useful, but true. That is, it should actually be the case that differences in the item scores depend on the targeted attribute, represented in the model as a latent variable, so that sensibly constructed functions of these item scores (like sum scores or more complicated estimators) can be interpreted as measures of the attribute in question.

In the psychometric developments over the past century or so, the specification and elaboration of such models have come to be viewed as 'technical' issues, to be handled by specialists who are better at statistics than at substantive psychology. This is not always equally productive because, even though the usefulness of latent variable models for scaling and such stands beyond doubt, their importance for the study of test validity is truly monumental and therefore deserves serious attention from substantively interested scholars. The reason for this is that such models code a necessary condition for interpreting the test scores as measures in the first place, namely, that the item scores measure the same attribute. The fact that latent variable models are underused in the social sciences (Borsboom, 2006) and are hardly ever even mentioned in treatises on construct validity indicates, in our view, that few researchers realize what their importance for validity really is.

In our view, in fact, establishing the *truth* of such a model would *clinch* the question of validity. This may raise some eyebrows between psychometricians and construct validity theorists, and understandably so. Current psychometric dogma has it that the best one can ever do is to ascertain the goodness of fit of a latent variable model against a given dataset, and that such goodness of fit only indicates that *a* latent variable may be responsible for the covariation among observables, but not *which* latent variable this may be. This is, however, only the case if one detaches the measurement model from substantive theory, i.e., if one views a latent variable as an anonymous technicality called 'theta'.

If one does not detach the substantive theory from the measurement problem, then clearly one *can* do better than inspecting goodness of fit indices and eyeballing residual plots, namely by investigating the processes that lead to item responses or test scores and *identifying what element of these processes is causing variation in each of the different items at the same time* (see Borsboom & Mellenbergh, 2007, for some ways in which this may be the case). If successful, such an investigation would clearly end up with a *substantive* specification of the common cause that underlies the item responses, not a purely technical one, and with a *substantive* justification for the structure of the latent space and the form of the item response functions. If successful, such a research program therefore *solves* the problem of test validity, because it by necessity becomes clear *what the items measure* and *how they measure it*. And that is all there is to know regarding validity.

Item response processes versus external correlations. The suppositions that (a) a reflective model is indeed required to sensibly speak of measurement, and (b) that such a model should be true rather than pragmatically useful or consistent with a particular dataset, raise the question of how such a model *could* be true. That is, if test validity concerns the sensitivity of a test to differences in the targeted attribute, then the question that immediately presents itself is how differences in this attribute are causally transmitted into the measurement outcomes. Questions concerning the actual causal relation or process responsible for variation in the measurement outcomes, however, are seldom asked in psychometrics or psychology at large. Perhaps this is because, in many cases, they present extraordinarily difficult problems for the conviction that we are actually engaged in a measurement process when doing our test theoretic work.

For instance, consider the individual differences literature, where factor analysis and its relatives are commonly used to investigate psychological properties having to do with personality, attitudes and ability. The construct validity doctrine has set the stage for a longstanding and ongoing quest for 'constructs' that are 'measured' by a series of observable 'indicators' in this field. A plethora of psychological constructs have emerged from these endeavors.

In such cases, on typically, one has a theoretical term, say, 'general intelligence' and a set of indicators, say items of the WAIS (Psychological Corporation, 1997), that supposedly measure the property that one thinks the theoretical term refers to. Now, the standard sequence of events is as follows: a principal components or factor analysis is performed, one factor is found to emerge from the analysis, and it is concluded that this factor can be no other than general intelligence (Carroll, 1993; Gustafsson, 1984; Mackintosh, 1998). Subsequently, the test scores are correlated with a number of relevant variables (in the context of intelligence research, these range from reaction times to job performance). If these correlations are in the right direction, this is taken as evidence that the test indeed measures general intelligence. Finally, heritabilities are computed and found to be impressively high. Often, inquiries stop about here, which is not altogether surprising because, within the construct validity framework, there is nowhere further to go (one may want to ponder this for a while). The only resources that current psychometric dogma in general, and construct validation practice in particular, have to offer are (a) inspecting the 'internal structure' of a test by fitting psychometric models or doing some classical test theory, and (b) correlating the test scores with a zillion external variables. Obviously, however, neither factor analysis nor the inspection of external correlations can, by themselves, provide an answer to the question of validity.

To see this, suppose some researcher performs a factor analysis and finds one factor on measurements obtained by balancing people against a set of old, inaccurate mechanical weight scales. Now suppose that for some reason the researcher is convinced that the test scores should be interpreted as a measure of length. If applied to the human population, the test results will show a reasonable correlation with bodily height, as measured with a meter stick—which supports the construct validity of the test score interpretation in terms of height—and will be predictive of a wide variety of phenomena theoretically related to bodily height.

Now imagine that another researcher interprets the test results as measures of weight and presents a comparable correlation with measurements that result from the application of an electronic weight scale. Given the magnitude of the correlation between height and weight in the human population, such a scenario is not unrealistic, especially if we are allowed to play around with reliability a little; furthermore, it is entirely possible that, if the researchers have at their disposal nothing but weak correlational data of the type that, say, intelligence researchers have, the external correlations of test scores with many other variables would be essentially the same for the electronic scale, the mechanical scale, and the meter stick. In particular, it is not clear that multi-trait-multi-method matrices would be sufficient to decide on the question which two instruments measure the same quantity. In fact, it is likely that the results of most currently fashionable validation strategies would be unequivocal, just as they are in psychology.

How could these scientists resolve their dispute? We can see only one answer: by investigating the processes through which the respective measurement instruments work. If pursued, such a program would likely point to the fact that behavior of the scales depends on objects' mass, while the height measure does not. The researchers thus would choose the interpretation of test scores in terms of weight because they have developed a good idea of how the mechanical and electronic scales work. The fact that we have a broadly correct explanation of how differences in weight result in differences in measurement is thus more convincing than any differences in correlation with external variables (see also Zumbo, 2007, on the importance of explanation in validity theory).

In fact, the entire idea that one can figure out what a test measures merely by looking at correlations (no matter how many) is, we think, mistaken. And what is missing in psychology, when it comes to the question of test validity, is exactly what is present in the above example but absent in validation research concerning tests for intelligence, abilities, and personality; namely, a good theory of how differences in the targeted attribute are responsible for differences in the measurement outcomes. Although such a theory can serve as excellent input for a factor model and for inspecting correlation structures, it is unlikely to be the output of such practices if they are carried out without being informed by substantive theory. Thus, one particularly important issue that we think should receive much more attention in validation research is the development of process theories that connect targeted attributes to test scores.

Interindividual differences and intraindividual processes. Naturally, we are not the first to point to the importance of developing process theories. Calls for such approaches have been repeatedly made by various scholars, including construct validity theorists (e.g., see Embretson, 1994; Leighton & Gierl, 2007; Snow & Lohman, 1989). However, as far as we know there are only a few researchers that have tackled this problem with some success, in the sense that they were able to specify how intraindividual processes may lead to interindividual differences in test scores (for a theoretical example, see Tuerlinckx & De Boeck, 2005; and for an empirical example, Jansen & Van der Maas, 1997, 2002; see also Borsboom & Mellenbergh, 2007, for a discussion of how these examples relate to validity).

For many important tests in psychology, tracking item response processes and relating them to individual differences has proven a tall order. This has to do with some general and enduring problems in psychology, as discussed in various sources (Borsboom, Mellenbergh, & Van Heerden, 2004; Cronbach, 1957; Lykken, 1991; Meehl, 1978). One of these issues, in our view, is of central importance to the issue of test validity. This concerns the relation, or lack thereof, between the structure of intraindividual processes and of individual differences.

To see this, one may consider the easiest way in which a measurement model could be true, which arises when one assumes that the structure of the time-dependent behavior of a single subject is isomorphic to the structure we find in the analysis of individual differences. Such a situation would obtain if the development of, say, depression in an individual would consist of that individual moving upwards along a latent continuum so as to increase the probability of depression symptoms in accordance with the item response theory model that is found in the analysis of individual differences (i.e., when a model is fitted to data that arise by administering a depression scale to many people at a single time point; see Aggen, Neale, & Kendler, 2005). This would be the case if all individuals functioned according to the same dynamical laws, so that the difference between any two time points for one individual is qualitatively the same as a corresponding difference between two individuals at one time point (see Hamaker, Nesselroade, & Molenaar, 2007; Molenaar, 2004). For many measurement systems in physics, this is clearly the case: for instance, the differences in thermometer readings of a number of substances, which differ in temperature, depend on the same attribute as the differences in thermometer readings of a single substance, when it increases in temperature. Thus, the within-substance model matches the between-substances model. In other words: the attribute that causes thermometer readings to rise or fall for a single substance is qualitatively the same attribute that causes thermometer readings to differ across substances at a single time point—namely, temperature.

There is little reason to assume that such a simple scheme holds for psychological attributes typically subjected to measurement procedures. Certainly, the fit of a model to individual differences data says virtually nothing about the adequacy of that model for individual change: between-subjects differences do not necessarily equate to within-subjects differences. For instance, it could well be that John's performance on IQ measures is determined by both speed of information processing and neural efficiency (i.e., John represents a two-factor model), and Paula's performance is determined by speed of information processing, neural efficiency and working memory capacity (i.e., Paula represents a three-factor model), while the analysis of individual differences between the Johns and Paulas of this world would fit a single factor model nearly perfectly. For as Molenaar, Huizenga, and Nesselroade (2003) demonstrated, different data generating structures in the intra-individual space can easily result in a one-factor model for between-subjects differences (see also Hamaker, Nesselroade, & Molenaar, 2007, for an explanation of why this is so). Hence, if a one-factor model fits between-subjects data, it is at best premature to conclude that this is evidence for an isomorphic structure 'in the head' of individual people (Borsboom, Kievit, Cervone, & Hood, in press).

Therefore it is a stretch to assume that the fit of a between-subjects model to individual differences serves to substantiate statements like 'extraversion causes party-going behavior in individuals' (McCrae & Costa, 2008, p. 288) or similar claims (see Borsboom et al., in press, for a more extensive discussion of many similar examples). Such a statement implies that Samantha is a passionate party-crasher because she is extraverted while Nicole rather stays at home with her favorite romantic comedy because she is insufficiently extraverted to behave otherwise. However, this likely oversimplifies processes that result in some people being party-lovers and others being party-avoiders. Perhaps Nicole is in fact extraverted (e.g., likes to meet new people, enjoys social interaction, etc.) but does not like to go to parties because she hates loud music and alcohol. Perhaps Samantha forces herself to go to parties in an attempt to overcome her fear of closed spaces packed with people. Certainly the dynamics of their behavior are rather more complicated than a typical measurement model presumes.

With the exception of some basic learning and conditioning theory, we know hardly anything about the time-dependent structure of processes that govern people's behavior. We know even less about how these processes connect to item response behavior, i.e., how people answer items like those administered in typical psychological tests. However, if one pauses to think about these issues for a moment, it appears quite unlikely that the individual differences variables we find in applied psychometrics have isomorphic counterparts in individual people; counterparts that could steer their mental and behavioral processes so as to eventually culminate in, say, ticking a response category on an answer sheet of a personality questionnaire (Borsboom, Mellenbergh, & Van Heerden, 2003). One supposes that something different must be going on.

Now this need not be a problem for psychology; rather it represents a fruitful avenue for theoretical and empirical research. However, it does represent a problem for the interpretation of test scores as measures. Clearly, if such an interpretation is warranted, it must be for different reasons than those that lead us to consider thermometers valid measures of temperature. That is, thermodynamic laws apply generally, to all substances at all time points, and therefore a causal explanation of individual differences in thermometer readings for different substances can be predicated on the hypothesis that, in each of these substances, the same property is responsible for the same behavior in the thermometer. In normal circumstances, the expansion of mercury in a fixed column, which leads us to perceive the thermometer readings to rise, *always* results from the transfer of kinetic energy from the particles in the measured substance to the particles in the mercury column. There is no other way.

But in psychological testing, there are many different ways of generating item responses. Even in low level skills, like addition or multiplication, one can discern different strategies of coming up with the right answer (left aside those of coming up with the wrong one). In more complex phenomena, such as those that should be expected to underlie the phenomena of interest in the study of attitudes, personality, or psychopathology, as well as complex skills like those involved in playing chess or solving Raven test items, there are myriads of processes that run in parallel, likely to be intertwined in complex ways. It is not clear whether in such cases we can sensibly speak of measurement, especially since many of the more interesting cases of psychological testing might require an altogether different way conceptualizing the relation between test scores and theoretical terms—an issue we turn to next.

Causal networks. In our above ponderings, we assumed that, in some way, a psychometric model adequately pictures the situation in the real world—so that it makes sense to think about the test scores as measures: a one-factor model for general intelligence, for instance, should then refer to a single variable in the real world (e.g., speed of information processing) that causes differential performance on IQ tests, hopefully in the same way between people as within them. But what if we are wrong? What if the psychometric factor in a factor model does in fact not refer to a linearly ordered property that causes variation in IQ-scores? If this is the case, then we have a serious problem on our hands, namely that it may be altogether mistaken to think about the relation between test scores and psychological attributes as one of measurement.

Results presented by Van der Maas et al. (2006) show that, in the case of general intelligence, such a situation may be actual rather than hypothetical: these authors showed that a dynamical model *without any latent variables*, and a fortiori without the factor *g*, easily rivals the theory of general intelligence in explaining empirical phenomena. More specifically, Van der Maas et al. (2006) simulated data based on a dynamical model in which cognitive processes interact beneficially during development. This is called *mutualism.* The mutualism model results in the same positive manifold (i.e., positive correlations between cognitive tasks) that is consistently seen in IQ data and, in a factor analysis, always yields a dominant first factor or principal component. Hence, the mutualism model yields typical IQ data but does not contain an overarching psychometric factor *g* that refers to a construct of general intelligence. This is food for thought, because the measurement of intelligence through IQ-tests is one of the primary and best researched examples of psychological measurement—in fact, one could argue that many other measurement systems are copied from the intelligence example.

A similar situation may be true for another broad class of psychological constructs, namely mental disorders (e.g., see Borsboom, 2008; Cramer, 2008). A reflective model is often hypothesized to account for the relationship between a construct, for example depression, and its indicators (e.g., the symptoms of depression). An important consequence of assuming such a reflective model is that the attribute measured explains all systematic covariation between individual symptoms (i.e., local independence; see for instance Lord & Novick, 1968). However, such a model might not paint the most adequate picture of mental disorders (Borsboom, 2008). For example, consider two symptoms of depression, as mentioned in the *Diagnostic and Statistical Manual of Mental Disorders* (American Psychiatric Association, 1994), sleep disturbance and fatigue. According to a reflective model, a high correlation between those two symptoms is entirely explained by the measured attribute, i.e., depression. However, it would appear rather more plausible to assume that a direct relationship exists between those symptoms: If you don't sleep, you get tired. It is not difficult to see that many such relations may exist between symptoms of mental disorders. If one accepts this possibility, then a *causal network* in which symptoms stand in direct causal relationships toward one another could be the model that best describes the phenomenon of mental disorders. As in the mutualism example, one would have a model without a latent variable and thus, without a unitary psychological attribute that underlies the distinct symptoms. This would be an interesting situation, because it necessitates a complete reconsideration of the way test scores function. In particular, it is not obvious that one should think about the relation between symptoms and syndromes as one of measurement (Borsboom, 2008, proposes instead to view this relation as a mereological one; i.e., the symptoms do not measure the network, but are part of it).

Heritability and phenotypic heterogeneity. Perhaps the most often cited evidence for the reality of traits like general intelligence and extraversion concerns their high heritability. The heritability of IQ-scores, for instance, was found to be 70-80% in adulthood (Bouchard et al., 1990; Posthuma, de Geus, & Boomsma, 2001; Posthuma, 2002), and of liability to depression around 50-70% (Kendler et al., 2001; McGue, & Christensen, 2003). Similar figures hold for many other psychological variables; see Boomsma, Busjahn, and Peltonen (2002) for an overview. It is often thought that such figures provide evidence for the reality of psychological attributes, coded as latent variables in commonly used measurement models, and therefore substantiate the claim that test scores should be interpreted as measures. In our view, however, such evidence is hardly a smoking gun, as it does not provide us with a sensible answer to the question of how such attributes influence the test scores.

For instance, high heritability of test scores is in no way informative of their homogeneity. One may add up scores on measures of height, IQ, and eye color, and start looking for genetic basis of the newly defined phenotype; all three characters are highly heritable (Bräuer & Chopra, 1978; Bouchard et al., 1990; Silventoinen et al., 2003), so when the scores on their respective measures are added up, the resulting composite is necessarily highly heritable as well—not because its components reflect a single property or are influenced by the same underlying cause, but merely because all three components are highly heritable in themselves. Therefore, the fact that something is heritable does not tell us anything about the homogeneity of its structure—in fact, in most extreme cases, each of the items on a given highly heritable composite could be measuring a different highly heritable characteristic.

The situation is worsened if one assumes that the elements that make up the composite stand in causal relations to each other. In such a case, each element of the composite may send out an effect to the other elements, thereby propagating genetic effects from any one element to all others. In addition, the strength of the causal relations between the different elements may itself be subject to genetic influences; e.g., sleep deprivation may more easily lead to fatigue, loss of concentration, and depressed mood in some people as compared with others, and these individual differences in the strength of the causal links may stand under the influence of genetic structures.

It is interesting to note that such a state of affairs would be in accordance with the fact that researchers have consistently failed to find a noteworthy contribution of any single gene explaining variation in any given psychological trait. For instance, the variation in composite measures such as full scale IQ has been found to be affected by many genes (Gosso, 2007; Plomin et al., 2008). Conversely, no single gene has been found to account for a substantial proportion of the variance in general intelligence (De Geus, Wright, Martin, & Boomsma, 2001; Nokelainen & Flint, 2002; Payton, 2006; Plomin, Kennedy, & Craig, 2006 Posthuma et al., 2005). In light of this, it seems reasonable to consider the possibility that IQ-scores might be complex composites, comprising distinct elements, or measures thereof, that depend on a heterogeneous collection of processes, possibly with mutualistic connections. A similar situation may obtain in the field of psychopathology research, where studies in search of genes associated with depression (association studies of monoaminergic candidate genes, genes related to neurotoxic and neuroprotective processes, studies of gene-environment interactions etc.) have so far failed to come up with a gene that would explain more than a minor part of the variance (Levinson, 2006). Thus, although heritability estimates are, for most psychological test scores, quite impressive, their evidential strength with respect to the thesis that the tests in question measure a single attribute is limited.

In conclusion, three often cited sources of evidence for the measurement hypothesis—the fit of latent variable models to test scores, the presence of significant external correlations, and the high heritabilities of these test scores—should not be considered definitive on the question of whether we are entitled to interpret our test scores as measures and our tests as measurement instruments. The reason is that none of these lines of evidence addresses the question of how the measurement instrument picks up variation in the targeted attribute and transmits such variation into the measurement outcomes. That, and nothing else, is the smoking gun of test validity. Now, if one ponders the way that tests are structured and the way in which variation in test scores is likely to arise, then it becomes altogether unclear whether we should conceive of the relation between test scores and theoretical terms in terms of measurement. This may seem to be a negative result, but we do not think this is so. It invites us to think about alternative ways of theorizing about the genesis of test score variation.

One supposes that there may be more fruitful alternatives to the theory-observation relation than the almost mandatory methodological outlook in psychology, which has arisen out of the construct validity doctrine coupled with conventional psychometric wisdom. This outlook invariably requires one to interpret one's test scores as measures indicative of a psychological construct, but never makes the parallel requirements of explicating what one means by the notion of measurement and in what way one's psychological attributes may be taken to exist or have causal effects. Therefore, it propagates a situation where researchers entertain shadowy notions of constructs, measurement, and validity, leading them to adopt a monolithic methodological strategy in the analysis of test scores, as coded in conventional test theoretic procedures. This strategy is scarcely motivated by subject matter. Rather, it represents a set of methodological dogmas that may be entirely inappropriate in view of the subject matter of psychology. In our view, it is time to leave these dogmas behind; in this sense, sensible theorizing about test scores is yet to begin.

DISCUSSION

Construct validity theory is at odds with the way in which many, if not most, researchers interpret validity. This raises the question of who has the better validity concept: construct validity theorists, who think that validity is a property of test score interpretations that reflects how strongly these interpretations are supported by the evidence, or the rest of the inhabitants

of the scientific world, who think that validity is a property of tests that signals whether these tests measure what they should measure. In the present
chapter, we have argued against the construct validity view and in favor of
test validity as it is normally understood.

In our view, and in contradiction to the theoretical mainstream in validity theory (e.g., Kane, 2006; Messick, 1989), it is a mistake to view validity as
a property of test score interpretations. Construct validity in no way restricts
the type of test score interpretation to be considered, thereby leaving the
possibility open to consider the construct validity of *any* test score interpretation that one whishes to make. Such a view easily leads to paradoxical
situations where tests score interpretations that deny the validity of tests can
nonetheless have high construct validity. Relatedly, it is a mistake to think of
validity as a function of evidence. Most important, such a view implies that
the construct validity of a test score interpretation is dependent on time:
If one adheres to construct validity theory, one would have to agree that a
test score interpretation that turns out to be wrong actually was valid up
until the moment the falsifying evidence became available. According to
the general view that a test is valid if it actually measures what it is supposed
to measure, this makes no sense. If a test turns out to measure nothing at
all or something completely different from what was once thought, it was
never valid in the first place. Therefore a theory of validity that concerns
test score interpretations and relies on evidence for these interpretations
is inadequate.

In addition, we think it is hardly possible to consider the validity of test
score interpretations in terms of measurement without spelling out what
one means by the term 'measurement'. And since it appears that the realist, causal interpretation of measurement has, at the moment, no serious
rivals, the test score interpretation 'test X measures attribute Y' must be
interpreted as requiring the presence of a causal effect of the attribute
on the test scores. If this is indeed granted, then it follows that there is
one and only one necessary condition for test validity, and that is that the
test has the property of picking up variation in the targeted attribute, and
transmitting it into variation in the test scores. This, however, is clearly a
property of the measurement instrument itself, not of the interpretations
of the measurement outcomes. In addition, whether a measurement instrument actually measures what the researcher intends it to measure is
ultimately a question of truth, not of evidence. Thus, following this line of
reasoning, we arrive at a position almost fully orthogonal to the dominant
view in construct validity theory.

To avoid any confusion caused by the ambiguous use of the word construct, we recommend abandoning this term along with the theory it lends
its name to. We carve up the world in a way that naturally corresponds to
the ordinary semantics of measurement. On the one hand we have a psy-

chological attribute that we hypothesize to exist in the world, and to cause variation in our measurement outcomes. That is the thing we want to measure. On the other hand we have the theoretical term that we use in our theories and that, if we are lucky, in fact picks out the psychological attribute in question. If we can explain how the psychological attribute acts to cause variation in our measurement outcomes, we can truly say something about the validity of our measurement instrument. This requires us to investigate the structures and processes that make up the psychological properties we are interested in and to show that these properties are picked up by the test. In essence, this means that we need to construct a psychometric model that is *psycho*metric rather than psycho*metric*. Rather than substanceless models, preferred for their philosophical or statistical niceties, psychometric models should be formal theories of test behavior. The task of validation then comes down to testing these theories in whatever way necessary.

Thus, in our view, psychometric theories are central to validation. Construct validity theory, however, has it that even though one may fit psychometric models if one so desires, establishing test validity always requires one to do 'something else' as well, and, interestingly, this something else may also be done without ever even raising the question of which measurement model should be considered. This means that one could support construct validity in the *absence* of a measurement model. This, in our view, is predicated on a mystical view of what measurement is—a view that is so vague that it may serve to leave the issue of validity forever undecided. The fact that construct validity theorists rejoice in claiming that validation is 'neverending', 'open-ended', etc. therefore may not indicate philosophical or methodological sophistication, but rather unwittingly illustrate how deeply misguided construct validity theory really is.

Moreover, the idea that test validity *cannot* be settled, deeply ingrained in the writings of construct validity theorists, blurs the difference between clearly successful and clearly doubtful cases of measurement. Whether one likes it or not, it is a fact of life that one can go to a hardware store and buy a hygrometer for two dollars. If one wants to know how and why that instrument measures humidity, one can look it up in the manual. Clearly such cases of measurement have something that psychology does not have, and we should be interested in what it is. In this respect, hiding behind the complexities of confirmation theory or philosophy of science is in nobody's interest. Surely one can make up all kinds of problems involved in the function of hygrometers, but these are of a completely different order as compared to those in psychology. The difference between the hygrometer manual and the WAIS manual is simply that the former offers an explanation of how differences in humidity are transmitted into differences in the measurement readings, whereas the latter does not offer an explanation of how differences in general intelligence are transmitted into differences in IQ-scores.

The legacy of construct validity theory is that people have come to think that theories about how intelligence relates to other properties, or the utility of IQ-scores in predicting college performance, or the correlations between IQ-scores and other IQ-scores, all prevalent in test manuals like that of the WAIS, can be a substitute for the missing corpus of process theories. As long as this remains the case, the validity of psychological tests will be in doubt.

AUTHOR NOTE

Send correspondence to Denny Borsboom, Department of Psychology, Faculty of Social and Behavioral Sciences, University of Amsterdam, Roetersstraat 15, 1018 WB Amsterdam, The Netherlands, e-mail: d.borsboom@ uva.nl. The work of Denny Borsboom and Angélique Cramer is supported by NWO innovational research grant 452-07-005. The work of Annemarie Zand Scholten is supported by NWO research grant 400-05-055. The work of Sanja Franic is supported by a Nuffic Huygens Scholarship Grant and a Ministry of Science, Education and Sports of the Republic of Croatia grant for postgraduate training abroad.

REFERENCES

Aggen, S. H., Neale, M. C., & Kendler, K. S. (2005). DSM criteria for major depression: Evaluating symptom patterns using latent-trait item response models. *Psychological Medicine, 35*, 475–487.

American Psychiatric Association. (1994). *Diagnostic and Statistical Manual of Mental Disorders (DSM-IV)*. Washington DC: APA.

Barker, P., & Goldstein, B. R. (1992). Distance and Velocity in Kepler's Astronomy. *Annals of Science, 51*, 59–73.

Batitsky, V. (1998). Empiricism and the myth of fundamental measurement. *Synthese, 116*, 51–73.

Bollen, K., & Lennox, R. (1991). Conventional wisdom on measurement: A structural equation perspective. *Psychological Bulletin, 110*, 305–314.

Boomsma, D. I., Busjahn, A., & Peltonen, L. (2002). Classical twin studies and beyond. *Nature Reviews Genetics, 3*, 872–882.

Borsboom, D. (2005). *Measuring the mind: Conceptual issues in contemporary psychometrics*. Cambridge: Cambridge University Press.

Borsboom, D. (2006). The attack of the psychometricians. *Psychometrika, 71*, 425–440.

Borsboom, D. (2008). Psychometric perspectives on diagnostic systems. *Journal of Clinical Psychology, 64*, 1089–1108.

Borsboom, D., & Dolan, C. V. (2007). Theoretical equivalence, measurement, invariance, and the idiographic filter. *Measurement, 5,* 236–263.

Borsboom, D., Kievit, R., Cervone, D. P., & Hood, S. B. (in press). The two disciplines of scientific psychology, or: The disunity of psychology as a working hypothesis. In J. Valsiner, P. C. M. Molenaar, M. C. D. P. Lyra, & N. Chaudary (Eds.), *Developmental process methodology in the social and developmental sciences.* New York: Springer.

Borsboom, D., & Mellenbergh, G. J. (2007). Test validity and cognitive assessment. In J. Leighton, & M. Gierl (Eds.), *Cognitive diagnostic assessment for education: Theory and applications* (pp. 85–115). Cambridge: Cambridge University Press.

Borsboom, D., Mellenbergh, G. J., & Van Heerden, J. (2003). The theoretical status of latent variables. *Psychological Review, 110,* 203–219.

Borsboom, D., Mellenbergh, G. J., & Van Heerden, J. (2004). The concept of validity. *Psychological Review, 111,* 1061–1071.

Bouchard, T. J., Jr., Lykken, D. T., McGue, M., Segal, N. L., & Tellegen, A. (1990). Sources of human psychological differences: The Minnesota Study of Twins Reared Apart. *Science, 250,* 223–228.

Bowler, P. J., & Morus, I. R. (2005). *Making modern science.* Chicago: University of Chicago Press.

Bräuer, G., Chopra, V. P. (1978). Estimating the heritability of hair colour and eye colour. *Journal of Human Evolution London , 9,* 627–630.

Bridgman, P. W. (1927). *The logic of modern physics.* New York: Macmillan.

Carnap, R. (1950). *Testability and meaning.* New Haven, CT: Whitlock's.

Carroll, J. B. (1993). *Human cognitive abilities: A survey of factor-analytic studies.* New York: Cambridge University Press.

Cliff, N. (1992). Abstract measurement theory and the revolution that never happened. *Psychological Science, 3,* 186–190.

Cramer, A. O. J. (2008). Lack of empathy leads to lack of remorse? Psychopathy as a network. *Newsletter of the Society for the Scientific Study of Psychopathy, 2,* 2–3.

Cronbach, L. J. (1957). The two disciplines of scientific psychology. *American Psychologist, 12,* 612–684.

Cronbach, L. J., & Meehl, P. E. (1955). Construct validity in psychological tests. *Psychological Bulletin, 52,* 281–302.

Domotor, Z., & Batitsky, V. (2008). The analytic versus representational theory of measurement: A philosophy of science perspective. *Measurement Science Review, 8,* 129–146.

Edwards, J. R., & Bagozzi, R. P. (2000). On the nature and direction of relationships between constructs and measures. *Psychological Methods, 5,* 155–174.

Embretson, S. (1994). Applications of cognitive design systems to test development. In C. R. Reynolds (Ed.), *Cognitive assessment: A multidisciplinary perspective* (pp. 107–135). New York: Plenum Press.

Gearhart, C. A. (1985). Epicycles, eccentrics, and ellipses: The predictive capabilities of Copernican planetary models. *Archive for History of Exact Sciences,* 207–222.

Geus, E. J. C., de, Wright, M. J., Martin, N. G., & Boomsma, D. I. (2001). Editorial: Genetics of brain function and cognition. *Behavior Genetics, 31,* 489–495.

Gosso, M. F. (2007). *Common genetic variants underlying cognitive ability.* Unpublished doctoral dissertation. Vrije Universiteit Amsterdam, The Netherlands.

Gustafsson, J. E. (1984). A unifying model for the structure or intellectual abilities. *Intelligence, 8,* 179–203.

Hamaker, E. L., Nesselroade, J. R., & Molenaar, P. C. M. (2007). The integrated trait-state model. *Journal of Research in Personality, 41,* 295–315.

Jansen, B. R. J., & Van der Maas, H. L. J. (1997). Statistical tests of the rule assessment methodology by latent class analysis. *Developmental Review, 17,* 321–357.

Jansen, B. R. J., & Van der Maas, H. L. J. (2002). The development of children's rule use on the balance scale task. *Journal of Experimental Child Psychology, 81,* 383–416.

Jensen, A. R. (1998). *The g factor: The science of mental ability.* Westport, CT: Praeger/ Greenwood.

Kane, M. T. (2001). Current concerns in validity theory. *Journal of Educational Measurement, 38,* 319–342.

Kane, M. T. (2006). Validation. In R. L. Brennan (Ed.), *Educational measurement* (4th ed., pp. 17–64). Westport: National Council on Measurement in Education and American Council on Education.

Karabatsos, G. (2001). The Rasch model, additive conjoint measurement, and new models of probabilistic measurement theory. *Journal of Applied Measurement, 2,* 389–423.

Kendler, K. S., Gardner, C. O., Neale, M. C., & Prescott, C. A. (2001). Genetic risk factors for major depression in men and women: similar or distinct heritabilities and same or partly distinct genes. *Psychological Medicine, 31,* 605–616.

Krantz, D. H., Luce, R. D., Suppes, P., & Tversky, A. (1971). *Foundations of Measurement, Vol. I.* New York: Academic Press.

Leighton, J., & Gierl, M. (Eds.). (2007). Cognitive diagnostic assessment for education: Theory and applications. Cambridge: Cambridge University Press.

Levinson, D. F. (2006). The genetics of depression: A review. *Biological Psychiatry, 60,* 84–92.

Loevinger, J. (1957). Objective tests as instruments of psychological theory. *Psychological Reports, 3,* 635–694.

Lord, F. M., & Novick, M. R. (1968). *Statistical theories of mental test scores.* Reading, MA: Addison-Wesley.

Luce, R. D., Krantz, D. H., Suppes, P., & Tversky, A. (1990). *Foundations of measurement, Vol. III.* New York: Academic Press.

Lykken , D.T. (1991). What's wrong with psychology anyway? In D.Cicchetti & W. M. Grove (Eds.), *Thinking clearly about psychology. Volume 1: Matters of public interest.* Minneapolis: University of Minnesota Press.

Maas, H. L. J. van der, Dolan, C., Grasman, R. P. P. P., Wicherts, J. M., Huizenga, H. M., & Raijmakers, M. E. J. (2006). A dynamical model of general intelligence: The positive manifold of intelligence by mutualism. *Psychological Review, 113,* 842–861.

Mackintosh, N. J. (1998). *IQ and human intelligence.* Oxford: Oxford University Press.

Maraun, M. D., & Peters, J. (2005). What does it mean that an issue is conceptual in nature? *Journal of Personality Assessment, 85,* 128–133.

McCrae, R. R., & Costa, P. T., Jr. (2008). Empirical and theoretical status of the Five-Factor Model of personality traits. In G. Boyle, G. Matthews, & D. Saklofske (Eds.), *Sage handbook of personality theory and assessment* (Vol. 1, pp. 273–294). Los Angeles: Sage.

McGue, M., & Christensen, K. (2003). The heritability of depression symptoms in elderly Danish twins: occasion-specific versus general effects. *Behavioral Genetics, 33,* 83–93.

Meehl, P. E. (1978). Theoretical risks and tabular asterisks: Sir Karl, Sir Ronald, and the slow progress of soft psychology. *Journal of Consulting and Clinical Psychology, 46,* 806–834.

Messick, S. (1989). Validity. In R. L. Linn (Ed.), *Educational measurement* (pp. 13–103). Washington, DC: American Council on Education and National Council on Measurement in Education.

Molenaar, P. C. M. (2004). A manifesto on psychology as ideographic science: bringing the person back into scientific psychology, this time forever. *Measurement, 2,* 201–218.

Molenaar, P. C. M., Huizenga, H. M., & Nesselroade, J. R. (2003). The relationship between the structure of interindividual and intraindividual variability: A theoretical and empirical validation of Developmental Systems Theory. In U. M. Staudinger & U. Lindenberger (Eds.), *Understanding human development: Dialogues with lifespan psychology* (pp. 339–360). Dordrecht: Kluwer Academic Publishers.

Narens, L., & Luce, R. D. (1986). Measurement: the theory of numerical assignments. *Psychological Bulletin, 99,* 166–180.

Nokelainen, P., & Flint, J. (2002). Genetic effects on human cognition: lessons from the study of mental retardation syndromes. *Journal of Neurology, Neurosurgery and Psychiatry, 72,* 287–296.

Payton, A. (2006). Investigating cognitive genetics and its implication for the treatment of cognitive deficit. *Genes, Brain and Behavior, 5,* 44–53.

Pearl, J. (2000). *Causality: Models, reasoning, and inference.* Cambridge: Cambridge University Press.

Plomin, R., DeFries, J. C., McClearn, G. E., & McGuffin, P. (2008). *Behavioral genetics* (5th ed.). New York: Worth.

Plomin, R., Hill, L., Craig, I. W., McGuffin, P., Purcell, S., Sham, P., Lubinski, D., Thompson, L. A., Fisher, P. J., Turic, D., & Owen, M. J. (2001). A genome-wide scan of 1842 DNA markers for allelic associations with general cognitive ability: a five-stage design using DNA pooling and extreme selected groups. *Behavioral Genetics, 31,* 497–509.

Plomin, R., Kennedy, J. K. J., & Craig, I. W. (2006). The quest for quantitative trait loci associated with intelligence. *Intelligence, 34,* 513–526.

Popper, K. R. (1959). *The logic of scientific discovery.* London: Hutchinson Education.

Posthuma, D. (2002). *Genetic variation and cognitive ability.* Unpublished doctoral dissertation. Vrije Universiteit Amsterdam, The Netherlands.

Posthuma, D., Geus, E. J. C., de, & Boomsma, D. I. (2001). Perceptual speed and IQ are associated through common genetic factors. *Behavioral Genetics, 31,* 593–602.

Posthuma, D., Luciano, M., Geus, E. J. C., de, Wright, M. J., Slagboom, P. E., Montgomery, G. W., Boomsma, D. I., & Martin, N. G. (2005). A genome-wide scan for intelligence identifies quantitative trait loci on 2q and 6p. *American Journal of Human Genetics, 77*, 318–326.

Psychological Corporation (1997). *WAIS-III WMS-III Technical Manual.* San Antonio, TX: Harcourt Brace & Co.

Rasch, G. (1960). *Probabilistic models for some intelligence and attainment tests.* Copenhagen: Paedagogiske Institut.

Silventoinen, K., Sammalisto, S., Perola, M., Boomsma, D. I., Cornes, B. K., Davis, C., Dunkel, L., De Lange, M., Harris, J. R., Hjelmborg, J. V., Luciano, M., Martin, N. G., Mortensen, J., Nistico, L., Pedersen, N. L., Skytthe, A., Spector, T. D., Stazi, M. A., Willemsen, G., & Kaprio, J. (2003). Heritability of adult body height: A comparative study of twin cohorts in eight countries. *Twin Research, 6*, 399–408.

Snow, R. E., & Lohman, D. F. (1989). Implications of cognitive psychology for educational measurement. In R.L. Linn (Ed.), *Educational measurement* (pp. 263–311). Washington DC: American Council on Education and National Council on Measurement in Education.

Stegmüller, W. (1979). *The structuralist view of theories: A possible analogue of the Bourbaki programme in physical science.* New York: Springer-Verlag.

Suppe, F. (1974). *The structure of scientific theories.* Urbana: University of Illinois Press.

Suppes, P., Krantz, D. H., Luce, R. D., & Tversky, A. (1989). *Foundations of measurement, Vol. II.* San Diego, CA: Academic Press.

Tuerlinckx, F., & De Boeck, P. (2005). Two interpretations of the discrimination parameter. *Psychometrika, 70*, 629–650.

Van Fraassen, B. C. (1980). *The scientific image.* Oxford: Clarendon Press.

Zumbo, B. D. (2007). Validity: Foundational issues and statistical methodology. In C. R. Rao & S. Sinharay (Eds.), *Handbook of statistics, Vol. 26: Psychometrics* (pp. 45–79). Amsterdam: Elsevier.

PART III

APPLICATION ORIENTED

CHAPTER 8

VALIDITY IN ACTION

State Assessment Validity Evidence for Compliance with NCLB

William D. Schafer, Joyce Wang, and Vivian Wang

ABSTRACT

This chapter describes validity evidence required in peer reviews for compliance with NCLB requirements for state assessment systems and makes recommendations about acceptable validity evidence. We first examined available 2007 Title I peer review outcomes for each state in order to identify what are the most salient elements of validity documentation in actual use. In addition, we studied validity evidence from five state peer review reports and summarized peer reviewers' comments. We also reviewed the validity evidence contained in their technical reports by states whose assessment systems had been approved by the U.S. Department of Education. Finally, we discuss several features in the assessment and accountability program review process that pose some unique challenges in developing evidence for establishing validity and describe a source of validity evidence that seems appropriate for this use.

The Concept of Validity, pages 173–193
Copyright © 2009 by Information Age Publishing
All rights of reproduction in any form reserved.

1   INTRODUCTION

The main objectives of this project were to review the evidence that state testing programs provide to the United States Department of Education on the validity of their assessments, to examine in greater detail the validity evidence that certain successful states provided for their peer reviews, and to make recommendations for improving the evidence supporting validity for state assessments. To address these objectives, we first examined the available 2007 Title I peer review results for each state. This was done in order to identify the most salient aspects of validity documentation that are in actual use in evaluating statewide tests of educational attainment. We then studied a convenience sample of five state peer review reports and summarized peer reviewers' comments on validity evidence. We also evaluated the validity evidence submitted in technical reports by a sample of states whose assessment systems had been approved by the U.S. Department of Education. Finally, we discussed some features of assessment and accountability program reviews that seem to pose some unique challenges for establishing validity.

The structure of this report is as follows. The second section introduces the methodology, including data sources and procedures. The standards for classification and peer review results are presented in the third section. The fourth section presents a discussion of some features of the nature of validity evidence for compliance reviews.

2   METHODOLOGY

2.1   Data Sources

The data we used in this study were 2007 Decision Letters on Each State's Final Assessment System Under No Child Left Behind (NCLB) from U.S. Department of Education (USED). These are publicly available at the web site, http://www.ed.gov/admins/lead/account/nclbfinalassess/index.html. We also used the peer review reports for five selected states. Because the specific states are irrelevant for our purposes, they will remain anonymous. In addition to the above two sources, we also examined the technical reports for selected states that have received full approval from the Peer Review processes. All the technical reports were downloaded from the official department of education web sites of each state.

2.2 Procedures

Our first step was to examine the "Decision Letters on Each State's Final Assessment System Under No Child Left Behind (NCLB)," state by state. Briefly, the process is that each state submits its evidence as outlined by the USED (2004). This has been revised since we collected our data; the current guidance is available at http://www.ed.gov/policy/elsec/guid/saaprguidance.pdf, and includes revisions made after our initial work was completed in order to include guidance for alternate assessments based on modified academic achievement standards. Following each submission, the USED convenes a panel of peers (independent assessment professionals with varied backgrounds) who review the evidence submitted by the state and complete peer-review reports that are advisory to the USED and are shared with the states. After reviewing the advice in the peer reports, the USED determines which elements are adequately met and which require further work, either in the procedures used by the state, or in the evidence it presents, or both. These outcomes are communicated to the states in the form of Decision Letters. In the Decision Letter for each state, the USED provides the state's approval status, and the necessary further evidence a state must provide in order to document its compliance with NCLB. It is the Decision Letter, and not the peer report, that defines what a state needs to do if it has not been fully approved.

States who have resubmitted their modified evidence undergo a further peer review of the new evidence. Therefore, each of the states may have more than one peer review report and more than one approval letter. In this report, we collected all the available data (Decision Letters) from the USED website from January 1, 2007 to May 30, 2008.

This study was restricted to the validity evidence that states submitted. States were asked to provide further evidence on validity if the initially reported validity evidence of their assessment system was not sufficient. Thus, we focused on the lack of validity evidence for each and when specifically identified in the Decision Letter, we considered it as necessary validity evidence for the assessment system in this report. Then, we classified the evidence into the five types in the *Standards for Educational and Psychological Testing* (AERA/APA/NCME, 1999). We focused primarily on two sections of the Peer Review Guidance, Section 4 (Technical Quality) Critical Element 4.1 (Validity), Critical Element 4.3 (Fairness and Accessibility), Critical Element 4.6 (Accommodations), and Section 5 (Alignment).

3 RESULTS

3.1 Classifications

After examining the decision letters and considering the 1999 *Standards for Educational and Psychological Testing* (AERA/APA/NCME, 1999), we identified five broad categories of evidence used to determine validity: (1) evidence based on test content, (2) evidence based on student response process, (3) evidence from internal structure, (4) evidence based on the assessment's relation to other variables, and (5) evidence based on consequences of testing. The classifications of evidence into these five categories were our own; states were not asked to provide them. Below we describe the guidelines we used, adapted from AERA/APA/NCME (1999).

3.1.1 Evidence Based on Test Content

This refers to consistency between the coverage of the test (including administration, tasks, and scoring), and the content domain the test is supposed to represent.

The evidence includes the surface aspects of validity illustrated by a good content match, and the more substantive aspects of validity that clarify the "real" meaning of a score. Thus, the state should specify the purposes of the assessments, the types of use to which the scores will be put, and ensure that the anticipated decisions that will be based on the results of the assessment are consistent with the purposes for which the assessments were designed. The foregoing justifies the domain of the assessment; in state assessments, the domain is described in the academic content standards at each grade level.

In addition, the state should ensure that the measurement of the knowledge and skills in the academic content standards fits the grade-level expectations (content alignment). In other words, it should be documented that the test items sample the content domain appropriately.

Another aspect of content evidence has to do with inferences about student competencies from the test scores. On statewide tests, this sort of evidence is usually presented in terms of achievement level descriptors (ALD's). The USED requires each state to differentiate at least three levels of performance, which can be associated with basic, proficient, and advanced; some states use more than three levels. For each level beyond the lowest, states conduct studies to set minimum scores for students to be classified into that level as well as descriptions of what students at those levels can be expected to know and do. Along with reports of these studies, the ALD's are in terms of the content domain of the test and themselves constitute further evidence about the nature of the inferences that are anticipated from the various ranges of test scores.

3.1.2 Evidence Based on Student Response Process

This refers to consistency between the activities the test demands on the part of examinees and the processes the test is supposed to represent.

For statewide tests, this evidence concerns whether the test items represent the intended cognitive processes of examinees in an appropriate way. Evidence based on response process would document the consistency between the activities the test demands of examinees and the psychological processes the test is supposed to represent.

3.1.3 Evidence Based on Internal Structure

This refers to the consistency between the structure of the construct(s) that are supposed to be represented by the test and the relationships of the test items and scales with each other.

This type of evidence includes relationships among items within and across subscales and the consistency between subscale relationships and understandings about the construct or content domain. Evidence based on internal structure is normally correlational, including item-scale relationships between both the scale the item is assigned to as well as the other scales on the test, as well as scale-to-scale relationships. Methods that are designed to study groups of relationships, such as factor analyses, are also commonly used. The concern that should be addressed is whether the test structures are consistent with the sub-domain structures of the academic content standards.

3.1.4 Evidence Based on the Assessment's Relationship with Other Variables

This refers to consistency between scores on the test and scores on other assessments, including other tests of the same, similar, and dissimilar content/process domains and assessments of domains the test may be intended to be predictive of or otherwise associated with.

The *Standards* differentiate three classifications of this sort of evidence: (A) convergent and discriminant evidence, (B) test-criterion relationships, and (C) validity generalization.

(A) *Convergent and Discriminant Evidence.* Convergent evidence refers to relationships between scores on the test and scores on other tests that assess similar constructs. Generally, larger correlations between the scores provide more positive convergent evidence. In other words, multiple measures of a same trait should converge (correlate strongly) across these measurements. On the other hand, discriminant evidence refers to relationships between scores on the test and scores on other tests that assess dissimilar constructs. Lower correlations provide more positive discriminant evidence. That is, measures of different traits should correlate less than do measures of the same trait.

(B) *Test-Criterion Relationships.*   This refers to two relationships between the test and other measures of the same trait, called concurrent studies, and measures of traits that have a predictive relationship with the test, called predictive studies. In other words, this evidence shows the degree to which a test is associated with a criterion measure.

In concurrent studies, we study relationships between scores on the test and scores on other tests (criterion measures) that are gathered at the same time. For example, at the time of testing, teachers could be asked to share their students' grades, which could be related to the test scores.

In predictive studies, we obtain a test score (e.g., aptitude) first and then wait to assess a second trait that the test is intended to predict (e.g., achievement). In other words, we study relationships between scores on the test and scores on other tests that are gathered at a later time. In the context of statewide testing, predictive evidence could be generated by correlating test scores with scores on tests of the same content areas in other years, for example.

(C) *Validity Generalization.*   This refers to studying whether and how test-criterion correlations differ across different contexts, such as for different people, different criteria, or different settings. Validity generalization is a form of meta-analysis that can be used to combine and analyze data from several studies. For example, a study of the concurrent validity coefficients of statewide tests could be conducted across states using each state's technical manual and the magnitudes of the coefficients could be related to such variables as grade level, academic content area, and degree of alignment.

3.1.5   Evidence Based on Consequences of Testing

This refers to evidence derived from the effects of testing. Messick (1989) indicated that the consequential basis of validity has two component parts and that they are distinct from the evidentiary basis of validity. The first component, the consequential basis of test interpretation, is the appraisal of the value implications of the construct, of the theory underlying test interpretation, and of the ideologies in which the theory is embedded. The second component, the consequential basis of test use, is the appraisal of both potential and actual social consequences of applied testing. It should be pointed out that, while some feel that consequential evidence has to do with an evaluation of the positive and negative effects of testing (and often use the label, "consequential validity"), others restrict the meaning of "consequential evidence of validity" to the implications of the effects of decisions made using a test's scores, about support for the inferences that have been (and can be expected to be) made from those scores (Kane, 2006).

3.2 State-by-State Decision Letters

We first reviewed all the states' decision letters available at the USED web site. Table 8.1 presents the sorts of evidence about validity that were required of various states by the USED along with the states whose letters

TABLE 8.1 Examples of Necessary Additional Validity Evidence for 19 States

Evidence Type	Evidence Required	States
Evidence based on test content	1. Clarification of the impact (if any) of the standard-setting activity on content validity. (New Jersey)	Alabama
	2. Documentation of the standard setting process and final results. (Alabama)	DC
	3. Evidence that the State has provided documentation of the standards-setting process, including a description of the selection of judges, methodology employed, and final results. (Hawaii, Louisiana, Mississippi, New Hampshire, New Mexico, Oregon, Wisconsin)	New Jersey
	4. Information regarding basic validity and reliability (i.e., consequential validity, item interrelationships and structural consistency, criterion validity and standards setting procedures). (Hawaii)	Hawaii
	5. Evidence of the accuracy of teacher-provided ratings of the Alternate Assessment. (North Dakota)	Louisiana
	6. Technical quality documentation for the standards setting. (Pennsylvania)	Mississippi
	7. Assessments, including the alternate assessment, are measuring the knowledge and skills described in the academic content standards and not knowledge, skills, or other characteristics that are not specified in the academic content standards or grade level expectations. (South Dakota)	New Hampshire
	8. Documentation of the demographics of standards-setting panelists. (Virginia)	North Dakota
	9. Technical quality documentation for the standards-setting in reading and mathematics at grades 3, 5, 6, and 8. (Washington)	Oregon
	10. Clear explanations of design and scoring (Wyoming)	Pennsylvania
	11. Clear blueprints, item specifications, and test development procedures. (Wyoming)	South Dakota
	12. Consistency between test administration practices and the standards-setting process (reading, writing, and mathematics). (Wyoming)	Virginia
		Washington
		Wisconsin
		Wyoming

(continued)

TABLE 8.1 Examples of Necessary Additional Validity Evidence for 19 States (continued)

Evidence Type	Evidence Required	States
Evidence based on response processes	1. Assessment items are tapping the intended cognitive processes and that the items and tasks are at the appropriate grade level. (South Dakota)	South Dakota
Evidence based on internal structure	1. Evidence that its assessments yield reliable scores that are consistent with the structures inherent to the state's academic content standards. (DC) 2. Data (such as inter-item correlations) that confirms that scoring and reporting structures are consistent with the subdomain structure of the content standards. (New Jersey) 3. Interpretation or analysis to accompany data summaries of the inter-correlations of subdomains. (Puerto Rico) 4. Justification of score use given the threat to validity represented by the inter-component correlations that show higher correlations between content areas than between components within content areas. (Wyoming)	DC Hawaii New Jersey Puerto Rico Wyoming
Evidence based on relations to other variables	**A. Convergent and discriminant evidence:** 1. Evidence to show the state has evaluated the relationships between test performance and other relevant, external variables. This is essential to show convergent and divergent validity. (DC) **B. Test-criterion relationships:** 1. Criterion-related validity evidence. (Alabama) 2. An analysis of (consequential and) concurrent validity. (Puerto Rico) 3. Reliability and validity information for the operational assessments, including data supporting concurrent...validity. (Wyoming) **C. Validity Generalization:** None	Alabama DC Puerto Rico Wyoming
Evidence based on consequences of testing	1. Information regarding basic validity and reliability (i.e., consequential validity...). (Hawaii) 2. An analysis of consequential (and concurrent) validity. (Puerto Rico) 3. Plans for, or results from, analyses of consequential validity. (New Jersey) 4. A plan and a timeline for studies of intended and unintended consequences. (North Dakota, Illinois) 5. Complete validity information for the operational test and reliability and validity information for the alternate assessments, including data supporting...consequential validity. (Wyoming)	Hawaii Illnoins New Jersey North Dakota Puerto Rico Wyoming

included that evidence. The evidence is subdivided by type of evidence. It should be remembered that these items were required over and above the evidence submitted by the states, so the list is not exhaustive.

As shown in Table 8.1, eighteen states were asked to provide the evidence based on test content, one state was asked to provide the evidence based on student response process, five states were asked to provide the evidence based on internal structure, and four states were asked to provide the evidence based on the relations to other variables. The three sources of relationships-with-other-variables evidence are: (1) convergent and discriminant, one state was asked to provide this evidence; (2) test-criterion relationships, three states were asked to provide this sort of evidence; (3) Validity generalization, none of the states was asked to provide this kind of evidence, but validity generalization is a form of meta-analysis that is used to combine and analyze data from several studies and is normally well beyond the scope of most state testing programs. Finally, six states were asked to provide the evidence based on the consequences of test interpretation and use.

In addition, twenty-three states were asked to provide studies to ensure their standards and assessments are aligned.

It should be emphasized that thus far, the evidence that has been described may be thought of as important, even mandatory. Although not all states were asked to provide each particular type, there are two reasons why mandatory evidence might not have been required of a state in the decision letters. First, the state may already have provided that evidence. In that case, the decision letter would not have cited it. Second, although the USED makes an effort to be consistent in what they require of states, it is always possible that one type of evidence is required of a particular state when another state may not have submitted it, and it may not have been mentioned by the particular group of peers in their review process of that state. Thus idiosyncrasies may arise in what is supposed to be a fair process, and it is almost inevitable that they will. Over time, it is likely that states will be asked for validity evidence more consistently, and it would not be surprising to see states asked to submit evidence from sources more, rather than less broadly in the future.

3.3   Peer Review Reports

The USED peer review process involves development of a report by a peer review team, with recommendations to USED that may or may not be followed. One feature of this report is a description of the evidence that the state has submitted. For a state that received approval on the first round, there is only one such report, but if a state does not receive approval, additional rounds of evidence are submitted and there are additional peer review reports. Realizing that the decision letters presented for any state only the required evidence that was missing, and did not constitute an exhaustive list of the evidence that is necessary, we wanted to use the peer review reports to review the evidence that was deemed adequate for each state.

For several reasons, it was impossible to review all these reports. While they are shared with the states, they are not available publicly. We therefore did not have access to all the reports. Additionally, the sheer number of reports would have been rather daunting. Fortunately, we had access to five states' reports and were able to use them as a convenience sample. All reports for each state that we reviewed were available to us.

The state submissions may or may not have included evidence that was unnecessary for USED purposes. Therefore, while our review of the decision letters could have been incomplete of all the evidence that is necessary to establish validity for USED purposes, the results of this analysis may be over-inclusive of the necessary evidence. Nevertheless, since it was the only data source available to us, we used it.

In this section we describe the evidence submitted in the five state reports using the five categories of evidence as above. The states are not discussed separately. Rather, all evidence for the purposes of establishing validity that was submitted is noted, no matter how many or few states submitted it.

The peer review guidance includes a requirement for a description of the purposes of the assessments as evidence. This is a common element in developing a validity argument (Kane, 2006) and each state included such a discussion. However, it does not fall within the various categories of evidence, so it is omitted below.

3.3.1 *Evidence Based on Test Content*

The primary vehicles for content evidence of validity are test blueprints and alignment reports. The former describes the process by which the test domain is sampled and the latter are an evaluation of how well that process worked for a particular form. An alignment review typically includes criteria such as Categorical Concurrence (that each content strand is associated with enough items to support a subscore report), Range of Knowledge (the number of content elements in each strand that have items associated with them), and Balance of Representation (the distribution of items across the content elements within each strand). Although rather generic criteria are applied to alignment reports (that is, they do not represent the goals of a particular content area at a particular grade), they have been used successfully to document success in content representation as well as to generate recommendations for improvement that seem to make sense to other professionals as well as those associated with the particular testing program.

The achievement levels implied by the cut score standards have also been used to support validity. In one case, the achievement level descriptions were compared with the strand structure of the content standards to document that the testing program captures a balanced representation of the content. The same sort of analysis has been performed for the rubrics and scoring tools used to evaluate student constructed responses.

3.3.2 *Evidence Based on Response Processes*

The same two vehicles of content evidence also apply to process evidence. While blueprints may or may not include a process dimension (many do not), virtually all alignment studies include a fourth component that can be called Depth of Knowledge, which related the cognition tapped by each item to that implied in the statement of the element in the content standards the item is associated with.

3.3.3 *Evidence Based on Internal Structure*

Evidence of internal structure was generated mostly by dimensional analysis at the item level and by intercorrelations among the subtest scores. Both these are empirical. The specific sorts of dimensional analysis evidence that were presented include item-subtest correlations, item-test correlations, and factor analyses. Intercorrelations among subtests were evaluated according to whether they were sufficiently large to be scaled together in a total score but at the same time were sufficiently low to be reported with differential meaning. This sort of evidence is commonly found in technical manuals.

3.3.4 *Evidence Based on Relations to Other Variables*

Correlations between external, such as nationally marketed tests were presented. These were always correlations of the same trait, i.e., reading to reading and math to math. It would also have been interesting to show that each trait correlated more strongly with the same trait than with the other trait, and it should have been easy to develop that evidence, too, but it was not presented. Other external variables included student demographics and course-taking patterns.

Another sort of evidence is based on fairness and accessibility goals. This includes accommodations for disabilities and limited English proficiency (those that are acceptable, choosing among them, and implementing them), as well as bias studies, such as differential item functioning (DIF) and passage reviews. We classify it here since it involves other variables, but realize that its nature may not be relational. Also in this area are adherence to universal design principles (Thompson, Johnstone, & Thurlow, 2002) and monitoring of consistent test administration procedures.

3.3.5 *Evidence Based on Consequences of Testing*

There was very little evidence based on consequences provided by the states. One did evaluate change in dropout and graduation rates in a longitudinal analysis, but there was no systematic effort in any of the states to generate researchable questions around the areas of intended and unintended consequences.

4 TECHNICAL MANUALS

While reviewing the Decision Letters for states, we found some states were asked to provide technical reports in the peer review process. Thus, we tried to review the technical reports for states that have received approval status to review the validity evidence that appears in them. According the decision letters (01/01/07–05/30/08), two states have received the full approval status in the first round of peer review process: Delaware and Massachusetts and ten states have also received the full approval status in their second round or third round of peer review process: Alabama, California, Georgia, Kentucky, Maine, Missouri, Montana, New York, North Dakota, and Rhode Island. Considering the data available from the websites, five states were selected for this paper: Delaware, Massachusetts, Missouri, North Dakota, and Rhode Island.

The validity evidence shown in states' technical reports were as follows.

4.1 Evidence Based on Test Content

The empirical validity evidence based on test content in Delaware's technical reports were presented in two aspects: the summary findings from Delaware Student Testing Program (DSTP) Administration Student Survey, and the summary of revisiting/ establishing cut scores for DSTP Reading, Writing, and Mathematics.

Massachusetts provided the degree to which Massachusetts Comprehensive Assessment System (MCAS) items align to the Massachusetts Curriculum Framework learning standards for each content area and grade level. They provided the detailed test construction process examined by the Assessment Development Committees (ADCs) and Bias Committee. In addition to the MCAS, Massachusetts also provided validity evidence based on test content for their MCAS-Alt.

Missouri uses construct validity as the central concept for the Missouri Assessment Program (MAP) validation process. Evidence for construct validity is comprehensive and integrates evidence from both content and criterion related validity. Thus, in Missouri's technical report, they addressed the content-development process that is intended to minimize construct-irrelevant variance and construct under-representation (2007, 2007MAP technical report).

For North Dakota, validity evidence based on test content was provided through the following procedures: (1) attention during the item development and item selection process; (2) item writers and test developers following published guidelines (e.g., *Guidelines for Bias-Free publishing, Reflecting Diversity: Multicultural Guidelines for Educational Publishing Professionals*) for reducing or eliminating bias, and (3) avoiding the use of items with poor statistical fit (2007, 2008 NDSA technical report).

For Rhode Island, components of validity evidence based on the test content included item alignment with content standards; item bias; sensitivity and content appropriateness review processes; adherence to the test blueprint; use of multiple item types; use of standardized administration procedures, with accommodated options for participation; and appropriate test administration training (2007, NECAP 2006-2007 Technical Report).

4.2 Evidence Based on Student Response Processes

Rhode Island described additional studies that might provide evidence based on student response processes in a future report. For example, think-aloud protocols could be used to investigate students' cognitive processes when confronting test items (2007, NECAP 2006–2007 Technical Report). For other states, evidence based on student response processes was not clearly specified in the technical reports, although alignment reports may contain this sort of evidence.

4.3 Evidence Based on Internal Structure

Delaware provided the inter-correlation matrix among sub-domains to show evidence based on internal structure.

According to the Massachusetts's technical report, statistical analyses were conducted to provide evidence based on internal structure. These analyses included: (1) classical item statistics (item difficulty and item-test correlation), (2) differential item functioning analyses, (3) a variety of reliability coefficients, (4) standard errors of measurement, and (5) item response theory parameters and procedures(2007, 2007 MCAS Technical Report).

Missouri provided the fit of their IRT models and the unidimensionality of IRT models using principal component analyses (PCA).

North Dakota examined the unidimensionality of each grade-level NDSA test using principal component analysis (PCA).

In Rhode Island's technical report, evidence on internal structure was included in discussions of scaling and equating, item analyses, and reliability. The internal structures of the tests were presented using statistics, such as item difficulty, differential item functioning analyses, reliability coefficients, SEM, multidimensionality hypothesis testing and effect size estimation, and IRT parameters and procedures (2007, NECAP 2006-2007 Technical Report).

4.4 Evidence Based on Relations to Other Variables

Massachusetts conducted two separate studies to provide evidence based on relations to other variables. The first study was to examine the relationship between MCAS and performance on the Metropolitan Achievement Test (MAT-7) at grade 10. The second study was to examine the relationship between MCAS scores and the Stanford Achievement Test (SAT-9) scores at grade 4, 8, and 10 (2007, 2007 MCAS Technical Report).

Missouri provided convergent validity and divergent validity to show evidence based on relations to other variables. For convergent validity, they use Principal Components Analyses to justify that there is a dominant dimension underlying the items/tasks in each test and those scores from each test represent performance primarily determined by that ability. For divergent validity, they presented the correlations between the Mathematics, and Communication Arts scale scores for students who took both of the MAP subject area tests in 2007 (2007, 2007 MAP technical report).

North Dakota provided convergent validity and divergent validity to show evidence based on relations to other variables. For convergent validity, they analyzed internal structure by evaluating how well the relationships among test items conform to the constructs the test purposes to measure. For divergent validity, they computed the correlations between Mathematics, Reading, and Science scale scores for students who took either both or all three NDSA subject area tests in 2007.

For Rhode Island, evidence based on relations to other variables was represented in two ways: (1) cross-tabulations of NECAP test scores with teacher judgments and questionnaire data, and (2) correlating NECAP scores with scores on the Iowa Test of Basic Skills (ITBS). In addition, Rhode Island also provided evidence of convergent and discriminant validity by using the multi-trait/multi-method matrix (2007, NECAP 2006-2007 Technical Report).

4.5 Evidence Based on Consequences of Testing

Massachusetts provided evidence that their reporting structures are consistent with the sub-domain structures of its academic content standards.

They also claimed that the consequences of MCAS testing are consistent with the purposes of the MCAS program because educators in the state: 1) Evaluate the performance of students, schools, districts, and the state based on the Massachusetts Curriculum Framework content standards and the MCAS performance standards; 2) Improve classroom instruction and student academic achievement by providing data that assist local educators in improving curriculum design and instruction; 3) Relate MCAS test scores to AYP requirements, in concert with other evidence, to determine NCLB federal funding; 4) certify students for eligibility to earn a high school diploma(2007, 2007 MCAS Technical Report).

Missouri provided evidence that MAP test scores could be appropriately used for different levels. For example, MAP test scores may be used by classroom teachers as evidence of student achievement in the content areas. At the aggregate level, MAP scores may be used by district and school administrators for planning curriculum. At state level, MAP test scores are appropriate to use for accountability programs associated with No Child Left Behind and the Missouri School Improvement Program (2007, 2007 MAP technical report).

North Dakota did not clearly specify validity evidence based on test consequences in their technical report; however, they provided analysis to show the validity evidence that support the intended uses and interpretations of the test scores for the North Dakota State Assessment (NDSA).

For Rhode Island, evidence on the consequences of testing was addressed in two ways: scaling and equating as well as score reporting. Each of these provided the public with test score information. Scaled scores simplify reporting across content areas, grade levels, and successive years by using achievement levels as reference points for mastery at each grade level, another. They also used NAEP test trends as evidence of the consequences of testing (2007, NECAP 2006-2007 Technical Report).

5 SYNTHESIS OF EVIDENTIARY NEEDS FOR VALIDITY

It is not clear that we can use these studies to generate a list of the necessary evidence that a state should present in order to evaluate the validity of its assessments. As soon as we do so, surely it will be challenged, and likely with reasonable justification. Nevertheless, such as listing would be quite helpful to states, at least to establish a minimum for their regulatory submissions. With that in mind, it seems reasonable to submit the following in each evidence area. It should be assumed that each tested content and grade combination, as well as test series (i.e., regular assessment, alternate assessment) is independent and needs to be justified separately.

5.1 Content Evidence

- The content standards.
- The test blueprint.
- The item (and passage) development process.
- The item categorization rules and process.
- The forms development process.
- The results of alignment studies.

5.2 Process Evidence

- The test blueprint (if it has a process dimension).
- The item categorization rules and method (if items are categorized by process).
- The results of alignment studies.
- The results of other studies, such as think-alouds.

5.3 Internal Structure Evidence

- Subscore correlations.
- Item subscore correlations.
- Dimensionality analysis.

5.4 Evidence Based on Relations with Other Variables

5.4.1 Convergent Evidence

- Correlations with independent, standardized measures.
- Correlations with within-class variables, such as grades.

5.4.2 Discriminant Evidence

- Correlations with standardized tests of other traits (e.g., math with reading).
- Correlations with within-class variables, such as grades in other contents.
- Correlations with irrelevant student characteristics (e.g., gender).
- Item-level DIF studies.

5.5 Consequential Evidence

- Purposes of the test.
- Uses of results by educators.
- Trends over time.
- Studies that generate and evaluate positive and negative aspects from user input.

6 VALIDITY EVIDENCE IN THE ACCOUNTABILITY CONTEXT

One view of validity is that it focuses on the degree or quality of support for proposed interpretations and uses of test scores (Kane, 2006). Traditionally, the emphasis is on a particular test, or perhaps a set of test forms. Much of the evidence that has been discussed so far capitalizes on well-known methods for study of the validity of a particular test form.

But in the context of compliance review of state assessment and accountability systems, the object of study is actually a process by which tests are developed, used, and hopefully evaluated rather than on a particular test form; a given test form is important only to the extent that it is representative of forms that have been, are, and will be developed. Moreover, the process is not static; programs are expected to engage in a continual process of self-evaluation and improvement.

6.1 Process Evidence

It may or may not prove useful to distinguish between product evidence and process evidence, the former focusing on a particular test and the latter on a testing program. We will review and extend some suggestions for process evidence that were originally proposed in the context of state assessment and accountability peer reviews (Schafer, 2005). The goal of the original discussion was to suggest ways that states could both study and then organize their documentation of their assessment and accountability actions for reviewers.

First, what is a process? Here, a process will be defined as a recurring activity that takes material, operates on it, and produces a product. This could be as large as the entire assessment and accountability program, or as small as, say, the production of a test item. One challenge in developing process evidence is to organize the activities of a program into useful process definitions. If this sounds a bit like project management to you, you're getting the right idea. Some examples will follow, but first it would be helpful to discuss the nature of process evidence.

6.2 Elements of Process Evidence

Four elements of process evidence were discussed. These are Process, Product, Evaluation, and Improvement. Each should be included in the documentation of the validity of the process.

- *Process.*   The process is described. The inputs and operating rules and any other important characteristics are laid out.
- *Product.*   The results of the process are presented or described.
- *Evaluation.* The product is evaluated. Is it adequate, can it be improved, should it be improved (e.g., do the benefits of improvement justify the costs)?
- *Improvement.*   The recommendations from the evaluation are considered for implementation in order to improve the process. Ideally, a formal process is documented in a report. (Anecdotally, this is often the least appreciated step by those who prepare materials for submission to review, and even perhaps by those who implement assessment and accountability programs.)

6.3 Examples of Process Evidence

Three examples of these sorts of process evidence follow. They vary markedly in scope, small to large, in order to illustrate the development of process evidence in different contexts within an assessment and accountability program.

- Bias and Sensitivity Committee Selection.
    - *Process.* Desired composition, generation of committee members, contacting potential members, proposed meeting schedule, etc.
    - *Product.* Committee composition, constituencies represented.
    - *Evaluation.* Comparison of actual with desired composition, follow up with persons who declined, suggestions for improvement.
    - *Improvement.* Who has responsibility to consider the recommendations generated by the evaluation, how they go about their analysis, how change is implemented in the system, examples of changes that were made in the past to document responsiveness.

- Alignment.
  - *Process.* Test blueprint, items, item categorizations, sampling processes.
  - *Product.* Test form.
  - *Evaluation.* Alignment study.
  - *Improvement.* Review of study recommendations, plan for future.
- Psychometric Adequacy.
  - *Process.* The analyses that are performed.
  - *Product.* Technical manual.
  - *Evaluation.* Review by a group such as a TAC, recommendations for the manual as well as the testing program.
  - *Improvement.* Consideration of recommendations, plan for future.

In these examples there are two layers of judgment, and they are typically independent. The first is a review by an internal group or perhaps a vendor. The review makes recommendations about improvement. These are then considered by a second layer of review. In many cases, this would be an excellent way for a state to use its Technical Advisory Council (TAC).

6.4   Documentation of Process Evidence

For review purposes, each of the four steps needs to be documented. The review can then include both the processes that have been documented (for completeness) and the activities (for adequacy). If this is done, the state should receive back from the process very pointed either requirements or recommendations for improvement, but if the documentation is incomplete, the review will be performed on what is an ambiguous submission, and likely will not be as helpful as it could be.

6.5   Criteria for Process Evidence

Since process evidence by definition describes processes, it should be judged by how well it describes processes that support interpretations based on future assessments that are consistent with the purposes of the assessment program. These criteria seem appropriate:

- Data are collected from all relevant sources.
- The data are reported completely and efficiently.
- The reports are reviewed by persons with all the appropriate areas of expertise.

- The review is conducted fairly.
- The needed results of the reviews are reported completely and efficiently.
- Recommendation based on the reviews are suggested in the reports.
- There is appropriate consideration given to the recommendations.
- Actions based on past reports are presented as evidence that the process results in improvement.

7 LIMITATIONS

There are several limitations in this study. First, the Decision letters available on the website did not include the all fifty-two states at the time of our study. Thus, only 34 states were included in this study.

Second, we concluded the necessary validity evidence based on the lack of the validity evidence for each state in this study. We only examined a small, convenience sample of states submissions, and those were only examined based on the peer review reports. One might consider examining the actual validity evidence based on what evidence states actually provided in a future study. It might be possible, for example, to examine the technical reports and other evidence for those states that have received the approval status in the peer review process.

NOTE

This project was funded by the Maryland State Department of Education (MSDE) under a contract with the University of Maryland College Park (UMCP) through the Maryland Assessment Research Center for Education Success (MARCES). The opinions expressed are the responsibility of the authors and do not necessarily represent those of MARCES, MSDE, or UMCP.

REFERENCES

AERA, APA, and NCME. (1999). *Standards for educational and psychological testing.* Washington, DC: AERA.

Delaware Department of Education. (2007). Student Testing Program Technical Report–2006. Retrieved May 20, 2008 from http://www.doe.k12.de.us/programs/aab/Report_and_documents/Technical_Reports.shtml

Kane, M. T. (2006). Validation. In R. L. Brennan (Ed.), *Educational Measurement* (4th ed., pp. 17-64). Westport, CT: Prager.

Messick, S. (1989). Validity. In R. L. Linn, *Educational Measurement,* (3rd edition, pp. 13-103). New York: Macmillan.

Messick, S. (1994). The interplay of evidence and consequences in the validation of performance assessments. *Educational Researcher,* 23(2), 13-23.

Michigan Department of Education. (2008). MEAP Technical Report, 2005–2006. Retrieved May 20, 2008 from http://www.michigan.gov/mde/0,1607,7-140-22709_31168_40135-172664—,00.html

Missouri Department of Education. (2008). Missouri Assessment Program Technical Report, 2007. Retrieved July 20, 2008 from http://www.dese.mo.gov/divimprove/assess/tech/Final%20MAP%20Tech%20Report.pdf

New York Department of Education. (2008). New York State Testing Program: English Language Arts/Math Technical Report,2007. Retrieved July 20, 2008 from http://www.emsc.nysed.gov/osa/pub/reports.shtml

North Dakota Department of Education. (2008). North Dakota State Assessment Fall 2007 Administration Technical Report. Retrieved July 20, 2008 from http://www.dpi.state.nd.us/testing/assess/index.shtm

Rhode Island Department of Education. (2008). New England Common Test Program 2006-2007 Technical Report. Retrieved July 20, 2008 from http://www.ride.ri.gov/assessment/NECAP.aspx

Schafer, W. D. (2005). *A reviewer's perspective on NCLB peer reviews of state assessment systems: Suggestions for states.* Large Scale Assessment Conference, Council of Chief State School Officers, San Antonio.

Thompson, S. J., Johnstone, C. J., & Thurlow, M. L. (2002). *Universal Design Applied to Large-Scale Assessment (Synthesis Report 44).* Minneapolis, MN: University of Minnesota.

U. S. Department of Education. (2004, April 28). *Standards and assessments peer review guidance.* Washington, DC: Author.

U.S. Department of Education. (2007). Decision Letters on Each State's Final Assessment System Under No Child Left Behind (NCLB). Retrieved October 13, 2007, from http://www.ed.gov/admins/lead/account/nclbfinalassess/index.html

CHAPTER 9

THE CONCEPT OF VALIDITY IN THE CONTEXT OF NCLB

Robert L. Linn

ABSTRACT

Validity is the most fundamental consideration in the evaluation of the appropriateness of claims about, and the uses and interpretations of assessment results. A comprehensive validation program for state assessments used for purposes of NCLB requires systematic analysis of the myriad uses, interpretations and claims that are made. A key use of assessment results for NCLB is the identification of schools as either making or failing to make adequate yearly progress. Validation of this use requires evidence that schools that make AYP or better or more effective than schools that fail to make AYP. It is argued that evidence to support the conclusion that the two categories of schools differ in relative effectiveness has seldom been part of validation programs for state assessment, but such evidence is critical for an adequate validation of the primary use of state assessment results for purposes of NCLB.

INTRODUCTION

There is a broad consensus among specialists in educational measurement that validity is the most important consideration in the evaluation of tests.

The Concept of Validity, pages 195–212
Copyright © 2009 by Information Age Publishing
All rights of reproduction in any form reserved.

Although Lissitz and Samuelsen (2007) have recently argued for a different conceptualization of validity, there is also fairly general agreement that it is the inferences made from test scores and the uses that are made of the scores rather than the test per se that is validated. Since test scores may be interpreted in different ways and be subject to a variety of uses, it follows from this prevailing perspective that a given test may have relatively good validity when the results are interpreted in a particular way and used for a specified purpose, but have little or no validity for some other interpretation and use. Thus, validation must focus on specific interpretations and uses of test scores.

PREVAILING CONTEMPORARY VIEWS OF VALIDITY

The *Standards for Educational and Psychological Testing* developed by a joint committee of the American Educational Research Association (AERA), the American Psychological Association (APA), and the National Council on Measurement in Education (NCME), hereafter referred to as the *Test Standards* (AERA, APA, & NCME, 1999), represents the most authoritative statement of professional consensus about expectations for the development and evaluation of tests.[1] According to the *Test Standards,* validity "is the degree to which evidence and theory support the interpretations of test scores entailed by the proposed uses of tests" (AERA, APA, & NCME, 1999, p. 9).

Because validity depends on the particular interpretations and uses of test scores, it naturally follows that it is important to identify the intended uses and the interpretations that are involved in those uses. "Validation logically begins with an explicit statement of the proposed interpretation of test scores, along with a rationale for the relevance of the interpretation to the proposed use" (AERA, APA, & NCME, 1999, p. 9).

The conceptualization of validity articulated in *Test Standards* builds upon the thinking of major validity theorists such as Cronbach (1971, 1980, 1988, 1989) Kane (1992), Messick (1975, 1989), and Shepard (1993). The conceptualization also represents a gradual evolution of the perspectives on validity that were articulated in earlier editions of the *Test Standards.*

Messick's (1989) chapter, in the third edition of *Educational Measurement,* for example, which Shepard (1993) described as the "most cited authoritative reference on the topic (p. 423) began with the following definition.

> Validity is an integrated evaluative judgment of the degree to which empirical evidence and theoretical rationales support the *adequacy* and *appropriateness* of *inferences* and *actions* based on test scores or other modes of assessment. (Messick, 1989, p. 13, emphasis in original)

Kane's (2006) chapter on validity in the most recent edition of *Educational Measurement* presents a conceptualization of validity that builds upon the evaluative approach that was articulated by Messick (1989) and in the 1999 *Test Standards*. As well as his own earlier work on an argument-based view of validity (Kane, 1992) and Cronbach's (1989) discussion of the role of argument in test validation. Kane (2006) conceptualized validation as the process of developing two types of argument that he calls the *interpretive argument* and the *validation argument*. The "*interpretive argument* specifies the proposed interpretations and uses of test results by laying out a network of inferences and assumptions leading from the observed performances to the conclusions and decisions based on the performances" (Kane, 2006, p. 23). The evaluation of the *interpretive argument* is called the *validation argument*. The *validation argument* brings evidence and logical analysis together for the purpose of evaluating the claims and propositions of the *interpretive argument*.

A systematic analysis of the various uses, interpretations, and claims that are made about test results is needed to develop a comprehensive validation program for a test. An interpretive argument needs to be developed for each interpretation and the uses entailed in a particular interpretation. Kane (2006) proposes that interpretive arguments be judged in terms of their clarity, coherence, and plausibility. The interpretive argument can be used to guide the collection of evidence relevant to the particular interpretations, and claims used to support uses of the assessment results. That evidence needs to be accumulated and organized into relevant validity arguments (Kane, 2006).

Shepard (1993) calls for "a coherent framework for prioritizing validity questions" (p. 444). She expands on Cronbach's (1989) suggestion that there are five types of perspectives[2] that are relevant to a validity argument and on Kane's (1992) discussion of validity arguments. She asks, "What does the testing practice claim to do? . . . What are the arguments for and against the intended aims of the test?" and "What does the test do in the system other than what it claims?" (Shepard, 1993, p. 429). For each such question it is helpful to consider the level of stakes that are involved in the use or interpretation of results and then to give the highest priority to those areas with the highest stakes.

The conceptualization of validity in the *Test Standards* as elaborated by the work of Messick (1989), Shepard (1993), and Kane (2006) provides a firm foundation for the evaluation of a testing program. It is the conceptualization that will be used in this paper to identify the validation efforts that are needed to support the use of tests for purposes of meeting the requirements of the No Child Left Behind (NCLB) Act.

NCLB TESTING REQUIREMENTS

Although most states had testing requirements in place prior to the enactment of the NCLB, there was considerable variability in the nature of the state testing programs and in the uses that were made of the results. NCLB has greatly increased the commonalities at least for tests of mathematics and reading or English language arts in grades 3 through 8. States were required to adopt grade-specific content standards in mathematics and reading or English language arts and they had to develop tests that were aligned with those standards.[3] Those tests have to be administered each year to students in grades 3 through 8 and one grade in high school.

The test results were used to hold schools accountable for student achievement. Schools receiving federal funds under NCLB must make adequate yearly progress (AYP) or be subject to a series of corrective actions that become more severe with each additional year that a school does not make AYP.[4] Making AYP not only requires that students in the school score above set targets each year in both mathematics and reading or English language arts, but at least 95% of the eligible students had to be assessed in each subject.[5]

States had to adopt student academic achievement standards that would identify at least three levels of achievement (usually called basic, proficient, and advanced) and set intermediate performance targets (called annual measurable objectives) each year that would lead to all students performing at the proficient level or above by 2014. Exclusions of students from assessments that were once commonplace are not allowed on tests used to meet the requirements of NCLB. Students with severe cognitive disabilities for whom the regular assessment is inappropriate, for example, must be assessed with an alternate assessment.

NCLB assessment results must be reported not only for the student body as a whole but also must be separately reported for racial/ethnic subpopulations, economically disadvantaged students, students with disabilities, and students with limited English proficiency. To make AYP, schools must assess at least 95% of eligible students in each subgroup that is large enough to allow disaggregated reporting in both mathematics and reading or English language arts. Furthermore, the annual measurable objective must be met in each subject for every reportable subgroup for the school to make AYP. Large schools with diverse student bodies can fail to make AYP in many different ways, but there is only one way to make it and that is to exceed the 95% participation rate requirements and the annual measurable objective in each subject for every reportable subgroup.

PRIMARY USE AND INTERPRETATION OF TEST RESULTS FOR NCLB

The primary use of test results that is required by NCLB is for the purpose already described, that is, to determine whether or not schools (and school districts) make AYP. The use of student test results to identify schools that need improvement and are therefore subject to various types of corrective actions or sanctions while other schools are identified as making adequate yearly progress rests on an implicit assumption that the observed school-to-school differences in student achievement are due to differences in school quality. For example, an inference is made in the NCLB accountability system that a school that makes adequate yearly progress (AYP) is better or more effective than a school that fails to make AYP (Linn, 2006). The validity of the school quality inference needs to be evaluated.

Validation of School Quality Inference

There are many reasons other than differences in school quality that may result in one school making AYP while another school does not. If school A makes AYP while school B fails to make AYP in a given year, it could be that school A is more effective than school B. But, it may be that students in school A were higher achieving in earlier years than students in school B. Moreover, it might also be that school B is serving a large number of students with disabilities or a large number of English language learners while school A has few, if any, students facing such challenges. School A may have a homogeneous student body while school B has a diverse student body that requires several different subgroups of students to meet targets. The fact that the school that has fewer challenges makes AYP while the school with greater challenges fails to make AYP does not justify the conclusion that the first school is more effective that the second school. The first school might very well fail to make AYP if it had a student body that was comparable to the one in the second school.

Individual student results from state assessments are used to provide information to parents and teachers, but it is the results at the school level for the student body as whole that are of primary concern for purpose of NCLB. Zumbo and Forer (in press) have argued persuasively that different approaches to validation are needed when inferences from test results are made at different levels of aggregation (e.g., individual, school, school district). "At the very least, systematic and coherent evidence (validation evidence) needs to be assembled to support inferences at various levels. Furthermore, *the level of validation evidence needs to be in line with the level of inferences*" (Zumbo & Forer, in press, p. 7 of typescript, emphasis in original).

Zumbo and Forer go on to argue that evidence at the individual student level is not only insufficient to support inferences at an aggregate level such as schools, but it may be misleading. Strong validity evidence at the individual student level may give a false sense of confidence about the validity of inferences at a different level.

Evaluating the validity of inferences about the quality of schools from test-based accountability results requires the elimination of potential explanations of the observed student test results other than differences in school quality. Ruling out alternative explanations for differences in the achievement of students in different schools poses the biggest challenge to validating the inferences about differences in school quality. As Raudenbush (2004a) has argued, the conclusion that school A is more effective than school B requires an inference that the schools and their instructional programs have caused the observed differences in achievement. The validity of such a causal inference, however, depends on the degree to which many competing explanations can be eliminated. Differences in achievement at the start of the school year, for example, would provide an explanation of the differences in test performance at the two schools in the spring that resulted in one school making AYP while the other school failed to make AYP.

There are many plausible explanations other than differences in school quality that might explain the differences in student performance on tests administered toward the end of the school year. For example, students at the school with the higher scores on the state assessment might have received more educational support at home than students at school B. The student bodies attending different schools can differ in many ways that are related to performance on tests, including language background, socioeconomic status, and prior achievement.

"Test results will reflect not only...the impact of participation in different programs or treatments, but also the characteristics of those tested....Valid interpretations may depend upon additional considerations that have nothing to do with the appropriateness of the test or it's technical quality, including the study design, administrative feasibility, and the quality of other data" (AERA, APA, & NCME, 1999, p. 163). Differences in the characteristics of students attending different schools, for example, call into question the validity of inferences about school effectiveness based on AYP. Potentially relevant student characteristics that are not taken into account in the interpretation of assessment results for purposes of NCLB include student motivation and parental support as well as prior student achievement.

Growth Models and School Quality Inferences

The difficulty in justifying inferences about school quality from assessment results at a single point in time has contributed to the interest in growth models. The longitudinal tracking of individual students across years provides a stronger basis for eliminating competing explanations for school differences in performance other than differential school quality than do accountability systems that rely on current status measures. Prior achievement during the span of grades for which students test results are included in the longitudinal tracking is no longer a viable explanation for differences among schools because that prior achievement is taken into account in analyses of the longitudinal student achievement data.

Although the use of growth models to judge school quality makes it possible to eliminate many alternative explanations for between school differences and thereby make the causal conclusion that differential school effectiveness explains the performance differences, strong causal claims still are not warranted (see, e.g., Raudenbush, 2004b; Rubin, Stuart, & Zanutto, 2004). Rubin et al. (2004) argued that growth model results "should not be seen as estimating causal effects of teachers or schools, but rather as descriptive measures" (p. 113).

Direct evidence regarding instruction in the schools needs to be obtained to evaluate the implicit assumption that schools with different student achievement outcomes differ in terms of the quality of their instructional offerings. This is needed regardless of whether the school accountability relies on measures of current status or on measures of student growth. Surveys of teachers and principals could be used along with direct observations and the collection of instructional artifacts to obtain evidence regarding the nature of and quality of instruction in schools that are rated high or low based on student performance. For example, classroom assessments might be collected from a sample of schools that do and do not make AYP and the relationship of the classroom assessment tasks could be compared to the state assessment in terms of content coverage and the level of cognitive demand of the assessment tasks. Teacher reports of instructional coverage of the content of the standards could also be evaluated for the two categories of schools.

Validation of the interpretation that school differences in student achievement are due to differences in school quality is not easy. Rather, it is a demanding undertaking, similar to research efforts that try to establish causal connections in situations where randomized experiments are impossible. The difficulty of the task, however, is not an excuse for ignoring the validation challenge posed by the central interpretation and use of assessments required by the NCLB accountability system.

NCLB PEER REVIEW

The U.S. Department of Education has a peer review process that requires states to submit evidence regarding a number of characteristics of the assessments that a state uses for purposes of NCLB. The Department has published *Standards and Assessments Peer Review Guidance* (U.S. Department of Education, 2004) in which the requirements for peer review are articulated. The *Peer Review Guidance* specifies that state assessments "Must be valid and reliable for the purposes for which the assessment system is use and be consistent with recognized professional standards (U.S. Department of Education, 2004, p. 3).

The *Peer Review Guidance* relies heavily on the *Test Standards*. Indeed, the *Test Standards* are introduced with the following statement. "The *Standards for Educational and Psychological Testing* (1999) delineates the characteristics of high quality assessments and describes the processes that a State can employ to ensure its assessments and use of results are appropriate, credible and technically defensible" (U.S. Department of Education, 2004, p. 32). Although the *Peer Review Guidance* does not mention the interpretation of assessment results as an indication of the relative quality of schools, that interpretation is implicit in the primary use of the results to determine whether or not a school has made AYP.

The *Peer Review Guidance* identifies several categories of validity evidence with reference to the *Test Standards*. In particular, the *Peer Review Guidance* requires states to collect evidence related to assessment content, evidence based on relationships of assessments with other variables, evidence based on student response processes and evidence related to the internal structure of assessments. Although not discussed under the general validity heading, the *Peer Review Guidance* also requires states to submit evidence of the alignment of their assessments with their content standards and the alignment results clearly have a bearing on aspects of validity related to the content of the assessment. In addition, the *Peer Review Guidance* calls for evidence regarding the consequences of uses and interpretations of state assessments.

CONSEQUENCES OF TESTS USED FOR PURPOSES OF NCLB

As Brennan (2006) has noted, the role of consequences in validity is a contentious topic, but as Brennan goes on to argue, consequences are necessarily a part of validity because it is "almost universally agreed that validity has to do with the proposed interpretations and uses of test scores" (p. 8). Consequences are worthy of consideration, in part, because of the contentious nature of the need to consider consequences as part of validation and, in part, because validation efforts such as those mounted by states either for their own purposes or to meet the NCLB peer review requirements, have rarely attended to consequences. Furthermore, as was just noted, the *Standards* and *Assessments Peer Review Guidance* (U.S. Department of Education, 2004, p. 33) explicitly requires states to consider the consequences of the state's interpretation and use of assessments as part of the validation process.

The *Test Standards*, which as has already been noted are highlighted in the *Peer Review Guidance* as an important resource for states in ensuring that their tests are technically defensible, address the issue of consequences. After noting that assessments are "commonly administered in the expectation that some benefit will be realized from the intended use of the scores," the *Test Standards* go on to conclude that a "fundamental purpose of validation is to indicate whether these specific benefits are likely to be realized" (1999, p. 16).

As was implied by Brennan (2006), the inclusion of consequences as part of validation is controversial (see, for example, Linn, 1997; Mehrens, 1997, 1998; Popham, 1997; Shepard, 1997). However, as Kane (2006, p. 54) has recently noted there is, in fact, nothing new about giving attention to consequences in investigations of validity. What is relatively new is the salience of the topic and the breadth of the reach that is no longer limited to immediate intended outcomes (e.g., students perform better in classes following the use of a placement test). The inclusion of broader social consequences and the inclusion of negative unintended, as well as positive intended, consequences led to objections by some measurement experts (see, e.g., Green, 1990; Mehrens, 1997: Popham, 1997; Wiley, 1991).

The objections have more to do with the question of whether consequences should be a part of validity than they do with the question of whether or not consequences are relevant to an evaluation of a use or interpretation of assessment results. There is broad consensus regarding the importance of investigations of consequences as part of the overall evaluation of particular interpretations and uses of assessment results (Cronbach, 1980, 1988; Kane, 2006; Linn, 1994, 1997; Linn, Baker, & Dunbar, 1991; Shepard, 1993, 1997), but some authors have maintained that such an evaluation is outside the scope of validity.

Regardless, of whether consequences are considered a part of validity or as part of a broader evaluation of test uses and interpretations, the *Peer Review Guidance* makes it clear, as has already been noted, that states are expected to attend to consequences.

> In validating an assessment, the State must also consider the consequences of its interpretation and use. Messick (1989) points out that these are different functions and that the impact of an assessment can be traced either to an interpretation or to how it is used. Furthermore, as in all evaluative endeavors,

States must attend not only to the intended outcomes, but also to unintended effects. (U.S. Department of Education, 2004, p. 33)

The Department's position with regard to responsibility for evaluating consequences of the uses and interpretations of assessments seems consistent with the prevailing view that validation should be a broadly conceived evaluative process.

Evidence Regarding Consequences of Uses of State Tests

Discussions of the consequences of assessments usually distinguish between intended positive consequences and unintended negative consequences. Although both types of consequences are relevant to the evaluation of the validity of an assessment program, what is a positive effect for one observer may be a negative effect for someone else (see, for example, Mehrens, 1998). Narrowing the curriculum provides an obvious example. Narrowing may be viewed as a positive outcome by those who want instruction to have a sharper focus on the material in the state content standards, but it may be viewed as a negative outcome for those that worry that important concepts and content areas (e.g., science, history or music) may be short changed.

Because there is not universal agreement about whether particular outcomes are positive or negative, separation into intended positive and unintended negative consequences serves little purpose. Whether they are combined or treated separately conceptually, however, it clearly is undesirable to make a sharp distinction in data collection. Questionnaires are often used to collect evidence regarding the consequences of an assessment program. Questions that sharply distinguish positive and negative effects can be leading and should be avoided. It is better to have questions stated in a neutral fashion so that respondents are free to express either positive or negative opinions. Neutral statements also can reduce the confounding effects of social desirability.

State tests that are used for NCLB as well as for state defined purposes are intended to have a number of consequences. They are intended to focus instruction on the knowledge, skills, and understandings that are specified in the state content standards. They are intended to motivate greater effort on the part of students, teachers, and administrators and they are intended to lead to improved learning and to a closing of gaps in achievement among subgroups of students (see, e.g., Lane & Stone, 2002, for a discussion of these and other intended consequences of state tests).

It is far easier to talk about the desirability of obtaining evidence that uses of an assessment have particular consequences than it actually is to be able to make a convincing case one way or the other. As Mehrens (1998) has noted "consequence implies a cause and effect relationship" (p. 5), but evidence can seldom, if ever, be gathered in a manner that unambiguously demonstrates a causal connection (see also, Reckase, 1998). Although it may be impossible to obtain evidence that demonstrates an irrefutable causal connection between the uses of assessments and the various intended positive outcomes, there are a variety of ways that evidence can be obtained that makes such causal links more or less plausible.

Lane and her colleagues (Lane & Stone, 2002; Lane, Parke, & Stone, 1998) provided a framework for evaluating the consequences of assessments that builds on several years of research investigating the consequences of Maryland State Performance Assessment Program (MSPAP) that was reported in a series of technical reports. Their approach is consistent with Kane's (2006) conceptualization of validity as argument. They began by identifying a set of propositions that are central to the interpretive argument (e.g., "school administrators and teachers are motivated to adapt the instruction and curriculum to the standards" and "students are motivated to learn as well as to perform their best on the assessment") (Lane & Stone, 2002, p. 27). For each proposition they then identified relevant types of consequential evidence and data sources (e.g., teacher, administrator, and student questionnaires; classroom artifacts such as classroom assessments; and assessment results) that can be used to obtain that evidence.

For example, using teacher and principal questionnaires, Lane and Stone (2002) suggested that teacher and principal familiarity with content standards and state assessments can be evaluated. The questionnaires can also be used to probe teacher beliefs and attitudes toward standards and assessments, and to assess teacher and principal morale. The match of instruction and curriculum to content standards can be assessed both by the use of questionnaires and by the collection of classroom artifacts such as classroom assessment tasks and test preparation materials. Changes in instruction reported by teachers and students can be related to changes in performance on state assessments (Lane & Stone, 2002, p. 27).

In his American Educational Research Association Division D Vice Presidential Address, Mehrens (1998) reviewed the available evidence regarding the consequences of assessments. Although not presented as a framework for new data collection, he summarized the evidence in terms of five broad categories that might be used as a framework for posing questions about consequences of assessments and collecting relevant evidence. The five categories derived from Mehrens' review are (1) curricular and instructional reform, (2) teacher motivation and stress, (3) student motivation and self concept, (4) changes in student achievement, and (5) public awareness of student achievement.

Curricular and instructional reform. As suggested by Lane and Stone (2002), both teacher questionnaires and the collection of instructional artifacts such as classroom test items can provide relevant evidence regarding intended reforms in curriculum and instruction. Several of the studies reviewed by Mehrens (1998) used teacher questionnaires to obtain evidence regarding perceived effects of assessments on curriculum and instruction.

Other studies reviewed by Mehrens relied on interviews (a combination of interviews and questionnaires or focus groups). The collection of instructional artifacts as suggested by Lane and Stone (2002) appears to be less common according to the set of studies reviewed by Mehrens, but was used effectively in the work of Lane and her colleagues in the Maryland MSPAP studies that were conducted after the Mehrens (1998) review.

Teacher motivation and stress—student motivation and self concept. Questionnaire surveys of teachers and principals have been the most common way of investigating the perceived effects of assessments on teacher motivation and feelings of stress as well as student motivation and self concept. Qualitative studies have also been conducted, however. Sometimes teacher reports are relied upon to evaluate not only their perceptions of their own motivation, but their perceptions of the effects assessments have on student motivation. As Mehrens (1998) notes, however, teacher reports of effects of assessments on student motivation while possibly accurate reflections of their beliefs do not provide direct evidence of actual effects on students. Student questionnaires, student focus groups or student interviews can provide more direct evidence of student reactions to assessments.

Student achievement. Since assessment programs are expected to contribute to improved learning it is natural that trends in achievement provide one source of evidence that is relevant. Similarly, trends in the gaps in achievement among racial/ethnic groups are relevant to the proposition that the combination of standards, assessments, and the disaggregated reporting of results will reduce the magnitude of achievement gaps.

A recent study examined trends in achievement on state assessments for all 50 states (Center on Education Policy, 2007, available at http://www.cep-dc.org/). The Center on Education Policy (CEP) study also examined the trends in gaps in achievement between black and white students, between Hispanic and white students, and between low income and not low income groups. Although trend results were not available for all states due to recent changes in the assessment programs in some states, and the results were not uniform across states where trend results were available, more states showed increases in achievement since NCLB became law than had flat or declining achievement. For the states where gaps trends could be ascertained, there were also more states where the gaps decreased than where they increased or remained unchanged.

Although the overall results based on state assessments are positive, the report makes it clear that it is not possible to make a casual attribution of either the tendency for there to be gains in achievement or for the gaps to narrow to NCLB, or, for that matter, to any particular intervention such as the adoption of state content standards or the use of state assessments. As the 2007 CEP report acknowledges, there are a number of plausible explanations for the trends that were observed in state assessment results. The possibilities identified in the report include the possibility that there has been increased learning, that there has been a narrow teaching to the test, that the tests have become more lenient, or that the composition of the student population has changed (CEP, 2007, pp. 41–42).

One way to try to evaluate whether apparent improvements in state test results reflect increased learning or simply artificially inflated test scores is to investigate the degree to which the results generalize to other indicators of student achievement. The trends on a state assessment can be compared to trends on other tests such as a norm-referenced test, a college admissions test, or the National Assessment of Educational Progress (NAEP) (see, e.g., Hamilton, 2003; Koretz, 2005 for discussions of this issue).

NAEP trend results were compared to state assessment trends by CEP (2007). The comparisons showed that the gains found on the many state assessments were not reflected in the changes in NAEP results. NAEP and state assessment results often diverged and the correlation of the two sets of results across states were relatively low in both reading and mathematics at both grades 4 and 8. Although it was concluded that "NAEP results should not be used as a 'gold standard' to negate or invalidate state test results" (CEP, 2007, p. 61), the lack of agreement does raise questions about the reasons for the lack of generalizability of the state trends.

Alternate Assessments

One of the strongest rationales for the creation and use of alternate assessments for students with severe cognitive disabilities is that the inclusion of those students in the assessment and accountability system will encourage greater attention to the academic learning of those students. The focus on the teaching of academic skills to students with severe cognitive disabilities that is encouraged by alternate assessments is presumed to be beneficial for the students in question and to provide them with academic knowledge and skills that they would not otherwise have. An investigation of the consequential aspects of validity of alternate assessments would start with an evaluation of the extent to which these expected positive effects of alternate assessments are realized in practice.

Focus groups involving teachers and parents as well as interviews of teachers and of parents could help identify the perceived changes in the education of students with disabilities that stem from the inclusion of these students in alternative assessments. Parents are a particularly relevant source of information for students with disabilities because of their active involvement as members of IEP teams.

Comparisons of alternate assessment results obtained over the course of several years could provide an indirect indication of change in curriculum and instruction for participating students. Tracking changes in assessment results could also be used as an indicator of the effects of alternate assessment on the achievement of this population of students.

Consequences of End-of-Course Tests

Because they are more narrowly focused than, say, a general high school mathematics test that may be expected to cover content dealing with numbers and operations, measurement, geometry, algebra, and probability and statistics, end-of-course tests can go into greater depth in the circumscribed content of the course. End-of-course tests are generally expected to increase the focus and rigor of high school courses. A natural starting place for an evaluation of the consequences of end-of-course tests is with a careful examination of the curriculum and instruction offered in the courses in question.

Questionnaire surveys of teachers and of students and the collection of instructional materials such as classroom assignments and tests could be used to provide evidence regarding the scope and rigor of a course. Ideally, a comparison would be made of the rigor of the curriculum and instruction in the courses before and after the introduction of an end-of-course test. In most cases, however, it is unlikely that surveys will be conducted prior to the introduction of an end-of-course test. Thus, in practice it is likely to be necessary to ask participants to provide retrospective reports to have a basis of comparing curriculum coverage and instruction before and after the end-of-course test becomes operational. Focus groups provide an alternative to or a supplement to the use of questionnaires. Getting information about changes in curriculum and instruction that are linked to the end-of-course tests may be accomplished more readily in some cases through the use of focus groups than the use of structured questionnaires.

The particular effects of end-of-course tests are likely to depend on the uses that are made of the results. For example, the impact may be different for tests that are part of graduation requirements than ones that only contribute a small percentage to course grades. It is plausible, however, that end-of-course tests might discourage some students form taking the courses where the tests are given when the courses are not required for graduation. On the other hand, if passing an end-of-course test is required for graduation, it may affect graduation and dropout rates. Thus, information about changes in course taking patterns, in dropout rates, and in graduation rates should be monitored as part of the evaluation of the consequences of end-of-course tests.

CONCLUSION

There are two major validity issues that have not been addressed for tests used by states for purposes of meeting the requirements of NCLB. The first of the issues that needs to be addressed concerns the interpretation of test results that are used to classify schools as either making or failing to make AYP. That use depends on an inference that schools that make AYP are better or have more effective instructional programs than schools that fail to make AYP. The second issue concerns the consequence of the uses and interpretations of the results of tests that are uses for purposes of NCLB.

Validation of the school quality inferences related to AYP status requires that evidence be accumulated that can buttress the causal claim that differences in the quality of instruction account for schools either making or failing to make AYP. Alternative explanations related to prior differences in student achievement, differences in student body characteristics, and differences in support outside of school need to be ruled out. Evidence also needs to be obtained to show that the instructional practices differ for schools that make AYP from those of schools failing to make AYP. Obtaining support for the causal claim will not be easy, but without such support it is impossible to argue that the primary use of tests for meeting NCLB requirements has adequate validity.

Validation of the myriad uses and interpretations of tests used by states to meet the requirements of NCLB is a nontrivial undertaking. Although states have made substantial progress in accumulating evidence that is relevant to the evaluation of the validity of the uses and interpretations of their tests, questions about the consequences of the uses of assessment results have been given little, if any, attention despite the fact the *Peer Review Guidance* requires that evidence be provided regarding the consequences of the uses and interpretations of state tests.

There are a number of reasons that consequences have largely been ignored in validity investigations conducted or commissioned by states. The inclusion of consequences as a legitimate focus of validity investigations is controversial. Even if it is agreed that evidence of consequences should be gathered, either within a validity framework or as part of a more general evaluation of the uses and interpretations of assessment results, there are many challenges that must be confronted. The implicit causal connection that underlies a claim that an assessment has had a particular consequence, presents a major challenge. It is unrealistic to expect that a causal connection can be unambiguously established. The best that can be done is to present evidence that buttresses the plausibility that an assessment has a particular consequence.

There are a variety of techniques that can provide evidence that is relevant to judging the plausibility that assessment results have a specified set of effects. Questionnaires, interviews, observations, focus groups, the collection of data of record (e.g., course-taking patterns, graduation and dropout rates), and the collection of instructional artifacts (e.g., student assignments and classroom tests) can be used to collect the needed evidence. Once collected that evidence needs to be used in the development of a coherent validity argument.

NOTES

1. The three associations responsible for the *Test Standards* recently decided that it is time to revise the *Test Standards* once again and have appointed Barbara Plake and Lauress Wise as Co-Chairs of the revision committee. Although the revision will introduce changes and new ideas, the conceptualization of validity has evolved gradually from one edition of the *Test Standards* to the next. Hence, it seems unlikely that the revised *Test Standards* will make fundamental changes in the conceptualization of validity.
2. The five perspectives are (1) a functional perspective, (2) a political perspective, (3) an operationalist perspective, (4) an economic perspective, and (5) an explanatory perspective.
3. Starting in 2007–08, states also have to assess students in science in at least one grade in each of three grade level spans (elementary, middle, and high school. So far, however, no use of the science assessments as part of the NCLB accountability system has been specified.
4. A school that fails to make AYP two years in a row is classified as "needs improvement" and must offer school choice to students and some additional instructional services. Additional corrective actions are added for each additional consecutive year that a school fails to make AYP. Schools that fail to make AYP five years in a row may be restructured.
5. Exceptions to the requirement of meeting a fixed target each year are allowed for schools that meet safe harbor requirements of reducing the percentage of students who score below the proficient level by at least 10% compared to the previous year. Schools in states that have been approved for the pilot program to use growth in student achievement may also meet AYP by showing that their students are on track to be proficient by a specified year (usually within three years).

REFERENCES

American Educational Research Association, American Psychological Association, and the National Council on Measurement in Education. (1999). *Standards for educational and psychological testing.* Washington, DC: American Educational Research Association.

Brennan, R. L. (2006). Perspectives on the evolution and future of educational Measurement. In R. L. Brennan (Ed.), *Educational measurement* (4th ed., pp. 1–16). Westport, CT: American Council on Education/Praeger.

Center on Education Policy. (2007). *Answering the question that matters most: Has student achievement increased since No Child Left Behind?* Washington, DC: Center on Education Policy.

Cronbach, L. J. (1971). Test validation. In R. L. Thorndike (Ed.), *Educational measurement* (2nd ed., pp. 443–507). Washington, DC: American Council on Education.

Cronbach, L. J. (1980). Validity on parole: How can we go straight? *New Directions for Testing and Measurement, 5,* 99–108.

Cronbach, L. J. (1988). Five perspectives on validation argument. In H. Wainer, & H. Braun (Eds.), *Test validity* (pp. 3–17). Hillsdale, NJ: Lawrence Erlbaum.

Cronbach, L. J. (1989). Construct validation after 30 years. In R. L. Linn (Ed.), *Intelligence: Measurement theory and public policy (Proceedings of a symposium in honor of Lloyd G. Humphreys* (pp. 147–171). Urbana: University of Illinois Press.

Green, B. F. (1990). A comprehensive assessment of measurement. *Contemporary Psychology, 35,* 850–851.

Hamilton, L. (2003). Assessment as a policy tool. In R. L. Floden (Ed.), *Review of Research in Education, 27,* 25–68.

Kane, M. T. (1992). An argument-based approach to validity. *Psychological Bulletin, 112,* 527–535.

Kane, M. (2006). Validation. In R. L. Brennan (Ed.), *Educational measurement* (4th ed., pp. 17–64). Westport, CT: American Council on Education/Praeger.

Koretz, D. (2005). Alignment, high stakes, and the inflation of test scores. In J. L. Herman & E. H. Haertel (Eds.), *Uses and misuses of data in accountability testing. Yearbook of the National Society for the Study of Education* (Vol. 104, Part I, pp. 99–118). Malden, MA: Blackwell Publishing.

Lane, S., Parke, C. S., & Stone, C. (1998). A framework for evaluating the consequences of assessment programs. *Educational Measurement: Issues and Practice, 17*(2), 24–27.

Lane, S., & Stone, C. (2002). Strategies for examining the consequences of assessment and accountability programs. *Educational Measurement: Issues and Practice, 21*(1), 23–30.

Linn, R. L. (1994). Performance assessment: Policy promises and technical measurement standards. *Educational Researcher, 23*(9), 4–14.

Linn, R. L. (1997). Evaluating the validity of assessments. *Educational Measurement: Issues and Practice, 16*(2), 14–16.

Linn, R. L. (2006). Validity of inferences from test-based educational accountability systems. *Journal of Personnel Evaluation in Education, 19,* 5–15.

Linn, R. L., Baker, E. L., & Dunbar, S. B. (1991). Complex, performance-based assessment: Expectations and validation criteria. *Educational Researcher, 20*(8), 15–21.

Lissitz, R. W. & Samuelsen, K. (2007). A suggested change in terminology and emphasis regarding validity and education. *Educational Researcher, 36*(8), 437–448.

Mehrens, W. A. (1997). The consequences of consequential validity. *Educational Measurement: Issues and Practice, 16*(2), 16–18.

Mehrens, W. A. (1998). Consequences of assessment: What is the evidence? *Educational Policy Analysis Archives, 6*(13), 1–30.

Messick, S. (1975). The standard problem: Meaning and value in measurement and evaluation. *American Psychologist, 30*, 955–966.

Messick, S. (1989). Validity. In R. L. Linn (Ed.), *Educational Measurement* (3rd ed., pp. 13–103). New York: Macmillan.

Popham, W. J. (1997). Consequential validity: Right concern—wrong concept. *Educational Measurement: Issues and Practice, 16*(2), 9–13.

Raudenbush, S. W. (2004a). *Schooling, statistics, and poverty: Can we measure school improvement?* The ninth annual William H. Angoff Memorial Lecture. Princeton, NJ: Educational Testing Service.

Raudenbush, S. W. (2004b). What are value-added models estimating and what does this imply for statistical practice? *Journal of Educational and Behavioral Statistics, 29*(1), 120–129.

Reckase, M. D. (1998). Consequential validity form the test developers' perspective. *Educational Measurement: Issues and Practice, 17*(2), 13–16.

Rubin, D. B., Stuart, E. A., & Zanutto, E. L. (2004). A potential outcomes view of value-added assessment. *Journal of Educational and Behavioral Statistics, 29*(1), 103–116.

Shepard, L. A. (1993). Evaluating test validity. *Review of Research in Education, 19*, 405–450.

Shepard, L. A. (1997). The centrality of test use and consequences for test validity. *Educational Measurement: Issues and Practice, 16*(2), 5–8.

U.S. Department of Education. (2004, April 28). *No Child Left Behind. Standards and assessments peer review guidance: Information and examples for meeting requirements of the No Child Left Behind Act of 2001.* Washington, DC: U.S. Department of Education, Office of Elementary and Secondary Education.

Wiley, D. E. (1991). Test validity and invalidity reconsidered. In R. E. Snow & D. E. Wiley (Eds.), *Improving inquiry in social science: A volume in honor of Lee J. Cronbach* (pp. 75–107). Hillsdale, NJ: Erlbaum.

Zumbo, B. D. & Forer, B. (in press). Testing and measurement fro a multilevel view: Psychometrics and validation. In J. Bouvaird, K Geisinger, & C. Buckendahal (Eds.), *High stakes testing in education—science and practice in K–12 settings (Festschrft to Barbara Plake)* Washington, DC: American Psychological Association Press.

CHAPTER 10

VALIDITY IS IN THE EYE OF THE BEHOLDER

Conveying SAT Research Findings to the General Public

Krista D. Mattern, Jennifer L. Kobrin, Brian F. Patterson, Emily J. Shaw, and Wayne J. Camara

ABSTRACT

In March of 2005, a revised version of the SAT was administered for the first time. At the College Board, plans to study the validity of the new test began as soon as the changes to the test were announced. The journey to validate the revised SAT for use in college admission is newly underway, after collecting first-year college performance data on the first entering cohort of students that had taken the new SAT. This chapter will describe our experiences in mapping out the research agenda, targeting our sample, forging connections with institutions, and the many decisions we have made with regard to analyzing the data and reporting the results. Finally, we will describe how we have communicated and disseminated the results of our validity work to varied audiences including: measurement professionals, admission officers, high school staff, parents, students, and the media—and the les-

The Concept of Validity, pages 213–240
Copyright © 2009 by Information Age Publishing
All rights of reproduction in any form reserved.

sons we have learned throughout the process. In sum, we have found that conducting validity research is only half of the battle. An equal amount of effort should be devoted to educating various stakeholders on the appropriate interpretation of validity results so that they are properly understood, referenced, and utilized.

INTRODUCTION

In March 2005, the SAT was revised to incorporate a number of important changes. These changes were made to enhance the test's alignment with current high school curricula and emphasize skills needed for success in college (Lawrence, Rigol, Van Essen, & Jackson, 2003). The Verbal section of the test was renamed Critical Reading to reflect changes in emphasis and format. Foremost, analogies were removed and were replaced by more questions on both short and long reading passages from a variety of fields, including science and the humanities. The Math section of the revised test was changed to include items from more advanced mathematics courses such as second-year algebra and no longer includes quantitative comparison items.[1] The most notable change to the SAT was the addition of a Writing section that measures basic writing skills and includes multiple-choice questions on grammar and usage and a student-produced essay. The SAT is now three hours and forty-five minutes in length, compared to the prior length of three hours. Given these changes, it was essential that data from the revised test were collected and examined to guarantee that the validity of the SAT for use in college admission had been preserved, most notably as it relates to its validity for predicting first-year GPA (FYGPA).[2]

This chapter is organized into five sections. First we discuss how research to establish the validity of the SAT has evolved over time in accord with current notions of validity. The second section discusses how SAT validity evidence should be collected to ensure accurate and generalizable results as it relates to sampling and data processing. The third section discusses the numerous ways to analyze data, highlighting the methods and adjustments we chose to build a strong validity argument for the SAT. In the fourth section we describe different ways to present SAT validity evidence and how data presentation has often led to misinterpretation of results or lack of understanding. This highlights the need for researchers to seek ways to more effectively display and disseminate findings to the general public. The fifth section discusses some different ways that SAT research has been interpreted, or rather misinterpreted. In this section, the authors reiterate how all components—the definition of validity, the collection of validity evidence, analysis, and presentation—influence the interpretation of results. It is imperative that all components are accurately and thoroughly addressed to ensure that appropriate interpretations are made.

I DEFINING VALIDITY—THE COLLEGE BOARD'S FOCUS IN SAT VALIDITY RESEARCH

The SAT was first administered in 1926 and since that time, hundreds of research studies have focused on the validity of the SAT for a variety of uses, in a variety of contexts, and with a variety of student populations. The SAT is arguably one of the most, if not the most frequently studied and closely scrutinized standardized tests in existence. Although the purpose of the SAT and the intended inferences to be made from the scores have remained constant, the research on the validity of the SAT has paralleled the trends and conceptions of validity that have evolved over time. The purpose of the SAT is specific and direct: to measure a student's potential for academic success in college. The SAT is intended for use by college admission officers, in conjunction with other academic and non-academic information, to evaluate the potential of their applicants for success at their institution.

The earliest conceptions of validity were centered on the theory of prediction, and the widely accepted definition of test validity was the extent to which the test correlated with other measures (Brennan, 2006). The very first SAT validity study was conducted as soon as the students tested in 1926 earned their first college grades. In 1932, Carl Brigham described studies of nine student groups in six colleges. The validity coefficients ranged from 0.14 to 0.46, with a median of 0.34; multiple correlation coefficients for the SAT in combination with high school average or rank ranged from 0.42 to 0.65, with a median of 0.55 (Schrader, 1971).

In the first published technical manual of the SAT, Angoff (1971) noted, "the meaning of validity in the context of the Admissions Testing Program is not confined solely to *predictive* validity. Validity can mean an appropriate content balance as well (p. 8)." However, the chapter on validity in the 1971 technical manual covered only predictive studies. The newest version of the SAT Technical Manual, currently in preparation, describes studies running the gamut from relating SAT content to secondary school curricula, investigating the dimensionality of the SAT, and ruling out irrelevant constructs (e.g., effects of time limits, test length/fatigue, and the effects of coaching on SAT scores). This new technical manual reflects the major shift in the conception of validity over the last 50 years, one that now emphasizes gathering validity evidence in many different forms and integrating those various strands of evidence "into a coherent account of the degree to which existing evidence and theory supported the intended interpretation of test scores for specific uses" (AERA/APA/NCME, 1999, p. 17).

Kane (2006) defines validity as argument and defines validation as the process of evaluating the plausibility of proposed interpretations and uses, as well as the extent to which the evidence supports or refutes the proposed interpretations and uses. The proposed use of an SAT score is to predict how well a student will perform in his/her first year of college. There are other potential uses for SAT scores, such as placing students into college courses, diagnosing areas of strength and weakness, and perhaps others. There are some uses of SAT scores that are not supported by the College Board (e.g., ranking schools, districts, or states). However, given the intended primary purpose of the SAT, the most pressing validity argument is in support of its ability to predict college success. According to Kane (2006),

> ...the main advantage of the argument-based approach to validation is the guidance it provides in allocating research effort and in gauging progress in the validation effort. The kinds of validity evidence that are most relevant are those that support the main inferences and assumptions in the interpretive argument, particularly those that are most problematic. (p. 23)

In responding to the demands of our test users, the media, and the public at large, the College Board focuses most of its efforts on examining the relationship of the SAT with measures of college performance. In addition, the SAT is under constant scrutiny and the College Board is very often obligated to respond to criticisms through research. Thus, an equal amount of effort and resources are spent collecting evidence for what the SAT *does not* do, as is spent collecting evidence for what it does do. Indeed, Kane (2006) points out that the extent to which proposed interpretations and uses of test score can stand up to serious criticism is a central issue in validation (Cronbach, 1971; Messick, 1989; Moss, 1998; as cited in Kane, 2006).

The SAT validity research at the College Board is much broader than simply these predictive studies, but the research that gets the most attention is invariably predictive in nature. Despite the fact that predictive validity findings seem relatively straightforward, more work needs to be done in terms of communicating the results to the general public. As will be discussed later in this chapter, researchers at the College Board are continually working to devise new and innovative ways of communicating validity research findings to our constituents—our supporters, our skeptics, and the uninformed—in order to underscore the value of standardized admission tests and their ability to help colleges make better, more informed decisions about their students.

II COLLECTING VALIDITY EVIDENCE

The world will not stop and think—it never does, it is not its way; its way is to generalize from a single sample.
—Mark Twain

The first, and one of the largest challenges encountered in validating the most recent version of the SAT, was obtaining outcome or college performance data. While the College Board has millions of records of data on how students perform on the SAT and other exams taken during high school, there is very little information on what happens to students after they graduate from high school. In order to obtain these necessary data, colleges and universities across the United States were contacted and asked to provide first-year performance data based on the fall 2006 entering cohort of first-time students. In return, these institutions were offered a stipend[3] for the work involved in creating the data file for the national study and also received their own institution-specific admission validity report and matched data file with additional College Board data for use in their own research and evaluation of existing admission practices.

In an attempt to achieve a representative sample that would allow for generalizability of results, preliminary recruitment efforts were targeted at the 726 four-year institutions that received at least 200 SAT score reports from the College Board in 2005. These 726 institutions served as the population and available information on these schools was obtained from the College Board's Annual Survey of Colleges.[4] Various characteristics including control (public/private), region of the country, selectivity, and full-time undergraduate enrollment of these 726 institutions were used to form stratified target proportions of institutions to be recruited. Hundreds of institutions were contacted and informed about participating in the study via e-mail, phone calls or visits by College Board regional staff, online newsletters, conference presentations and exhibit booth informational materials. The desired sample size was between 75 and 100 four-year institutions.

There were two primary perceived barriers to an institution signing on to participate. The first was an understaffed or already overextended Institutional Research (IR) office and the second was apprehension about data security. The current legal climate regarding the Family Educational Rights and Privacy Act (FERPA) and the sharing of personally identifiable information (required for matching purposes) did play a role in recruiting participants. It was important for the College Board to reassure institutions that it was indeed legal to release such information to educational agencies or institutions for the purposes of developing, validating or administering predictive tests.[5] Upon request, the College Board created signed data sharing agreements for participating institutions that were reviewed by attorneys for all involved.

The institutions that chose to participate uploaded their data files to the College Board's free online Admitted Class Evaluation Service™ (ACES™) system after the 2006–2007 school-year concluded.[6] ACES allows institutions to design and receive unique admission validity studies to—among other things—evaluate existing admission practices. ACES served as the data portal for the study, securely transferring data from the institution to the College Board for aggregate analysis. The data collected from each institution included students' coursework and grades, FYGPA, and whether the students returned for the second year. These data were matched to College Board databases that included SAT scores as well as self-reported HSGPA and other demographic information from the SAT Questionnaire, which is a survey students complete during registration for the SAT. Ultimately, we received individual level data on 196,364 students from 110 colleges and universities from across the United States. Upon transmission from ACES to the College Board, all data were examined for inconsistencies and miscoding to ensure the integrity of the analyses described below. One check was for institutions with particularly high proportions of students with zero FYGPAs. This was incorporated into the data cleaning procedures to ensure that these FYGPAs were not miscoded as zero, when they should have been coded as missing.[7] Students in the sample that did not have a valid FYGPA from their institution were removed from the sample ($n = 6,207$, 3%). Similarly, students without scores on the revised SAT were not included ($n = 31,151$, 16%) as well as students who did not indicate their HSGPA on the SAT Questionnaire ($n = 7,690$, 4%). The final sample included 151,316 students. See Kobrin, Patterson, Shaw, Mattern, and Barbuti (2008) for a list of participating institutions.

Table 10.1 provides a comparison of the population described above to the actual sample of institutions that participated in this study. The sample is largely representative of the target population; however, there is some overrepresentation of New England and Mid-Atlantic institutions and under-representation of Southern institutions. As for selectivity, institutions admitting 50 to 75% of students are over-represented while institutions admitting more than 75% of students are under-represented in the sample. In terms of institution size, the sample is quite representative of the target population. Finally, there are more private institutions represented in the sample than in the target population.

In sum, the results of a validity study are only as good as the quality of the data. This is clearly dependent upon diverse institutional collaboration, sound matching procedures, and intense data cleaning and quality control. The College Board went to great lengths to recruit a diverse sample of institutions and to check the accuracy of data submitted and matched. Additionally, many local studies have been conducted but the generalizability of such information is suspect as the quote at the beginning of this section suggests. By including multiple institutions with specific institutional characteristics, we are able to conduct subgroup analyses such as the relationship between SAT performance and FYGPA at private institutions versus public institutions. Many more specific research questions can be answered with a rich data source, in addition to examining the overall validity of the SAT for predicting FYGPA.

TABLE 10.1 Percentage of Institutions by Key Variables: Comparison of Population to Sample

Variable		Population	Sample
Region of U.S.	Midwest	16%	15%
	Mid-Atlantic	18%	24%
	New England	13%	22%
	South	25%	11%
	Southwest	10%	11%
	West	18%	17%
Selectivity	Admits under 50%	20%	24%
	Admits 50 to 75%	44%	54%
	Admits over 75%	36%	23%
Size	Small	18%	20%
	Medium to Large	43%	39%
	Large	20%	21%
	Very large	19%	20%
Control	Public	57%	43%
	Private	43%	57%

Note: Percentages may not sum to one hundred due to rounding. With regard to institution size, small = 750 to 1,999 undergraduates; medium to large = 2,000 to 7,499 undergraduates; large = 7,500 to 14,999 undergraduates; and very large = 15,000 or more undergraduates.

III ANALYZING VALIDITY DATA

If you torture data long enough, it will tell you anything you want!
—Unknown Source

Choice of the Criterion

In the realm of undergraduate admission validity studies, the most common criterion variable is some composite of students' early college grades—for example first-year or first-term grade point average. First-year college grade point average is the most often used criterion because this measure is available soon after admission, it is often based on a relatively comparable set of required courses, and grading standards are usually more comparable in first-year courses than in upper-division courses (Burton & Ramist, 2001). Yet, long-term success in college is also an important criterion to many colleges and universities. Burton and Ramist (2001) reviewed studies predicting such longer-term measures including cumulative GPA, graduation, as well as some nonacademic measures of college success (e.g., post-college income, leadership). They found that SAT scores and high school records predicted these longer-term measures in a roughly similar manner as they predicted FYGPA.

A common caveat offered in the interpretation of validity studies on the SAT and other college entrance examinations is that the criterion measure, FYGPA, is not a reliable measure and there is difficulty in comparing FYGPA across different college courses and instructors. Berry and Sackett (2008) proposed a solution by examining the validity of the SAT at the individual course level. This analysis resulted in a correlation of 0.58 between SAT scores and course grade composite[8] compared to a correlation of 0.47 using FYGPA as the criterion. The correlation of HSGPA and course grade composite was 0.58 compared to 0.51 for FYGPA. Berry and Sackett concluded that the predictive validity of the SAT is reduced by 19% and the predictive validity of HSGPA is reduced by 12% due to "noise" added as a result of differences in course choice. Most notably, the common finding that HSGPA is a stronger predictor than SAT disappears when the composite of individual course grades is used as the criterion measure. However, if one's goal was to determine the relationship between the SAT and FYGPA as it is observed with all its idiosyncrasies related to course selection and variation in course difficulty, then such an approach would not be appropriate (Berry & Sackett, 2008).

Given the desire for comparability with prior studies and for ease of interpretability, we chose FYGPA as the criterion for the current SAT validity studies. Ultimately, the choice of a criterion variable for a validity study must strike a balance between timeliness in acquiring the data and fidelity in representing the construct we want to predict. Most important, in taking an argument-based approach to validation (Kane, 2006), the criterion variable that is chosen must sustain the interpretative argument.

Regression or Correlation

After having selected the criterion and gathered the data, the next major choice is which statistical method(s) to employ in the analyses of the data. Historically, correlation and linear regression have been common choices, despite their relatively strong assumption of linear relationships between the predictors and criterion. Willingham et al. (1990) delineated several ways that a college can think of the relationship between the SAT and FYGPA.

- The slope of the regression line shows the expected increase in FYGPA associated with increasing SAT scores.
- The correlation coefficient (sometimes, the regression weight) indicates the predictive power of an individual measure.

- The multiple correlation indicates the level of prediction afforded by two or more measures used in concert.
- The increment in prediction indicated by the difference between the correlation for high school grades alone and the multiple correlation based on high school grades and SAT (the partial correlation of SAT with FYGPA holding high school grades constant provides similar information).

The two main types of considerations that must be made when deciding the method(s) for analysis are technical—i.e., which types of analyses do the data support—and what we will call contextual; these include considerations based on the intended use of the results, their consequences, and other constraints. As for the first question of whether the nature of the data will support the type of analyses that are planned, different analyses require different assumptions. For example, certain assumptions implicit in the use of regression do not need to be made if correlation is employed. Both assume identically and independently distributed error terms but correlation does not require the assumption that each predictor is normally distributed (Lawley, 1943).

The next set of considerations is contextual. If the goal of the study is to generate claims at a high level of the extent to which an instrument is related with the criterion in general, then performing correlational analyses on a large, multi-institution sample may be preferred. Such a study would seek to neither inform admissions' policies, nor compare individual institutions. It may, however, evaluate the overall relationships between predictors and criterion, which was the goal of the current SAT validity study. Table 10.2 (reproduced from Kobrin et al., 2008) presents the overall correlational results, which similar to past research, reveal that both the SAT and HSG-

TABLE 10.2   Correlations of Predictors with FYGPA

Predictors	Raw R	Corrected R
HSGPA	0.36	0.54
SAT W	0.33	0.51
SAT CR	0.29	0.48
SAT M	0.26	0.47
SAT CR+M	0.32	0.51
SAT CR+M+W	0.35	0.53
HSGPA + SAT	0.46	0.62

Note: N = 151,316 from 110 institutions. Pooled within-institution correlations are provided. Correlations are corrected for range restriction. W = Writing, CR = Critical Reading, M = Math.

PA are strongly related to FYGPA. Specifically, HSGPA correlated 0.54 with FYGPA and the SAT correlated 0.53. Using both SAT and HSGPA resulted in a corrected correlation of 0.62, providing strong support for the use of both measures in the admission process.

Additionally, we can determine whether these relationships vary by institutional characteristics, such as size or selectivity. As shown in Table 10.3 (from Kobrin et al., 2008), the SAT is more predictive of FYGPA at private institutions, selective institutions, and small institutions as compared to HSGPA. This is in contrast with the overall results, which found that HSGPA was slightly more predictive of FYGPA as compared to the SAT.

On the other hand, if an individual college or university was interested in examining the validity of the SAT at its institution, or a university system was interested in comparing the varied admission policies of its multiple campuses, then it may be more appropriate to estimate linear regression models. As mentioned in the data collection section, each institution participating in the SAT validity study received an ACES validity report, which provided validity results based on that specific institution's data. These reports provided detailed information such as regression equations with the beta weights associated with each predictor along with bivariate and multiple correlations between all predictors and FYGPA. This information is useful in guiding local admission practices.

Among the studies where linear regression is appropriate, the use of multi-level or hierarchical linear modeling relaxes some assumptions of multiple linear regression and may allow for additional control. In particu-

TABLE 10.3   Raw and (Adjusted) Correlations of SAT and HSGPA with FYGPA by Institution Control, Selectivity, and Size (from Kobrin et al., 2008)

Institutional Characteristic		N	SAT		HSGPA		HSGPA + SAT	
Control	Private	45,786	0.39	(0.57)	0.37	(0.55)	0.48	(0.65)
	Public	105,530	0.34	(0.52)	0.36	(0.53)	0.45	(0.61)
Selectivity	Under 50%	27,272	0.39	(0.58)	0.36	(0.55)	0.47	(0.65)
	50–75%	84,433	0.34	(0.53)	0.35	(0.54)	0.44	(0.62)
	Over 75%	39,611	0.36	(0.51)	0.40	(0.54)	0.47	(0.60)
Size	Small	6,471	0.42	(0.60)	0.41	(0.57)	0.52	(0.67)
	Medium to Large	30,333	0.36	(0.55)	0.38	(0.55)	0.47	(0.63)
	Large	40,861	0.34	(0.53)	0.37	(0.55)	0.45	(0.62)
	Very Large	73,651	0.36	(0.53)	0.35	(0.53)	0.45	(0.61)

Note: Pooled within-institution correlations are presented. The adjusted correlations (in parentheses) are corrected for restriction of range. With regard to institution size, small = 750 to 1,999 undergraduates; medium to large = 2,000 to 7,499 undergraduates; large = 7,500 to 14,999 undergraduates; and very large = 15,000 or more undergraduates.

lar, a university system evaluating the admissions policies of its many campuses may do well to estimate a single multi-level model that allows for the same fixed effects that could have been estimated under regression but also explicitly incorporates variation across campuses when estimating the intercepts and slopes of each predictor. To date, HLM has not been widely used in validity studies for large-scale college admissions tests. Brown and Zwick (in press) used HLM to examine the variability in predictive validity of SAT and SAT Subject Test scores on first-year grade point average at the University of California (UC). Two of the authors of this chapter are working on a study employing HLM to examine the variability in the relationship of SAT scores and HSGPA with FYGPA across the 110 colleges and universities that participated in the SAT validity study in order to identify characteristics of the institutions that may account for this variability.

Choice of Predictors

The choice of predictors to be used in a validity study should be guided by knowledge of the subject matter and the population of interest and familiarity with the possible instruments or variables to be used. For example, studies have shown that historically the best set of predictors of FYGPA is the combination of HSGPA and SAT scores (Camara & Echternacht, 2000); however, individual institutions using additional criteria (e.g., personal essay, interviews, letters of recommendations) in the admission process should also examine these measures' relative utility to determine the appropriateness of their inclusion and the amount of weight they should receive in the decision process (see Section IV for a more detailed discussion of the topic).

Just as Messick (1980) describes evidence against counterclaims as the "hallmark of construct validation," so too should the order of entry of variables into a predictive model be chosen such that the research question or hypothesis is properly tested. For example, one of the goals of the SAT validity study was to validate the addition of the Writing section to the SAT; therefore, it was logical that HSGPA and the other two sections of the test were entered into the model first. The comparison of that model, with the one that includes the Writing section enables readers to make judgments about the incremental predictive validity of the writing section. We found that the multiple correlation increased by 0.01 when the Writing section[9] was added (refer to Table 10.4). Though the incremental validity of the Writing section was not large, in the next section we will discuss that even small increases in validity can be meaningful in terms of its impact on the academic outcomes. Additionally, other sources of validity evidence with regard to the addition of the Writing section to the SAT, such as its conse-

TABLE 10. 4   Incremental Validity of the SAT

Predictors	R1	R2	ΔR
HSGPA (Add SAT-CR + SAT-M)	0.54	0.61	0.07
HSGPA (Add SAT-CR + SAT-M + SAT-W)	0.54	0.62	0.08
SAT-CR + M (Add SAT-W)	0.51	0.53	0.02
HSGPA + SAT-CR + SAT-M (add SAT-W)	0.61	0.62	0.01

[a] When the incremental validity of HSGPA over SAT is computed, similarly small changes in R are found.

Note: R1 = (multiple) correlation between the predictor(s) not included in the parentheses and FYGPA. R2 = multiple correlation between all predictors included in the row and FYGPA. ΔR = the change in the multiple correlation when the additional predictors are added, or incremental validity.

quences on K–12 education have been examined, and the results suggest that the change has had a positive effect on the importance placed on writing in the nation's K–12 education system (see Noeth & Kobrin, 2007).

Multicollinearity

In the case where regression analysis is chosen, we must be careful of the statistical problem of multicollinearity—where two or more of the predictors are highly correlated or collinear. The order in which variables are entered into regression can make a great deal of difference with respect to how much variance of the dependent variable they appear to account for, especially for moderate or highly correlated predictors (Stevens, 1996). In multiple regression studies using HSGPA and SAT scores to predict FYGPA, HSGPA is usually entered into the regression model first, so it has the largest coefficient. Most institutions use HSGPA (or high school rank) and SAT scores simultaneously when making admissions decisions, yet the theoretical reason for entering HSGPA first is that this measure is readily available and all colleges require it, while the SAT or other tests require additional effort and expense. Because HSGPA is moderately correlated with SAT scores, the measure that is entered first into the regression accounts for the measures' common variance.

When predictors are correlated, interpretation of the sign and size of the regression parameter estimates may result in flawed conclusions, since multicollinearity can lead to inflated regression parameter standard errors and erratic changes in the signs and magnitudes of the parameters themselves, given different orders of entry of predictors into the model. The first problem may cause us to fail to infer a significant relationship between predictor and criterion when one does exist and the second may lead to an incorrect inference (a real-world example of this problem is discussed in Section IV).

As Pedhazur (1982) stated,

> It should be clear now that high multicollinearity may lead not only to serious distortions in the estimations of regression coefficients but also to reversals in their signs. Therefore, the presence of high collinearity poses a serious threat to the interpretation of the regression coefficients as indices of effects. (p. 246)

When predictors are correlated, the standardized weights (beta weights) cannot be interpreted as indices of the relationship of the predictors with the outcome variable. Thus, when multicollinearity exists, it is equally important to interpret structure coefficients as it is to examine regression weights. The structure coefficient is the zero-order correlation of predictors with the dependent variable, divided by the multiple correlation coefficient. In 1978, Thorndike (as cited in Burdenski, 2000) summarized the advantage of interpreting correlations such as structure coefficients over beta weights:

> It might be argued that the beta weights provide the required information, but such is not the case. The beta weights give us the relative contribution of each variable to the variance of the composite, but to the extent that the X variables are correlated, the one with the large correlation with the criterion will receive a large weight at the expense of the other... [and] a description in terms of the beta weights would give a false impression of the relationship. Therefore, when description of the composite of X variables is desired, it is necessary to compute the correlations of the X variables with the composite. (pp. 153–154)

Before conducting regression analyses, the extent to which multicollinearity exists should be diagnosed. There are cutoff values proposed for when multicollinearity is considered moderate or severe, but researchers are encouraged to make judgments in the context of their particular research setting and with a solid understanding of the nature of the data. As Cohen et al. (2003) indicate, even the commonly accepted cutoff values for these diagnostic statistics may be too lenient:

> ...The problems associated with multicollinearity differ in degree; they do not differ in kind. Thus, there is no good statistical rationale for the choice of any of the traditional rule of thumb threshold values for separating acceptable from unacceptable levels of multicollinearity... the values of the multicollinearity indices at which the interpretation of regression coefficients may become problematic will often be considerably smaller than traditional rule of thumb guidelines such as VIF = 10. (pp. 424–425)

Since correlation analyses are robust to multicollinearity, if we wish to retain all predictors despite their intercorrelation, then correlation may be used in place of regression. In the current SAT validity study, we wanted to include HSGPA and each of the three SAT sections, which are known to be highly correlated; therefore, we opted to perform correlation analysis with all predictors, rather than dropping predictors and performing regression analyses.

Corrections

No research study is without study artifacts, which subsequently influence the results (i.e., employing predictors and/or criteria that are not perfectly reliable leads to downwardly biased correlation coefficients). In terms of predictive validity research of admission tests, an artifact that is often encountered is range restriction, which happens when the variability of a set of predictors is reduced due to either direct or indirect selection on all or a subset of the predictors. Because applicants with higher SAT scores are more likely to be admitted, the range of SAT scores of admitted students is restricted as compared to the range for the whole applicant pool. Pearson (1902) and Aitken (1934) were among the first to recognize and begin to address the problem of restriction of range, and later, Lawley (1943) generalized Pearson's approach, resulting in the Pearson-Lawley multivariate correction for restriction of range.

If the goal of an admission test validity study is to estimate the correlations of the predictors with the outcome for the entire applicant pool, then it is not enough to simply present the correlations based on only the enrolled students. Such correlations tend to underestimate the true relationship due to the reduced variability discussed above. There is even evidence that the corrected correlations may still be conservative (lower) estimates of the true correlation (Linn, Harnisch, & Dunbar, 1981). For this reason, correlations in the SAT validity study were corrected for restriction of range using the Pearson-Lawley multivariate correction with the 2006 College-bound Seniors Cohort[10] as the population.

Other possible corrections that could have been employed in the current SAT validity study are corrections for unreliability of the criterion (also called attenuation, see, e.g., Muchinsky, 1996; Pedhazur & Schmelkin, 1991, p. 114) and for shrinkage (see, e.g., Pedhazur & Schmelkin, 1991, p. 446). All of the decisions about which corrections to apply, which population to correct to and others should always be made in the context of both the intended use of the study being carried out and of the existing research. Specifically in the context of college admission validity studies, where grades are used as the criterion, the added complication of differences in grading policies and variation in the difficulty of courses taken present challenges. Berry and Sackett (2008), Stricker et al. (1994), and Young (1993) describe ways to address these challenges by analyzing the data at the course level or by computing adjustments for course difficulty. Finally, regardless of which correction(s) are applied, reports of the research should include documentation of the procedures employed, along with the uncorrected correlations, as described in Standard 1.18 of the *Standards for Educational and Psychological Testing* (AERA/APA/NCME, 1999).

Aggregating Results

When we have data from more than one institution—even if we have data from multiple campuses of the same university system—we must take care in how we compute and report aggregate results. In particular, if the data suggest that there are different relationships between predictors and criteria across institutions, we must be especially careful in deciding how to weight and when to combine the correlations in order to yield the most interpretable and relevant results. If such differences exist between the relationships and we are performing regression analyses, then rather than estimating separate models and aggregating them, we should consider whether multi-level modeling may better serve our goals. For the current SAT validity study (Kobrin et al., 2008; Mattern et al., 2008), we computed separate restriction-of-range corrected bivariate correlation matrices for each institution (rather than computing correlations across institutions). We then used those separate matrices to compute the multiple correlations of the relevant predictors with the criterion and computed the average bivariate and multiple correlations, weighting by institution-specific sample sizes. Another approach used by Powers (2004) took a similar but slightly different tack, in that the institution-specific bivariate correlation matrices were pooled by sample size and multiple correlations were computed based on that pooled or meta-analyzed bivariate matrix of correlations.

Fairness

Equal in importance to gathering evidence of the overall predictive validity of the SAT, the *Standards* (AERA/APA/NCME, 1999) stresses the importance of assessing the fairness of a test. Specifically, the differential validity and prediction of the SAT, or whether the test functions differently for various subgroups of students (e.g., males vs. females), are characteristics of the test that should be assessed.[11] To assess differential validity, correlations between predictors and FYGPA were computed within institution for relevant subgroups (i.e., gender, ethnicity, best language spoken) and then averaged over institutions, weighting by subgroup-specific sample sizes (Mattern et al., 2008). In some instances, the sample sizes for the subgroups were quite small within each institution and as such we were extremely careful when reporting results on very small subgroups that may not be stable for the entire subpopulations of interest. We ultimately limited our analyses to institutions with at least fifteen students in the subgroup being analyzed, since that was the number of covariance parameters being estimated per institution and per subgroup. Similar to prior research (e.g., Bridgeman, McCamley-Jenkins, & Ervin, 2000; Ramist, Lewis, & McCamley-Jenkins, 1994; Young, 2001), the results revealed that the SAT and HSGPA are more predictive of FYGPA for females, white students, and students who indicate English as their best language (Mattern et al., 2008).

To assess the extent to which the SAT, as well as HSGPA, exhibits differential prediction, regression equations for each of the 110 institutions participating in the SAT validity study were calculated and the average residual by subgroup was computed across the entire sample. Also, in line with previous research, the main conclusions were:

- The SAT and HSGPA tend to underpredict FYGPA for females; however, the magnitude is larger for the SAT.
- The SAT and HSGPA tend to overpredict FYGPA for minority students; however, the magnitude is larger for HSGPA.
- The SAT Critical Reading and SAT Writing sections tend to underpredict FYGPA for students whose best language is not English. The SAT Math section accurately predicts their FYGPA. SAT and HSGPA both tend to overpredict FYGPA for students whose best language is English and another language; however, the magnitude is larger for HSGPA.

Specific details of the differential validity and prediction of the SAT in terms of FYGPA are provided in Mattern et al. (2008).

In sum, despite the seemingly clear-cut approach to test validity, many critical decisions need to be made when analyzing validity data, including the choice of the criterion, the analytic method(s), and statistical corrections to apply—all of which will influence the results and ultimately the interpretation of the results. As such, these decisions should be based on what will support the interpretive argument (Kane, 2006). Just as there are numerous ways to analyze validity data, there are also numerous ways to present validity findings, which also influence the interpretation.

IV. PRESENTING VALIDITY EVIDENCE

There are three kinds of lies: lies, damned lies, and statistics.
—Mark Twain

When the results of the first validity study on the new SAT were publicly released in June 2008 (Kobrin et al., 2008; Mattern et al., 2008), different constituencies had different, and often opposing, reactions to the results (refer to Table 10.2). Many were critical of the findings; specifically, Robert Schaeffer of FairTest rebuffed in a *New York Times* article, "It [the SAT] underpredicts college success for females and those whose best language is not English,[12] and over all, it does not predict college success as well as high school grades,[13] so why do we need the SAT, old or new?" (Lewin, 2008). Others reading the exact same studies viewed the results as quite positive and encouraging for the continued use of this tool in admission. For example, David Myerson, an associate professor at the School of Medicine at the University of Washington, responding to the previous article, stated "... the data don't support a conclusion impuging standardized tests, specifically the SAT..." (Garner, 2008) while others still weren't exactly sure what to make of the results. These divergent interpretations of the results underscore the fact that no matter how good a job one does to collect, analyze, and present validity evidence, it may fall on deaf ears (or, in some cases, biased ears) if the results are not effectively communicated to each of the many, and often quite heterogeneous, audiences that use that information.

Educational researchers, including the authors of this chapter, should strive to do a better job of communicating validity results in a more effective way. Correlation coefficients are probably not the best choice. Even those with doctorates in educational psychology or measurement have a hard time communicating what a correlation of a specific magnitude means beyond being small, moderate, or large (Cohen, 1988). We faced a similar problem once the new SAT validity results were released, receiving numerous inquiries with regard to what a correlation of 0.53 meant. In order to make the results more concrete, we created a graph that presented the mean FYGPA of students by SAT score band as shown in Figure 10.1.

By no means do we suggest that such types of analyses should replace the more rigorous, quantitative methods that we are accustomed to employing, but rather, they should supplement our research reports. In doing so, we can provide a more tangible explanation of the relationship between SAT performance and FYGPA (or any other predictor and outcome measure) than a correlation coefficient. The graph in Figure 10.1 clearly illustrates

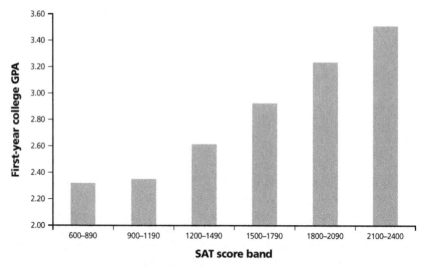

Figure 10.1 What does a correlation of 0.53 mean?

the positive monotonic relationship between SAT scores and FYGPA with students who scored between 600 and 890 on the SAT earning a mean FYG-PA of 2.32 compared to students who scored 2100 or higher had a mean FYGPA of 3.51. Such information is more readily comprehensible and thus may be of greater use to certain stakeholders. Other methods such as reporting odds ratios and utility analyses could also be employed to more readily demonstrate the value of the SAT in the admission process. For example, utility analyses could indicate the costs related to added remedial coursework or resources or retention losses associated with not using the SAT at an institution to make admission decisions. Given the very practical implications of validity research on the SAT and other tests, the ability to communicate validity research findings in a way that is meaningful to the general public should be a top concern and priority for researchers.

Another source of validity evidence that is often misconstrued is the relative utility of the SAT above HSGPA, or the incremental validity of the SAT (refer to Table 10.4). Typically, when SAT scores are added to a regression equation after HSGPA, the increase in R^2 is usually small (less than 0.10). Testing critics and others have suggested that such a small improvement in prediction is not worth the bother. In fact, misinterpretation of incremental validity findings has resulted in much criticism of the SAT by the media and others, and in some instances, institutions have decided to make the submission of standardized test results optional because they believe that the benefits (e.g., improved selection decisions) of the SAT don't outweigh the costs (e.g., reduced diversity). This widespread belief of the marginal utility of the SAT is apparent in recent news articles, such as the *New York Times* article previously mentioned (Lewin, 2008), and a report that was released by the National Association of College Admission Counseling (2008). In fact page 7 of the report states:

> The Commission encourages institutions to consider dropping the admission test requirements if it is determined that the predictive utility of the test or the admission policies of the institution (such as open access) support that decision and if the institution believes that standardized test results would not be necessary for other reasons such as course placement, advising, or research.

Though this report provides no guidance on the criteria for determining predictive utility, the belief that the SAT is not useful for college admission seems to resonate with many institutions. We would argue that before institutions can determine whether or not the SAT offers utility at their institution, they need to know how to interpret validity results. This is an area where we need to do a better job educating our stakeholders of the relative merit of the SAT as a tool in admission. The work by Bridgeman and colleagues (2004) is a step in the right direction.

In their straightforward approach, Bridgeman, Pollack, and Burton (2004) demonstrated that the seemingly very small increase in explained variance in FYGPA offered by the SAT after HSGPA is taken into account is actually quite meaningful when you look at the percent of students who succeed rather than the increment in R^2. Using a sample of 41 colleges that participated in the College Board's previous SAT validity study in 1994-95, the authors determined how many students at different SAT score levels reached different criteria of success in college (cumulative GPA of 2.5 or higher, and 3.5 or higher), after controlling for the selectivity of the college, the academic intensity of the students' high school curricula, and the students' high school grades. Figure 10.2 displays data from Bridgeman et al. (2004) and shows the percent of students who earned a cumulative college GPA greater than or equal to 3.5 for different SAT score levels, with academic intensity of high school courses taken by the student and HSGPA held constant. Approximately 14% of students with SAT scores between 800 and 1000 earned a 3.5 college GPA or higher compared to 77% of those with SAT scores greater than 1400. No students with an SAT score less than 800 earned a 3.5 even though these students included in this specific analysis all had a HSGPA that was higher than 3.70!

Our field is in dire need of more innovative, and perhaps, simpler ways of presenting validity results like Bridgeman et al.'s *Straightforward Approach* to effectively show that small changes in incremental validity can still have a meaningful impact on our ability to predict college outcomes. Additionally, we need to more effectively disseminate our results. More often than not, the traditional College Board research report is not very newsworthy and

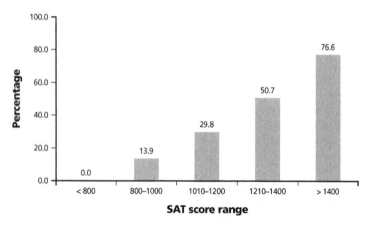

Figure 10.2 Percentage of students earning a cumulative college GPA of 3.5 or higher: Incremental validity of the SAT. *Note:* Academic intensity of high school courses and HSGPA were held constant across SAT score bands. Reproduced from Bridgeman et al., 2004.

doesn't reach a broad audience. Therefore, different, innovative reporting formats should be sought.

The perception of the incremental utility of the SAT has also been undermined by research at the University of California (UC) (e.g., Geiser & Studley, 2001). Examining UC data, Geiser and Studley (2001) found that SAT Subject Test[14] scores and HSGPA together account for 22.2% of the variance in FYGPA. Adding SAT scores into the equation improved the prediction by an increment of only 0.1%, thereby leading the researchers to support the use of SAT Subject Test scores and HSGPA, and not SAT scores.[15] However, they failed to mention that similar findings were found for the SAT Subject Test scores. Specifically, SAT scores and HSGPA together accounted for 20.8% of the variance. Adding SAT Subject Test scores improved the prediction by an increment of 1.5%. The reason for these finding is due to the fact that the SAT and SAT Subject Tests scores are highly correlated, which is an issue of multicollinearity as described in the previous section.

Another conclusion from the Geiser and Studley (2001) study was that after controlling for not only HSGPA and SAT Subject Test scores, but also parental education and family income, SAT scores did not improve the prediction of FYGPA. They claimed that the predictive power of the SAT essentially drops to zero when SES is controlled for in a regression analysis. As such, numerous articles in the public press have reported on the subject, using attention-grabbing headlines such as, "SAT measures money, not minds" (Grant, 2002), fueling animosity toward the test among guidance counselors, parents and students. The conclusion that SAT is a wealth test is misleading given the fact that the SAT's incremental validity was already essentially zero before any SES variables were added to the regression analysis. Additional research has been conducted, which refutes University of California's claims (i.e., Sackett et al., 2008; Zwick, 2002; Zwick, Brown, & Sklar, 2004). Specifically, Sackett et al. found that the SAT retained virtually all of its predictive power after controlling for SES with the correlation slightly dropping from 0.47 to 0.44.

Additionally, research should focus not only on the benefit(s) of using the SAT for college admission decisions but also frame research in terms of the cost of not using the SAT or using alternative measures in its place. Ironically, the NACAC report (2008) emphasized that institutions should conduct local validity studies to determine the predictive validity of the SAT at their institution to determine whether they should continue requiring it for admission; however, there was not a similar call for more validity research for other measures that are used in the admission process such as personal essays, interviews, and holistic file reviews. All measures used in the admission process should be held to the same rigorous standard if they are going to influence the decision making process. Compared to the amount of research devoted to validating the SAT and HSGPA; in reality, it is these other measures that require much more research and validation.

A meta-analysis on the predictive validity of letters of recommendation, personal statements, and interviews on graduate school performance provides some information on the subject (Kuncel et al., 2007). Based on seven studies and a sample size of 489, the correlation between recommendation letters and graduate school GPA was 0.14. Similar modest relationships were found between letters of recommendation and additional indicators of graduate school success such as attainment of PhD ($k = 15$, $N = 5,679$, $r = 0.19$), research productivity ($k = 3$, $N = 394$, $r = 0.10$), and faculty ratings ($k = 17$, $N = 1,991$, $r = 0.25$). These results suggest that subjective admission measures have less validity than the SAT and HSGPA and would result in worse selection decisions if they replaced objective, standardized measures, which has consistently been found in psychological research (cf. Highhouse, 2008). Also highlighted in the recent article by Highhouse (2008) on the effects of subjective ratings on selection was that using subjective measures in combination with standardized measures can result in worse selection accuracy than using the standardized measures alone. In addition to the lower predictive validity and reliability of subjective ratings, the extent to which these measures exhibit differential validity and prediction by gender and ethnicity is unknown and much more research is warranted if they are going to replace the SAT as the admission measure of choice.

As the quote by Mark Twain at the beginning of this section so succinctly implies, statistics are often presented in a way to advance one's agenda and not necessarily to advance knowledge. The numerous and often inaccurate articles published on the SAT are testament to this notion. As researchers of the SAT, we must work on more effectively presenting and disseminating our findings. However, the best we can do is present results accurately and in a way that is interpretable to all stakeholders. We cannot control how others may interpret the results for their own ends; therefore, it is ultimately up to the user to determine how to interpret and use the research findings.

V   INTERPRETING VALIDITY EVIDENCE

All things are subject to interpretation whichever interpretation prevails at a given time is a function of power and not truth.

—Friedrich Nietzsche

To summarize, the way that validity research is interpreted is largely a function of how the data are collected and analyzed and how the results are presented and disseminated. Traditionally, the College Board has taken an impartial stance with regard to interpretation of results, leaving it primarily up to the user. However, it has become clear that in doing so, others will make their own, potentially incorrect, inferences that influence readers who don't know how to interpret the results with invalid arguments.

This is apparent in the commanding influence of the media on the general public regarding their opinion of the SAT. Newspaper articles reach a larger audience than College Board Research Reports. Additionally, these popular articles are often written in a format that is more conducive to reading and digesting the information. Therefore, it is not surprising that the public has relied more on the media for their information than on well-designed research. Often these articles have compelling, emotional quotes by parents, students, administrators, or admission professionals that feel quite negatively toward the SAT and can excite the reader. These articles tend to include bold statements without pointing to the research that may support their point, leading the informed reader to wonder if the research actually exists. Alternatively, the uninformed reader may take the message at face value, not questioning the veracity of the information.

By presenting empirical data in a more straightforward manner and in a format that is more readily comprehensible, we hope to be more effective in transmitting the results of our research to constituents. Additionally, we need to continue to collect additional sources of validity evidence for the use of the SAT in college admission and relay these findings to all stakeholders. As mentioned in the beginning of this chapter, research on the SAT is much broader than predictive validity studies. For example, we have, and will continue to conduct research examining the internal structure of the SAT (e.g., Oh & Sathy, 2006), ensuring that the content of the SAT accurately reflects K–12 curriculum (for a review of the latest changes to the SAT see Lawrence, Rigol, Van Essen, & Jackson, 2003), and examining the consequences of the addition of the new Writing section to the SAT on K–12 education (Noeth & Kobrin, 2007). Acknowledging that factors other than academic ability are related to college success, the College Board is also conducting research on the development and validation of objective, non-cognitive measures that can supplement the SAT in the admission process. Such measures can help differentiate applicants on important dimensions such as leadership and perseverance, which are characteristics often subjectively and non-systematically inferred from recommendation letters and personal statements (Camara & Mattern, 2008). In the end, the accumulated evidence is intended to support the interpretations that the SAT is a valid measure of students' potential to succeed in college and that using the SAT in the admission process contributes to making fair and valid admission decisions.

NOTES

1. For this item type, students are asked to compare two quantities and determine which one is greater, if they are equal, or if it is indeterminable.
2. Hundreds of studies have been conducted assessing the validity of SAT scores prior to the most recent revisions in predicting college success (specifically, FYGPA), and the accumulated evidence has overwhelmingly substantiated their use (e.g., Bridgeman et al., 2000; Camara & Echternacht, 2000; Fishman & Pasanella, 1960; Hezlett et al., 2001; Morgan, 1989). Hezlett et al.'s (2001) meta-analysis found multiple correlations ranging from 0.44 to 0.62 between the verbal and mathematics sections of the SAT and FYGPA.
3. Institutions that had less than 1,500 students received a $2,000 stipend as compared to $2,500 for larger data files ($n \geq 1,500$).
4. The Annual Survey of Colleges is a yearly survey of colleges, universities, vocational/technical, and graduate schools with the objective to obtain information that is important for potential students.
5. FERPA permits educational institutions to disclose personally identifiable information from education records without parental or student consent to "organizations conducting studies for, or on behalf of, educational agencies or institutions for the purpose of developing, validating, or administering predictive tests." 20 U.S.C.A. § 1232g(b)(1)(F); *see* 34 C.F.R. § 99.31(a)(6)(i)(A). The legislative history of this provision recognizes that organizations such as the College Board and ETS need student data in order to validate tests that institutions of higher education use to predict the potential success of their applicants. Joint Statement in Explanation of Buckley/Pell Amendment, 120 Cong. Rec. 39862, 39863 (Dec. 13, 1974) ("Organizations such as the Educational Testing Service [and]...the College Entrance Examination

Board . . . develop and validate a number of tests which are used by institutions of higher education to predict the potential success of applicants for admission. These and other similar groups need student data in order to perform their function."). The organization must conduct the study in a manner that does not permit personal identification of students and their parents by persons other than representatives of the organization, and the organization must destroy the data when no longer needed for the purposes for which the study was conducted. 20 U.S.C.A. § 1232g(b)(1)(F); *see* 34 C.F.R. 99.31(a)(6)(ii).

6. Data files including retention to the second-year were submitted separately for those institutions uploading ACES first-year performance data files prior to September/October 2007. All ACES data files were uploaded by participating institutions by November 2007.

7. There were 118 cases where an institution indicated that a student had a zero FYGPA when they in fact had at least one non-failing letter grade in a course. It was suspected that these were cases where the school miscoded the student as having a zero FYGPA, so these FYGPAs were set equal to missing.

8. To determine the relationship between the SAT and course grade composite, the correlation between individual course grade and SAT were estimated, and then a weighted average of the correlations was computed. Based on the average number of courses that represent a student's first-year grade point averages (FYGPAs), the Spearman-Brown Prophecy formula was employed to estimate the correlation between SAT scores and course grade composite.

9. Out of the three SAT sections, the Writing section had the largest correlation with FYGPA ($r = 0.51$). The correlation was 0.48 for Critical Reading and 0.47 for Math.

10. The 2006 College-Bound Seniors Cohort represents high school graduates in the year 2006 who participated in the SAT program.

11. Additionally, all SAT items are pretested for differential item functioning. Any items exhibiting moderate DIF are excluded from operational forms to ensure measurement equivalence and those few items that are discovered to exhibit DIF after a full administration are excluded from scoring and/or equating, where appropriate.

12. See Mattern et al. (2008) for more information on the differential validity and prediction results of the revised SAT. It should be pointed out that HS-GPA also results in differential validity and prediction, and to a larger extent, for minority students as compared to SAT. That is, the HSGPA is a less fair measure than SAT scores for the prediction of FYGPA for ethnic/racial minorities.

13. The SAT is more predictive of college grades than HSGPA for all ethnic groups except for White students, for females, and for students whose best language is not English (Mattern et al., 2008). It is also more predictive for selective institutions and private institutions (Kobrin et al., 2008).

14. SAT Subject Tests are all one-hour multiple choice examinations designed to measure knowledge and skills in particular subject areas and are used by some institutions for admission and course placement. Currently, there are 20 tests. The University of California, previously required three SAT Subject Test: Writing, Mathematics, and an elective third test. Since the addition of the

Writing section to the SAT, the College Board has eliminated the SAT Subject Test in Writing.

15. A more recent study by the University of California (Agronow & Studley, 2007) reached the opposite conclusion where the results showed that the SAT was a better predictor of course grades than HSGPA.

REFERENCES

Aitken, A. C. (1934). Note on selection from a multivariate normal population. *Proceedings of the Edinburgh Mathematical Society*, 4, 106–110.

Angoff, W. H. (1971). *The College Board Admissions Testing Program: A Technical report on research and development activities relating to the Scholastic Aptitude and Achievement Tests*. New York: College Entrance Examination Board.

American Educational Research Association/American Psychological Association/ National Council on Measurement in Education. (1999). *Standards for educational and psychological testing*. Washington, DC: Author.

Agronow, S. & Studley, R. (2007, November). *Prediction of college GPA from new SAT test scores—A first look*. Paper Presented at the Annual Meeting of the California Association for Institutional Research (CAIR), Monterey, CA.

Berry, C. M., & Sackett, P. R. (2008, March). *The validity of the SAT at the individual course level*. Paper presented at the American Educational Research Association Conference, New York.

Brennan, R. L. (2006). *Educational measurement* (4th ed.). Westport, CT: American Council on Education/Praeger.

Bridgeman, B. McCamley-Jenkins, L., & Ervin, N. (2000). *Predictions of freshman grade-point average from the revised and recentered SAT I: Reasoning Test*. (College Board Research Report No. 2000-1). New York: The College Board.

Bridgeman, B., Pollack, J., & Burton, N. (2004) *Understanding What SAT Reasoning Test Scores Add to High School Grades: A Straightforward Approach*. (College Board Research Report No. 2004-4). New York: The College Board.

Brigham, C. (1932). *A study of error: A summary and evaluation of methods used in six years of study of the Scholastic Aptitude Test of the College Entrance Examination Board*. New York: College Entrance Examination Board.

Brown, T. L., & Zwick, R. (in press). Using hierarchical models in admissions test validity studies with multiple institutions or cohorts.

Burdenski, T. K. (2000). The importance of structure coefficients in multiple regression: A review with examples from published literature. In B. Thompson (Ed.), *Advances in social science methodology* (Vol. 6). Stamford, CT: JAI.

Burton, N. W., & Ramist, L. (2001). *Predicting success in college: SAT studies of classes graduating since 1980*. (College Board Research Report No. 2001-2). New York: The College Board.

Camara, W. J., & Echternacht, G. (2000). *The SAT I and high school grades: Utility in predicting success in college*. (College Board Research Note RN-10). New York: The College Board.

Camara, W., & Mattern, K. D. (2008, September). *Thinking outside the box: New predictors for college admissions.* Paper presented at the National Association of College Admissions Counseling, Seattle, WA.

Camara, W. J., & Schmidt, A. E. (1999). *Group differences in standardized testing and social stratification.* (College Board Report No. 99-5). New York: College Entrance Examination Board.

Cohen, J. (1988). *Statistical power analysis for the behavioral sciences* (2nd ed.). Hillsdale, NJ: Lawrence Earlbaum Associates.

Cohen, J., Cohen, P., West, S. G., & Aiken, L. S. (2003). *Applied multiple regression/correlation analysis for the behavioral sciences* (3rd ed.). Hillsdale, NJ: Lawrence Erlbaum.

Cronbach, L. J. (1971). Test validation. educational measurement. In R. L. Thorndike (Ed.), *American Council on Education* (2nd ed., pp. 443–507). Washington, DC: American Council on Education.

Fishman, J. A., & Pasanella, A. K. (1960). College admission selection studies. *Review of Educational Research, 30*(4), 298–310.

Garner, D. (2008, June 28). Validity of the SAT® for Predicting First-Year College Grade Point Average. *EdNews.* (Retrieved from http://www.ednews.org/articles/26852/1/Validity-of-the-SAT-for-Predicting-First-Year-College-Grade-Point-Average/Page1.html; accessed June 28, 2008).

Geiser, S., & Studley, R. (2002). UC and the SAT: Predictive validity and differential impact of the SAT I and SAT II at the University of California. *Educational Assessment, 8,* 1–26.

Grant, N. (2002, November 15). SAT measures money, not minds. Yale Herald. (Retrieved from: http://www.yaleherald.com/article.php?Article=1408; accessed November 7, 2008).

Hatch, N. O. (2008, June 29). A better measure than the SAT. *The Washington Post,* p. B7

Hezlett, S. A., Kuncel, N., Vey, M. A., Ahart, A. M., Ones, D. S., Campbell, J. P., & Camara, W. J. (2001, April). *The effectiveness of the SAT in predicting success early and late in college: A comprehensive meta-analysis.* Paper presented at the annual meeting of the National Council on Measurement in Education, Seattle, WA.

Highhouse, S. (2008). Stubborn reliance on intuition and subjectivity in employee selection. *Industrial and Organizational Psychology: Perspectives on Science and Practice, 1,* 333–342.

Kane, M. T. (2006). Validation. In R. L. Brennan (Ed.), *Educational measurement* (4th ed., pp. 18-64). Westport, CT: American Council on Education/Praeger.

Kobrin, J. L., Patterson, B. F., Shaw, E. J., Mattern, K. D., & Barbuti, S. M. (2008). *Validity of the SAT for Predicting First-Year College Grade Point Average.* (College Board Research Report No. 2008-5). New York: The College Board.

Kuncel, N., Cooper, S., Klieger, D., Borneman, Vannelli, & Ones, D. (2007). *Letters of recommendation, personal statements, and interviews.* Paper presented at the annual meeting of the Society of Industrial and Organizational Psychologists, New York.

Lawley, D. N. (1943). A note on Karl Pearson's selection formula. *Royal Society of Edinburgh, Proceedings, Section A, 62,* 28–30.

Lawrence, I. M., Rigol, G. W., Van Essen, T., & Jackson, C. A. (2003). *A historical perspective on the content of the SAT.* (College Board Research Report No. 2003-3). New York: The College Board.

Lewin, T. (2008, June 18). Study finds little benefit in new SAT. *New York Times.* (Retrieved From http://www.nytimes.com/2008/06/18/education/18sat. html?_r=1&ref=education; accessed June 18, 2008).

Linn, R. L., Harnish, D. L., & Dunbar, S. B. (1981). Corrections for range restriction: An empirical investigation of conditions resulting in conservative corrections. *Journal of Applied Psychology,* 66, 655–663.

Mattern, K. D., Patterson, B. F., Shaw, E. J., Kobrin, J. L., & Barbuti, S. M. (2008). *Differential validity and prediction of the SAT.* (College Board Research Report No. 2008-4). New York: The College Board.

Messick, S. (1989). Validity. In R .L. Linn (Ed.), *Educational measurement* (3rd ed., pp. 13–103). New York: Macmillan.

Messick, S. (1980). Test validity and the ethics of assessment. *American Psychologist,* 35, 1012–1027.

Morgan, R. (1989). *Analysis of the predictive validity of the SAT and high school grades from 1976 to 1985.* (College Board Research Report No. 89-7). New York: The College Board.

Moss, P. (1998). The role of consequences in validity theory. *Educational Measurement: Issues and Practice, 17*(2), 6–12.

Muchinsky, P. M. (1996). The correction for attenuation. *Educational and Psychological Measurement, 56*(1), 63–75.

NACAC. (2008, September). *Report of the commission on the use of standardized tests in undergraduate admission.* Arlington, VA: Author.

Noeth, R., & Kobrin, J. (2007). *Writing changes in the nation's K-12 education system (College Board Research* Note-34). New York: The College Board.

Oh, H., & Sathy, V. (2006). *Construct comparability and continuity in the SAT.* Unpublished statistical report. Princeton, NJ: Educational Testing Service.

Pearson, K. (1902). On the mathematical theory of errors of judgment, with special reference to the personal equation. *Philosophical Transactions of the Royal Society of London. Series A, Containing Papers of a Mathematical or Physical Character,* 198.

Pedhazur, E. J. (1982). *Multiple regression in behavioral research* (2nd ed.). New York: Holt, Rinehart, and Winston.

Pedhazur, E. J., & Schmelkin, L. P. (1991). *Measurement design and analysis: An integrated approach.* Hillsdale, NJ: Lawrence Erlbaum Associates.

Powers, D. E. (2004). Validity of Graduate Record Examinations (GRE) General Test Scores for Admissions to Colleges of Veterinary Medicine. *Journal of Applied Psychology,* 89(2), 208–219.

Ramist, L., Lewis, C., & McCamley-Jenkins, L. (1994). *Student group differences in predicting college grades: Sex, language, and ethnic groups.* (College Board Research Report No. 93-1). New York: The College Board.

Sackett, P., Kuncel, N. R., Arneson, J. J., Cooper, S. R., & Waters, S. D. (in press). *Socio-economic status and the relationship between the SAT and freshman GPA: An analysis of data from 41 colleges and universities* (College Board Report). New York: The College Board.

Schmidt, F., & Hunter, J. (1998). The validity and utility of selection methods in personnel psychology: Practical and theoretical implications of 85 years of research findings. *Psychological Bulletin, 124,* 262–274.

Schrader, W. B. (1971). The predictive validity of College Board admissions tests. In Angoff, W. H. (Ed.). *The College Board Admissions Testing Program:* A Technical report on research and development activities relating to the Scholastic Aptitude and Achievement Tests (pp. 117–145). New York: College Entrance Examination Board.

Stevens, J. (1996). *Applied multivariate statistics for the social sciences. Third edition.* NJ: Lawrence Erlbaum Associates.

Stricker, L. J., Rock, D. A., Burton, N. W., Muraki, E., & Jirele, T. J. (1994). Adjusting college grade point average criteria for variations in grading standards: A comparison of methods. *Journal of Applied Psychology, 79*(2), 178–183.

Thorndike, R. M. (1978). *Correlational procedure for research.* New York: Gardner.

Willingham, W. W., Lewis, C., Morgan, R., & Ramist, B. (1990). *Predicting college grades: An analysis of institutional trends over two decades.* New York: The College Board and Educational Testing Service.

Young, J. W. (2001). *Differential validity, differential prediction, and college admission testing: A comprehensive review and analysis.* (College Board Research Report No. 2001-6). New York: The College Board.

Young, J. W. (1993). Grade adjustment methods. *Review of Educational Research, 63*(2), 151–165.

Zwick, R. (2002). Is the SAT a "wealth test"? *Phi Delta Kappan,* 307–311.

Zwick, R., Brown, T., & Sklar, J. (2004, July 1). *California and the SAT: A reanalysis of University of California admissions data.* Berkeley: Center for Studies in Higher Education, UC Berkeley (Research & Occasional Paper Series, CSHE.8.04). (Available from: http://repositories.cdlib.org/cgi/viewcontent.cgi?article=1032&context=cshe; accessed November 13, 2007).

CHAPTER 11

CONTENT VALIDITY CONSIDERATIONS IN LANGUAGE TESTING CONTEXTS

Micheline Chalhoub-Deville

ABSTRACT

Lissitz and Samuelsen (2007a,b) call on measurement experts to give more prominence to content validity and the problems of test development. The chapter explores the issues associated with content validity by focusing on standards and tasks. The present chapter discusses the standards used for the development of tests for nonnative speakers of English in U.S. schools and those commonly relied upon to develop foreign language tests. Additionally, the chapter introduces critical arguments raised in explorations of context that have relevance for the discussion of tasks as a domain from which to sample for test development and validation. Ultimately, the analysis provides support to Lissitz and Samuelsen's call to focus increased attention on content validity, but also reveals the problems with such a narrow focus.

The Concept of Validity, pages 241–263
Copyright © 2009 by Information Age Publishing
241

INTRODUCTION

The centrality of construct validity seems to be in question once again (see Messick, 1989) for an historical account of earlier debates. Renewed deliberations of the role of construct validity appeared in the articles published in the 2007 special issue of *Educational Researcher*, edited by Lissitz, and the related conference, organized by Lissitz, at the University of Maryland (Ninth Annual Maryland Assessment Conference, October 2008). In their articles, Lissitz and Samuelsen (2007a,b) call on measurement professionals to rethink their focus on construct validation and instead concentrate attention on content validity and issues associated with test development. Lissitz and Samuelsen (2007b) state: "we are attempting to move away from a unitary theory focused on construct validity and to reorient educators to the importance of content validity and the general problem of test development" (p. 482).

I wholeheartedly support the need to focus attention on developing arguments and procedures closely associated with content validity. I contend, however, that an exclusive focus on content offers a fragmented and an incomplete perspective with respect to the theoretical rationale and empirical evidence needed to appropriately examine the qualities of test content, and the interpretation and uses of test scores, the consequences of proposed score interpretation and use, and theory refinement. I understand that these issues are a tall order for psychometricians and researchers to undertake, but as argued by many, the higher the stakes associated with a given testing program, the more extensive the documentation to "support the adequacy of inferences and actions based on test scores" is needed (Messick, 1989, p. 13).

The chapter seeks to expound on the concept of content and to explicate the difficulties associated with content validity. The areas of exploration include standards and tasks, in accordance with the operationalization of content presented by Lissitz and Samuelsen (2007a,b). For example, Lissitz and Samuelsen (2007a) write: "Test standards, in typical large-scale educational testing, have been written to try to specify the domain in question. A test then can be defined to measure that particular content defined by the standards..." (pp. 440–441). They add: "... the test is a combination of tasks and these tasks are the operational definition that is captured (or is supposed to be) by the name and description of the domain to be measured by the test" (p. 441). The concerns I have with respect to a focus on standards and/or tasks for the development of tests and for validation are numerous. I explore these concerns in the context of second/foreign language (L2) testing to exemplify the issues.

In their article, Lissitz and Samuelsen (2007a) do not elaborate on the concerns that arise when using standards and tasks as content domains for test development in any specific area of practice. The authors discuss content validity at a general level with minimal reference to areas of application. However, as Moss (2007) maintains, it is informative to explore these validation notions in specific contexts. She writes: "I should note ... that our current dialogue about how best to represent validity theory in educational measurement would be enhanced if we were to explore, comparatively, the implications of different choices in concrete contexts of practice" (Moss, 2007, p. 474). Obviously, I agree with Moss' contention and I put forward in this chapter an exploration of validity in terms of standards- and task-based assessments in language testing.

The present chapter is organized within a discussion of content standards and focuses specifically on the standards used for the development of tests for nonnative speakers of English in U.S. schools. I also address standards commonly relied upon to develop foreign language tests. Another topic focused upon in the chapter is tasks. Often the words *task* and *context* are used synonymously in the published literature. I, therefore, introduce critical arguments raised in explorations of context that have relevance for the discussion of tasks as a domain from which to sample for test development and validation. Ultimately, the analysis provides support to Lissitz and Samuelsen's (2007a,b) call to focus increased attention on content validity, but also reveals the problems with such a narrow focus.

STANDARDS FOR ENGLISH LANGUAGE PROFICIENCY TESTS: NCLB TITLE III

Before we proceed, essential terminology needs to be introduced. English as a second language (ESL) learners or English language learners (ELLs) are broad terms used to refer to those whose first language is not English. Limited English Proficient (LEP) is the federal government's designation for this student population. Many educators frown upon the use of the term LEP because it underscores the limitations of these students, and favor the more neutral term of ELL. It is worth noting that ELLs represent a large, and rapidly increasing, segment of school students. Roughly 10 million ELL students are enrolled in U.S. schools and about half of these students are identified as LEP. Additionally, it is expected that by 2015 this group will comprise 30% of all school-age students (Francis, Rivera, Lesaux, Kieffer, & Rivera, 2006).

As is commonly known, the No Child Left Behind (NCLB) of 2001 requires the testing of all students in public schools, including ELLs. NCLB Title III mandates assessments that specifically measure the language proficiency of LEP students. NCLB specifies several criteria that must be adhered to when developing these assessments. The assessments are required, among other things, to measure the four modalities of listening, speaking, reading, and writing, also comprehension (typically operationalized as a combination of listening and reading scores) at all grade levels. Also these Title III assessments are required to measure *academic* English language proficiency and to be aligned with language and content standards. These last requirements are the most relevant to the arguments in this section and are discussed below.

Academic language proficiency. A fundamental requirement for NCLB Title III assessment is to measure academic language proficiency (ALP) in English. This focus on ALP references an important differentiation in language use widely accepted in the L2 literature. Cummins (1979) distinguishes between two primary uses of language, i.e., Basic Interpersonal Communicative Skills (BICS) and Cognitive/Academic Language Proficiency (C/ALP). BICS refers to the language used in everyday communication among friends in social and informal settings and C/ALP denotes language typically observed in classroom settings, textbooks, and exams. NCLB does not provide guidance with regard to what aspects of English language proficiency to measure beyond the need to address so-called ALP. The L2 literature available at the time was also of limited help. Cummins (2001) presents the following description to elaborate C/ALP:

> Students must gain access to the language of literature, science, math, and other content areas.... academic language entails vocabulary that is much less frequent than that typically found in interpersonal conversation, grammatical constructions that are unique to text and considerably more complex than those found in conversation, and significant cognitive processing demands that derive from the fact that meanings expressed paralinguistically in conversation (e.g., gestures, facial expressions, intonation, etc.) must be expressed linguistically in text. (pp. 123–124)

The quote provides some guidance with regard to the domains of language use and ALP features but falls short in terms of the elaboration needed to develop test specifications for Title III assessments.

This was, nevertheless, the level of information available in the field in the early 2000s when test developers struggled to construct academic English language proficiency assessments. This problem has been articulated by numerous researchers, e.g., Butler and Stevens (2001), Bailey and Butler (2003), and Chalhoub-Deville and Deville (2008). In 2001, Butler and Stevens wrote: "There is an urgent need to systematically operationalize academic language across content areas by describing the language used in mainstream classrooms and on content tests and then translating that information into academic assessments and guidelines for teachers" (p. 424). Test developers looked to the published standards to detail the academic language use domain and develop the specifications for NCLB Title III assessments.

Standards. The alignment of assessments with the standards presents significant dilemmas. In this section, I explore the challenges encountered by developers of Title III assessments in the early 2000s. A major difficulty for test developers in the early 2000s was attempting to align tests with standards that had not been fleshed out yet. This endeavor was rendered even more complicated by the proliferation of language and content standards that had to be considered, the need to articulate the language demands that underpin descriptions in different subject areas, the lack of theoretical and empirical support for these standards, among other issues. These issues are discussed below.

Because in the early 2000s state standards were in many instances still under development, states and test developers looked to the professional standards for guidance and these presented their own set of shortcomings. Given the emphasis on academic language use, test developers had to consider not only the *ESL Standards for Pre-K–12 Students* (TESOL, 1997),[1] but also the content standards of math, science, English language Arts, social studies, etc. The dilemma this multiplicity of standards presented was how to reconcile the information from various content standards and create linkages among them. Established procedures to create these linkages were not available at the time and researchers were forced to improvise and create best-guess linkages.[2]

A related hurdle in aligning tests with subject-matter content standards relates to the fact that they were not developed with ELL educators or those developing ALP tests in mind. These standards were developed for educators of math, science, social studies, etc. and did not elaborate the language needed to perform in these subject areas. The standards did not describe the vocabulary, grammar, and other discourse features that ELLs have to learn in order to be able to meaningfully engage in these subject areas.

A persistent concern with the *ESL Standards* is their lack of theoretical and empirical support to be able to prescribe what students should know and do, and concomitantly be tested on, as they progress in their language proficiency across grade levels (Chalhoub-Deville & Deville, 2008; Wixson, Dutro, & Athan, 2003). With regard to the *ESL Standards*, which attempt to differentiate between social and academic language use, or Goal 1 and Goal 2 respectively, researchers (Bailey & Butler, 2003) document that the language and task features embedded in these two uses overlap considerably and that it is difficult to distinguish between them.

Additionally, the developers of the *ESL Standards* intended the descriptions across grade clusters to be suggestive and not prescriptive. They indicate that the "ESL standards are *guidelines* that state departments of education and local school districts can use to develop ESL curriculum frameworks" (1997, p. 15, emphasis added). In other words, the *ESL Standards* are intended to offer guiding principles and to assist in establishing goals and "benchmarks according to the educational setting, students backgrounds, goals of instruction program design..." (TESOL, 1997, p. 16). It is, therefore, inadvisable to maintain prescriptive qualities in terms of standard progression of learning that could be considered a norm for proficiency development and against which we assess students proficiency.

A very disturbing phenomenon commonly observed in various states is the reliance on the English Language Arts (ELA) standards to elaborate the ALP for ELLs. According to Kieffer, Lesaux, and Snow (2007), "in most states, the expectations for language minority students are derived from English Language Arts standards" (p. 9). This substitution of the ELA standards for the ALP specifications can have serious negative consequences. Fundamentally, a focus on ELA to the exclusion of other subject areas is an underrepresentation of the ALP construct and threatens what students should be learning and tested upon in order to document their ability to handle the language needed to perform school work.

Conclusion. I agree that a focus on content, operationalized via standards, is worthwhile. For one thing, this operationalizeation has pushed states, educators, and test developers to more closely attend to the alignment between content and assessment. But content standards do not afford developers straightforward solutions for designing standards-based assessments. As discussed above, developing ALP tests from language and content standards presents complex challenges, such as specifying a domain from which to build test specifications where ESL and content standards are reconciled. The process can also lead to the generalization of standards intended for one purpose, e.g., defining content coverage in ELA, to their use in other contexts, e.g., developing ALP tests or providing content specifications for language arts tests in other languages. Finally, it is important to recognize that the standards are not a fixed domain from which to sample. There is a dynamic, fluid, interactional process in terms of standards driving test development and test development driving standards. This fluidity creates difficulties for test development because it can mean aligning tests with a moving target. That said, such a fluid interaction should ultimately lead to more refined standards and assessments.

Given the difficulties associated with the standards themselves, test developers must consider other sources of information, e.g., classroom observations, textbook analysis, literature on language development, etc., to help inform the construction of test specifications. Additionally, the difficulties discussed here compel us to ponder the merit of relying only on standards-derived content validity as the source of evidence to document the quality of assessments. To illustrate, in their push for content validity, Lissitz and Samuelsen (2007a) state: "we are suggesting that an inquiry into the validity of a test should first concern itself with the characteristics of the test that can be studied in relative isolation from other tests, from nomothetic theory, and from the intent or purpose of the testing" (p. 437). In this quote, I especially question the sensibility of evaluating tests without consideration of test purpose. As stated and argued before, numerous states align their Title III assessments with ELA standards apparently without informed consideration of targeted purpose and population for given tests and standards. Despite an alignment between standards and assessments in such a situation, any validity arguments would be weak, at best. Evidence beyond the test itself or the relationship between the test and the standards can serve to support/contest claims made solely based on content validity.

FOREIGN LANGUAGE FRAMEWORKS

In addition to the standards used to develop ALP tests for ELLs in the school, the L2 field has numerous foreign language standards. The foreign language field has traditionally used the terms *scale* and *framework* to refer to hierarchies of descriptors. The earliest of these hierarchies was the one developed by the Foreign Service Institute (FSI) immediately after World War II to document, based on an interview procedure, the oral proficiency of military and civil service personnel in a variety of foreign languages (Omaggio Hadley, 1993). The success the FSI experienced prompted other agencies to employ a modified version of the system for their own uses. In 1968, the Defense Language Institute, the Central Intelligence Agency, and the Peace Corps produced a standardized hierarchal system based on the FSI descriptions, known as the Interagency Language Roundtable (ILR) scale. The ILR scale continues to be used today in the various government sectors. (The ILR framework can be downloaded from the internet: http://www.dlielc.org/testing/round_table.pdf.)

The government scale profoundly shaped other language hierarchies developed in the U.S. and around the world, e.g., The American Council on the Teaching of Foreign Languages (ACTFL) Guidelines, the Australian/or International Second Language Proficiency Ratings, the Canadian Language Benchmarks, and the Council of Europe Framework of Reference (CEFR). For more information on the historical development of the foreign language proficiency frameworks, see North (2000) and Chalhoub-Deville and Deville (2006). In the present chapter, I focus discussion on the U.S.-based ACTFL Guidelines and the Europe-based CEFR.

The ACTFL Guidelines. In the 1970s, the government hierarchy was modified for use in the K–12 and higher education sectors in the U.S. (Liskin- Gasparro, 1984). This work was prompted by the President's Commission on Foreign Language and International Studies report "Strength through Wisdom: A Critique of U.S. Capability" (1979) to President Carter, which recommended establishing a national assessment program in the

U.S. to document the proficiency of students in various foreign languages. Consequently, the *ACTFL Provisional Proficiency Guidelines* appeared in 1982 and were formalized in 1986. The most recent version of the ACTFL Guidelines was published in 1999 (see http://www.actfl.org/). The ACTFL Guidelines have proven to be quite popular and have been used increasingly as an organizing principle for language instruction, program articulation, textbook formulations, and assessment development for practically all modern languages taught in the U.S.

The ACTFL Guidelines (1999) represent a nine-level hierarchy that describes the structures, functions, and levels of accuracy expected of L2 learners as they perform specific tasks. Closely linked to the ACTFL Guidelines is the Oral Proficiency Interview (OPI). The OPI is a structured, face-to-face interview, regulated by an interlocutor/rater according to the descriptions outlined in the Guidelines at various proficiency levels (Omaggio Hadley, 1993). Notwithstanding the growth and success of the ACTFL Guidelines, the criticisms of the ACTFL Guidelines are numerous and well documented in the published literature (Bachman, & Savignon, 1986; Brindley, 1991; Chalhoub-Deville, 1997, 2001; Chalhoub-Deville & Deville, 2005, 2006; Chalhoub-Deville & Fulcher, 2003; Fulcher, 1996; Johnson, 2001; Lantolf & Frawley, 1985; North, 1993, 2000; Van Lier, 1989).

Briefly, the ACTFL Guidelines, have been criticized because they are committee-produced and scant research evidence is available to support their hierarchical descriptors. A related problem is the fact that the ACTFL Guidelines, which were originally developed to describe speaking performance, have been adapted to provide descriptions of the other modalities of listening, writing, and reading—and with similar lack of empirical and theoretical grounding. Researchers have also expressed serious reservations about the narrow aspects of communication features and tasks represented in ACTFL-based assessments and the sweeping generalizations made by the developers and users of the framework.

As we are reminded by Kane (2006b), "To define a theoretical term like intelligence [or foreign language proficiency] narrowly in terms of a specific measure [such as an OPI or a group of tasks], while interpreting it broadly in terms of the traditional notion of intelligence [or language use], is clearly unwarranted" (p. 442). In other words, while language frameworks such as the ACTFL Guidelines provide some useful descriptions, they do not constitute a substantive theory. They are operational definition of language use limited to the specific tasks put forth in the framework.

CEFR. The CEFR is currently the most exciting of all of these frameworks in terms of recent research, the flurry of development activities, and its increasing spread worldwide. The CEFR represents a variety of language frameworks used predominantly in Europe, but beginning to be influential worldwide. Similar to the ACTFL Guidelines, the CEFR is a hierarchical description of what language learners can do at different levels of proficiency. The CEFR provides holistic and multi-trait descriptions of tasks, situations, and language features typically observed at these various levels. The CEFR, similar to the ACTFL Guidelines, is quite entrenched in terms of its impact on instruction and assessment in Europe. As numerous researchers (Chalhoub-Deville & Deville, 2006; McNamara, 2003) have pointed out, these frameworks seem to be immune to the debates and criticisms leveled at them and they continue to take hold among practitioners.

Political support for the CEFR has propelled its broad use in Europe. For example, the CEFR is an important component of the Council of Europe's plan to advance multilingualism and multiculturalism among European citizens "in order to combat intolerance and xenophobia" (http://www.coe.int/T/E/Cultural_Co-operation/education/Languages/Language_Policy/ downloaded 11/4/2003).

To help with this effort, the Council of Europe has established the Europass Language Passport for individuals to document their language proficiency whether learned in a school/academic environment or independent of such formal institutions. The Europass language passport is critical for mobile Europeans wishing to work and study throughout Europe. The Language Passport relies on the CEFR to provide documentation of learners' language skills. "A grid is provided where [a learners'] language competences can be described according to common criteria accepted throughout Europe and which can serve as a complement to customary certificates" (http://www.coe.int/t/dg4/linguistic/Portfolio_EN.asp downloaded 2/18/2009). The CEFR, therefore, plays a vital role in serving a variety of sociopolitical, cultural, and economic goals important to European mobility and integration. A critical and potent corollary to this political push to use the CEFR is the support from the language testing community. The language testing community, e.g., The Association of Language Testers in Europe, has been a large promoter of the CEFR (Saville, 2002). Given the political push and the organized activities of groups such as ALTE, language programs and assessment products are increasingly being linked to the CEFR.

The CEFR seems to be overtaking all other frameworks in terms of research, development of materials, innovation, and access. These qualities have contributed to the appeal of the CEFR and its spread in different regions of the world. A recent conference of ALTE at the University of Cambridge (2008) shows that the CEFR is not only popular in Europe but its use seems to be spreading all over the world. The conference included presentations about testing projects using the CEFR in countries such as Japan, Korea, Columbia, among others.

Some of the criticisms of the ACTFL Guidelines are also leveled at the CEFR. The theoretical underpinnings of the CEFR have been questioned (Fulcher, 2003), but the framework is better anchored in empirical research (see North, 2000). However, and as with the ACTFL Guidelines, the number of CEFR categories is also influenced by tradition, politics, and practical demands. As Little (2006) writes with regard to determining the number of CEFR levels:

> There are six levels because there appears to be 'a wide, though by no means universal, consensus on the number and nature of levels appropriate to the organisation of language learning and the public recognition of achievement' (Council of Europe 2001a: 22f.). The results of the Swiss research project that developed the levels, on the other hand, 'suggest a scale of 9 more or less equally sized, coherent levels (ibid.: 31).... (p. 168)

Little indicates that the empirical research was moderated by the public perception of language development and achievement to determine the six CEFR proficiency levels.

Conclusion. Content frameworks, as operationalized by the ACTFL Guidelines and the CEFR, have benefitted the practice of foreign language learning and testing. These frameworks have contributed significantly to advancing curriculum, instruction, textbook content, and assessments (Liskin-Gasparro, 2003). These frameworks, nevertheless, lack a credible body of professional evidence to support their current formulations. While they offer a basis for the development of assessments, they lack what most researchers and developers consider to be a content domain based on accumulated theoretical knowledge and grounded research. Test developers would be prudent to rely on these frameworks as one source to consult for developing specifications. As stated earlier with regard to the standards, it is indispensable for test developers and researchers to focus their attention not only on the hierarchy of tasks but more broadly on the construct-related knowledge base in the field of application, e.g., language use.

Another relevant point is the multiple uses of the frameworks and the varied purposes, score interpretations and uses, as well as, the impact associated with assessments aligned with these frameworks. The notion of multiple uses prompted Messick (1989) to move validation beyond the test itself and more to an examination of the relationship between the test and its use. Messick writes: "content validity should not be viewed as residing in the test but, if anywhere, in the relation between the test and the domain of application" (p. 41). Given the wide-ranging applications and uses of these frameworks, it is virtually impossible for them to adequately serve the many purposes and represent concomitant domains, let alone allow a systematic examination of the relationship between framework-based tests and their specific real-life uses. In conclusion, validation is undermined if viewed solely in terms of frameworks-based tasks without consideration of the purpose and/or domain of application.

TASK AND CONTEXT

Lissitz and Samuelsen (2007a,b) also refer to content validity in terms of a domain of pertinent tasks. A reliance on tasks as the content domain from which to sample, however, presents multiple challenges that compel us to rethink fundamental practices in measurement. These issues are addressed in this section.

Often in the literature the terms *tasks* and *contexts* are used interchangeably (e.g., Bachman, 1990; Bachman and Palmer, 1996). While such practice is reasonable in some instances, the term context connotes a broader representation of content-related variables than task does. It is worthwhile examining how the non-measurement literature has addressed context. This literature can point to considerations rarely raised in the narrower focus on tasks.

Context. The following is one of my favorite quotes in the measurement literature: "when selecting or developing tests and when interpreting scores, consider context. I will stop right there, because those are the words, more than any others, that I want to leave with you: consider context" (Anastasi, 1989, p. 484). I wholeheartedly agree with the idea expressed by Anastasi and will explore in this section what the published literature examines with regard to context.

To explore the meaning and use of the term context, Rex, Green, Dixon, & the Santa Barbara Discourse Group (1998) reviewed articles published within a period of five years in literacy (*Journal of Literacy Research*), reading (*Reading Research Quarterly*), and teaching of English (*Research in the Teaching of English*) journals. Their review demonstrates that context is a vague and imprecise term, used generically with different meanings. Rex et al. report: "when we tried to examine what was meant by context, we found that the authors often left the term undefined..." (p. 407). The authors readily acknowledge that researchers are consistent in maintaining "that context, whatever that is, makes a difference" (p. 416), but they lament the complete lack of a coherent and cogent definition and use of the term.

Similar findings are observed by other researchers as well. For example, Gilbert (1992) reviews the definition of the term context in several research methods texts and qualitative studies and concludes that context is not a particularly well explicated term. Gilbert writes:

> Context has often appeared, if at all, as a general background which functions to set the scene so that the real drama can unfold in the subsequent account of particular people and events. The tendency has been to relate the figure to the ground, or the particular case to the general form, but it has not shown how the general is implicated in the very nature and operation of the particular. Consequently, where contextual reference is made for an explanatory purpose, it is often unsystematic, and the connections are not well theorized. (p. 39)

Gilbert concludes that the absence of a systematic representation of context is "a serious flaw, for qualitative researchers have argued that it is the holism and sensitivity to context that sets their approach apart from the selective abstraction of quantitative methods" (p. 39). Despite the lack of a definition of context and the absence of any articulated theory of the term, several conceptualizations that have appeared in the literature are informative and can be relevant to measurement and L2 researchers and testers.

Communicative interaction conceptualizations of context. It is not the intention in this chapter to elaborate on these ideas of context and present a coherent theory of the term and its usage. The main goal of the present discussion is to identify notions that expand upon the conventional notion of context and tasks. One useful representation of context is advanced by Gilbert (1992).

Gilbert identifies two uses of the term context in the qualitative methodological literature: an extensive and an intensive use. The extensive representation of context pertains to the broader societal system. Gilbert conceptualization could be summarized as the properties in the broader milieu that relate to, impact, and help explain the phenomenon under investigation. These include the values, beliefs, and assumptions operating in a given society. The intensive aspect of context pertains to the immediate sphere of interaction. It is a site-specific interpretation of whatever phenomenon is under investigation. For example, in a communicative interaction, intensive use refers to features of the immediate sphere in which participants find themselves, i.e., an emic perspective. The focus tends to be on the fluid features of the interaction as constructed by participants. In terms of language use, researchers have explored a interactions constructed moment-by-moment to achieve communication goals (Erickson & Shultz, 1981).

The intensive and extensive aspects of context are not mutually independent categories and it is important for research investigations to consider the interplay between them. The intensive practices are influenced by the broader, extensive elements, while the social milieu is constantly being shaped by the actions and conditions created by individuals. Figure 11.1 presents extensive and intensive uses along a continuum and depicts the interdependence of these two uses as overlapping categories. Additionally, Figure 11.1 shows that moment-by-moment communication falls at the intensive use end of the context continuum.

In terms of the moment-by-moment construction of discourse, Erickson and Shultz (1981) focus their attention and analyses on the dynamic features of interaction. The researchers argue that meaningful and appropriate communication necessitates recognizing the cues that identify the context one is engaged in, if and when the context changes, and the communicative behavior appropriate in each context. Erickson and Shultz em-

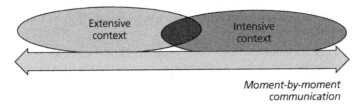

Figure 11.1 Useful representation of context.

phasize the importance of changes in communication signals to indicate how contexts can change from one moment to the next and can impact the direction and intention of the communication.

Frederiksen (1981) elaborates on the role played by participants' inferences in shaping communicative interactions. Inference, he argues, plays a central role in formulating "contextual frames," which encapsulate what each participant assumes to be the intent of the interaction and the resources needed for appropriate communication. Frederiksen argues against a conceptualization of contextual frames as a fixed, a priori set of structures with slots to be filled. Instead, he emphasizes that discourse participants jointly construct these frames and continually reformulate them as communication evolves and negotiation of meaning, topics, and turns occurs.

Context in language testing. A major figure in language testing, whose work continues to shape thinking, research, and test development activities, is Lyle Bachman. In his publications (e.g., Bachman, 1990; Bachman & Palmer, 1996), Bachman presents a Communicative Language Ability (CLA) model that elaborates the L2 construct in context. Chapelle (1998) writes that "Bachman (1990) composed a general interactionalist L2 construct definition, which includes 'both knowledge, or competence, and the capacity for implementing, or executing that competence in language use' in context (Bachman 1990, p. 84)" (p. 44). Language use in context features prominently in CLA (e.g., Bachman, 2002a,b). Additionally, based on this CLA conceptualization of language use in context, Bachman and Palmler's (1996) present a task framework, known as the target language use domain (TLU) checklist, to be used in test research and development projects. The TLU checklist draws attention to the importance of describing and replicating real life context features in test specifications.

As represented in Table 11.1, the CLA model and its derived TLU checklist include concepts, which are somewhat akin to how communicative interaction researchers (e.g., Erickson & Shultz, 1981; Fredriksen, 1981) define context. Nevertheless, and as summarized in Table 11.2, the perspectives that underline these two areas of investigation are different. The communicative interaction investigations of language use are viewed as emic, i.e., specific and local, while in language testing—or testing in general—the

TABLE 11.1 A Comparison of Context Representation in CLA/TLU and Communicative Interaction

Tests of L2 Use in Context	Communicative Interaction
• Target language use domain (TLU) checklist	• Moment-by-moment construction of communication
• External context	• Contextualization cues
– Discourse features	– verbal indicators
– Situation features	– nonverbal indicators
• Internal context/processes	• Inference/contextual frames
(Bachman, 1990; Bachman & Palmer, 1996)	(Erickson & Shultz, 1981; Frederiksen, 1981)

TABLE 11.2 Differences in Perspectives on Context Representation

Tests of L2 Use in Context	Communicative Interaction
• Generalized performance	• Emic orientation
• Static, fixed sample of use	• Fluid interaction
• Overall performance	• Moment-by-moment communication
• Individual representation	• Co-constructed by participants
• Predominantly cognitive external and internal contexts	• Socio-cognitive external and internal contexts

focus is on the generalization of circumscribed performances. Communication and conversational analysis researchers view interaction as fluid and unpredictable. In language testing, on the other hand, communication is depicted largely as static and fixed. Communicative analysis documents moment-by-moment interaction. Testing practices, however, tend to emphasize overall or macro aspects performance. In L2 testing, context features are predominantly cognitive and tend to emphasize the ability within an individual because ultimately we are interested in awarding individual scores. Communicative interaction views internal and external aspects of context as sociocognitive in nature and co-constructed by all participants.

In conclusion, given the shared focus and similarity of concepts explored with regard to context, one could superimpose terms from communicative interaction and language testing. Communicative interaction and L2 testing investigations are driven, however, by different orientations, needs, and uses. The communicative interaction conceptualizations offer notions that lead us to reconsider our traditional practices in testing, as explained below.

Tasks. Issues that have manifested themselves in explorations of context also arise when the focus is on tasks. The two major conceptualizations of context, described above, are most succinctly represented with regard to tasks by Snow (1994). Snow, the prominent educational psychologist, proposes four approaches to understanding tasks or, more specifically, person and task interaction (PxT). These approaches include Independent, Interdependent, Reciprocal, and Transactional interaction. The first two PxT approaches represent traditional, cognitively grounded testing practices, while the last two PxT representations are sociocognitive in their orientation. The following elaborates the four PxT approaches.

The first PxT approach is labeled Independent interaction, i.e., the person and task variables are viewed as independent from one another and examined separately. The Independent interaction approach is well represented in the ILR/ACTFL Guidelines. For example, in the area of reading, it is common practice to establish the difficulty of texts linguistically independent of readers. In the article "Proficient Texts or Proficient Readers" Bernhardt (1986), a well renowned reading researcher, vividly explicates the separation of task and person represented in the Independent interaction approach. In that article, Bernhart writes: "Despite some efforts to focus professional attention on readers . . . most of the current professional literature about second language reading describes text types and configurations. Primary documentation for this generalization is in the ACTFL Proficiency Guidelines themselves, one-half of whose descriptor statements delineate text characteristics—not what readers *do* when they try to comprehend" (Bernhardt, 1986, p. 25, emphasis in original). Bernhardt expresses strong concerns for the independent treatment of text and reader and argues that the two variables need to be considered in concert.

Snow's (1994) second interactional approach is Interdependent interaction. In the Interdependent PxT approach, person and task are considered in relation to one another. Researchers such as Bachman (2002b) and Chapelle (1999) operate within this approach. Bachman's (2002b), for example, argues that "difficulty does not reside in the task alone, but is relative to any given test-taker" (p. 462). As indicated above, Bachman (1990) and Bachman and Palmer (1996) propose a TLU checklist to describe task features. The TLU checklist documents the degree to which test tasks match those in relevant language use domains, i.e., real life. Bachman states that "the closer the correspondence between the characteristics of the test method and the essential features of language use contexts, the more 'authentic' the test task will be" (p. 112).

Unlike ACTFL, where tasks are assigned a difficulty level, Bachman makes use of the TLU checklist to delineate the features of the tasks without an assignment of inherent difficulty. It is the interaction of test-taker and task that results in an evaluation of performance. That said, this evaluation of performance depends on a stable conceptualization of the test taker and tasks.

Snow (1994) labels the third approach as Reciprocal interaction to denote that person and task variables are continuously acting to change one another. Work by interactionlists, also labeled co-constructionists (e.g., Kramsch, 1986; Johnson, 2001; Swain, 2001; Young, 2000), could be said to endorse this reciprocal interactional perspective. These interactionlists object to a conceptualization of L2 ability as a stable construct that resides within an individual and sits still as we measure it. Their argument is supported by task specificity studies. Task specificity findings, which indicate that students exhibit inconsistent performance across tasks are well documented in the language testing and general measurement literature (e.g., Brennan, 2001; Chalhoub-Deville, 1995a,b, 2001; Lee, Kantor, & Mollaun, 2002; Shavelson, Baxter, & Goa, 1993; Shohamy, 1984).

Based on my own research (Chalhoub-Deville, 1995a,b) and a review of the knowledge base in the field (see Chalhoub-Deville & Deville, 2005), Chalhoub-Deville and Tarone (1996) write that "the nature of the language proficiency construct is not constant; different linguistic, functional, and creative proficiency components emerge when we investigate the proficiency construct in different contexts" (p. 5). McNamara (1997) makes a stronger argument in his aptly titled article, "'Interaction' in second language performance assessment: Whose performance?" He calls on language testing researchers and practitioners to attend to the dynamically constructed performance by all participants involved in a communicative event.

The fourth approach, labeled Transactional interaction, indicates that person and task variables exist only in the relations and actions between them. A case could be made that tests of language for specific purposes, e.g., L2 use tests for pilots and air traffic controllers, are a good example of this Transactional interaction approach. The language and tasks observed in communication between pilots and air traffic controllers are very specific in nature and exist for the most part in relation to one another. The language is embedded in the types of tasks undertaken by these professionals and the tasks determine largely the language features.

Snow (1994) acknowledges that his aptitude work represents both Reciprocal and Transactional interactions. However, he cautions against an extreme version of a Transactional approach, which posits that research into person and task (context) independently yields no useful information at all. Snow's reservation and caution regarding an extreme version are supported by findings from learning research, which show that learners are able to transfer knowledge learned with specific tasks in one context to new contexts (Schoenfeld, 1999; Sfard, 1998).

In conclusion, Lissitz and Samuelsen (2007a,b) suggestion to focus on content, operationalized in terms of tasks, as the domain from which to sample for test development is useful. While they do not elaborate on how to translate tasks into test specifications, they clearly advocate a traditional, cognitive representation of tasks. For example, in discussing validity, Lissitz and Samuelsen (2007a) write: "The approach that is being developed should initially be focused on the content elements of the assessment... their relationships, and the student behavior and cognitions that relate to those elements as they are being processed (i.e., cognitive theories of cognitive processes" (p. 440). The present chapter, on the other hand, reviews wide-ranging conceptualizations of task. Some represent established testing practices and others necessitate a fresh look at these practices. The sociocognitive PxT interaction approaches deserve serious deliberation by measurement and language testing specialists to ascertain their significance and how best to incorporate them into development and validation practices.

Validation and theory development. The sociocognitive Reciprocal and Interactional interaction approaches present fundamental challenges to traditional language test development and validation practices. If we maintain that examinees' interactional performances are bound together and testing criteria should reflect this co-constructed performance, then we may need to reconsider the practice of awarding individual test scores. Also, the instability of performances across tasks compels us to rethink variability as error that confounds ability measures. Task specificity explorations as well as the work of sociocognitive researchers compel us to revisit variability and to consider what it denotes about the construct itself. A focus on a stable core of abilities, which has been the usual practice in testing, affords necessary but not sufficient information about the interactional nature of internal and external contexts, and ultimately about score interpretability. For more on this point, see Deville and Chalhoub-Deville (2006).

The Reciprocal and Interactional PxT approaches lead us to reconsider a generalized conceptualization of L2 ability and to question our established practices of providing scores that generalize across contexts. These approaches challenge the usefulness of a general conceptualization of language use and to underscore the need for local representations of L2 ability. They call for research within a framework of *ability-in language user-in context*, i.e., based on local theories (Chalhoub-Deville, 2003; Chalhoub-Deville & Deville, 2006). (This *ability-in language user-in context* representation follows Snow's (in Cronbach, 2002) notation). Local theories developed within a framework of *ability-in language user-in context* pay close attention to salient person and contextual features and their interconnections. In reflecting on Snow's thinking and research, Cronbach (2002) states: "Snow abandoned at an early date all visions of a synoptic theory or of theory that merely links up variables from refined but separate taxonomies of person characteristics and situation characteristics" (p. 234). He goes on to point out that for Snow "[a]dequate theories would give thorough treatment to behavior in situations of one or another type" (p. 234). It is worth mentioning that while investigations based on local theories will describe salient features in a given context, they will also highlight abilities that cross over to other contexts as well.

The challenge of developing local theories of L2 use and adapting testing practices to accommodate an *ability-in language user-in context* framework requires a dialogue across disciplines and necessitates collaborative teamwork. A collaboration among researchers in applied linguistics, language testing, cognitive psychology, and measurement would be a productive undertaking. Historically, language testers have been adept at crossing over into related disciplines. It is important for measurement specialists to do the same. A quote from Kane (2006b) that calls upon measurement specialists to engage in collaborative research is fitting. Kane writes:

> I think that it would be especially useful for psychometricians to join research groups as full participants who are actively engaged in all aspects of research projects. I am not talking about a consulting gig or an elegant reanalysis of some existing data set...but rather about participating in the preliminary analysis, hypothesis development, study design, and data collection, as well as the analysis and interpretation of the results. (p. 445)

Long term, meaningful collaborations between measurement professionals and pertinent research groups is necessary to undertake the challenges raised by a focus on standards and tasks as the content domain for test development and validation.

CONCLUSION

Lissitz and Samuelsen (2007a,b) call on measurement experts to give more prominence to content validity. The researchers question the usefulness of a unitary theory of validity and a construct-driven approach to validation. Lissitz and Samuelsen identify standards and tasks as good examples of domains from which to sample content when developing tests. The present chapter explores the complex domain representation of standards and tasks, problems associated with test development when relying on standards and tasks, and the limited conceptualization and narrow operationalization of context in measurement practices. The explorations presented in this chapter are discussed within the field of language testing.

The explorations strongly support the call by Lissitz and Samuelsen (2007a,b) to pay more attention to arguments and procedures associated with content validity and test development. Obviously, such attention is critical to enhancing the quality of our tests and the scores they yield. Nevertheless, I ultimately depart from the call by Lissitz and Samuelson to break away from the current focus in the field on construct-driven validation, as articulated by Messick (1989). I support comprehensive validation agendas that encompass "multiple sources of evidence" (Embretson, 2007, p. 454). Such validation plans are akin to what Kane (2006a) calls *interpretive arguments*, which describe "the network of inferences and assumptions leading from the observed performance to the conclusions and decisions based on the performances" (p. 23). Finally, I agree with the recommendation made by Moss (2007) to the committee in charge of the upcoming revisions to the *Standards* (AERA, APA, and NCME, 1999) that they compile examples of comprehensive validation agendas associated with a variety of commonly observed testing uses in "concrete contexts of practice" (p. 474). Examples from language testing contexts can help serve this purpose.

NOTES

1. New *ESL standards for Pre-K–12* (TESOL, 2006) have been published. The 2006 ESL Standards elaborate ALP in the content domains of science, math, English language arts, and social studies at all grade levels.
2. Researchers have been working to address these problems. For example, Bailey, Butler and Sato (2005) have been investigating the development of systematic standard-to-standard linkages, which is critical to show correspondence among the various standards as well as discrepancies that need to be resolved. Such research provides methical descriptions that delineate the academic language use domain from which to construct Title III tests for ELLs.

REFERENCES

Association of Language Testers in Europe (ALTE) Third International Conference. (2008, April). *Social and educational impact of language assessment.* Cambridge: University of Cambridge.

American Education Research Association, American Psychological Association, & National Council on Measurement in Education. (1999). *Standards for educational and psychological testing.* Washington, DC: American Psychological Association.

American Council on the Teaching of Foreign Languages. (1982). *ACTFL provisional proficiency guidelines.* Hastings-on-Hudson, NY: Author.

American Council on the Teaching of Foreign Languages. (1986). *ACTFL proficiency guidelines.* Hastings-on-Hudson, NY: Author.

American Council on the Teaching of Foreign Languages. (1999). *Revised ACTFL proficiency guidelines–speaking.* Yonkers, NY: Author.

Anastasi, A. (1989). Ability testing in the 1980's and beyond: Some major trends. *Public Personnel Management, 37,* 471–485.

Bachman, L. F. (1990). *Fundamental considerations in language testing.* Oxford: Oxford University Press.

Bachman, L. F. (2002a). Alternative interpretations of alternative assessments: Some validity issues in educational performance assessments. *Educational Measurement: Issues and Practice, 21,* 5–18.

Bachman, L. F. (2002b). Some reflections on task-based language performance assessment. *Language Testing, 19,* 453–476.

Bachman, L. F., & Palmer, A. S. (1996). *Language testing in practice.* Oxford: Oxford University Press.

Bachman, L. F., & Savignon, S. J. (1986). The evaluation of communicative language proficiency: A critique of the ACTFL Oral Interview. *Modern Language Journal, 70,* 380–390.

Bailey, A. L., & Butler, F. A. (2003). *An evidentiary framework for operationalizing academic language for broad application to K-12 education: A design document.* (CSE Report 611). Los Angeles: University of California, National Center for Research on Evaluation, Standards, and Student Testing (CRESST).

Bailey, A. L., Butler, F. A., & Sato, E. (2005). *Standards-to-standards linkage under Title III: Exploring common language demands in ELD and science standards.* (CSE Report 667). Los Angeles: University of California, National Center for Research on Evaluation, Standards, and Student Testing (CRESST).

Bernhardt, E. B. (1986). Proficient texts or proficient readers? *ADFL Bulletin, 17,* 25–28.

Brennan, R. L. (2001). *Generalizability theory.* New York: Springer-Verlag.

Brindley, G. (1991). Defining language ability: The criteria for criteria. In S. Anivan (Ed.), *Current developments in language testing* (pp. 139–164). Singapore: Regional Language Center.

Butler, F. A., & Stevens, R. (2001). Standardized assessment of the content knowledge of English language learners K-12: Current trends and old dilemmas. *Language Testing, 18,* 409–427.

Chalhoub-Deville, M. (1995a). Deriving oral assessment scales across different tests and rater groups. *Language Testing, 12,* 16–33.

Chalhoub-Deville, M. (1995b). A contextualized approach to describing oral language proficiency. *Language Learning, 45,* 251–281.

Chalhoub-Deville, M. (1997). Theoretical models, assessment frameworks and test construction. *Language Testing, 14,* 3–22.

Chalhoub-Deville, M. (2001). Task-based assessment: A link to second language instruction. In M. Bygate, P. Skehan, & M. Swain, (Eds.), *Researching pedagogic tasks: Second language learning, teaching and testing* (pp. 210–228). Harlow, UK: Longman.

Chalhoub-Deville, M. (2003). Second language interaction: Current perspectives and future trends. *Language Testing, 20,* 369–383.

Chalhoub-Deville, M., & Deville, C. (2005). A look back at and forward to what language testers measure. In E. Hinkel (Ed.), *Handbook of research in second language teaching and learning* (pp. 815–832). Mahwah, NJ: Lawrence Erlbaum Associates.

Chalhoub-Deville, M., & Deville, C. (2006). Old, borrowed, and new thoughts in second language testing. In R. L. Brennan (Ed.), *Educational measurement* (4th ed., pp. 516–530). Washington, DC: The National Council on Measurement in Education & the American Council on Education.

ub-Deville, M., & Deville, C. (2008). National standardized English language assessments. In B. Spolsky & F. Hults (Eds.), *Handbook of educational linguistics* (pp. 510–522). Oxford, UK: Blackwell Publishers.

houb-Deville, M., & Fulcher, G. (2003). The oral proficiency interview: A research agenda. *Foreign Language Annals, 36,* 498–506.

houb-Deville, M., & Tarone, E. (1996, March 23-26). *What is the role of specific contexts in second-language acquisition, teaching, and testing?* Unpublished manuscript version of this paper was presented at the Annual Meeting of the American Association for Applied Linguistics, Chicago, IL.

hapelle, C.A. (1998). Construct definition and validity inquiry in SLA research. In L. F. Bachman & A. D. Cohen (Eds.), *Second language acquisition and language testing interfaces* (pp. 32–70). Cambridge: Cambridge University Press.

Cronbach, L J. (Ed.) (2002). *Remaking the concept of aptitude: Extending the legacy of Richard E. Snow.* Mahwah, NJ: Lawrence Erlbaum.

Cummins, J. (1979). Cognitive academic language proficiency: Linguistic interdependence, the optimum ages question and other matters. *Working Papers on Bilingualism 19,* 197–205.

Cummins, J. (2001). Assessment options for bilingual learners. In J.V. Tinajero & S.R. Hurley (Eds.), *Literacy assessment of bilingual learners* (pp. 115–129). Boston: Allyn and Bacon.

Deville, C., & Chalhoub-Deville, M. (2006). Old and new thoughts on test score variability: Implications for reliability and validity. In M. Chalhoub-Deville, C. Chapelle, & P. Duff (Eds.), *Inference and generalizability in applied linguistics: Multiple research perspectives.* Amsterdam: John Benjamins Publishing Company.

Educational Researcher. (2007). Special issue: Dialogue on validity, *36,* edited by R. W. Lissitz.

Embretson, S. E. (2007). Construct validity: A universal validity system or just another test evaluation procedure? *Educational Researcher, 36,* 449–455.

Erickson, F., & Schultz, J. (1981). When is context? Some issues and methods in the analysis of social competence. In J. Green & C. Wallat (Eds.), *Ethnography and language in educational settings* (pp. 147–160). Norwood, NJ: Ablex.

Francis, D. J., Rivera, M., Lesaux, N., Kieffer, M., & Rivera, H. (2006). *Practical guidelines for the education of English language learners: Research based recommendations for instruction and academic interventions.* Available at http://www.centeroninstruction.org/files/ELL1-Interventions.pdf.

Frederiksen, C.H. (1981). Inference in preschool children's conversations—a cognitive perspective. In J. Green & C. Wallat (Eds.), *Ethnography and language in educational settings* (pp. 303–350). Norwood, NJ: Ablex.

Fulcher, G. (1996). Invalidating validity claims for the ACTFL Oral Rating Scale. *System, 24,* 163–172.

Fulcher, G. (2003). *Testing second language speaking.* London: Pearson Education Limited.

Gilbert, R. (1992). Text and context in qualitative educational research: Discourse analysis and the problem of contextual explanation. *Linguistics and Education, 4,* 37–57.

Johnson, M. (2001). *The art of non-conversation.* New Haven, CT: Yale University Press.

Kane, M. T. (2006a). Validation. In R. L. Brennan (Ed.), *Educational mea* (4th ed., pp. 17–64). Washington, DC: The National Council on M ment in Education & the American Council on Education.

Kane, M. T. (2006b). In praise of pluralism: A comment on Borsboom. *Psych ka, 71,* 441–445.

Kieffer, M. J., Lesaux, N. K., & Snow, C. E. (2007). Promises and pitfalls: Imp tions of No Child Left Behind for identifying, assessing, and educating lish language learners. In G. Sunderman (Ed.), *Holding NCLB accounta Achieving accountability, equity, and school reform* (pp. 57–74). Thousand Oa CA: Corwin Press.

Kramsch, C. J. (1986). From language proficiency to interactional competenc *Modern Language Journal, 70,* 366–372.

Lantolf, J. P., & Frawley, W. (1985). Oral proficiency testing: A critical analysis. *Mod ern Language Journal, 69,* 337–345.

Lee, Y-W., Kantor, R., & Mollaun, P. (April, 2002). *Score dependability of the writing and speaking sections of New TOEFL.* Paper presented at the annual meeting of the National Council on Measurement in Education (NCME), New Orleans, LA.

Liskin-Gasparro, J. E. (1984). The ACTFL proficiency guidelines: A historical per- spective. In T. V. Higgs, (Ed.), *Teaching for proficiency: The organizing principle* (pp. 11–42). Lincolnwood, IL: National Textbook Company.

Liskin-Gasparro, J. E. (2003). The ACTFL proficiency guidelines and the oral profi- ciency interview: A brief history and analysis of their survival. *Foreign Language Annals, 36,* 483–490.

Lissitz, R. W., & Samuelsen, K. (2007a). A suggested change in terminology and em- phasis regarding validity and education. *Educational Researcher, 36,* 437–448.

Lissitz, R. W., & Samuelsen, K. (2007b). Further clarification regarding validity and education. *Educational Researcher, 36,* 482–484.

Little, D. (2006). The Common European Framework of Reference for Languag- es: Content, purpose, origin, reception and impact. *Language Teaching, 39,* 167–190.

McNamara, T. (1997). 'Interaction' in second language performance assessment: Whose performance? *Applied Linguistics, 18,* 446–466.

McNamara, T. (2003). Looking back, looking forward: Rethinking Bachman. *Lan- guage Testing, 20,* 466–473.

Messick, S. (1989). Validity. In R.L. Linn (Ed.), *Educational measurement* (3rd ed., pp. 13–103). New York: American Council on Education/Macmillan.

Moss, P. A. (2007). Reconstructing validity. *Educational Researcher, 36,* 470–476.

Ninth Annual Maryland Assessment Conference. (2008, October). The Concept of Validity: Revisions, New Directions and Applications. University of Maryland, College Park, MD.

No Child Left Behind Act of 2001, Public Law No. 107-110.

North, B. (1993). *The development of descriptors on scales of language proficiency.* Wash- ington, DC: National Foreign Language Center.

North, B. (2000). *The development of a common framework scale of language proficiency.* New York: Peter Lang.

Omaggio Hadley, A. C. (1993). *Teaching language in context: Proficiency-oriented instruc- tion* (2nd ed.). Boston: Heinle & Heinle Publishers, Inc.

Green, J., Dixon, C., & the Santa Barbara Discourse Group. (1998). What counts when context counts?: The uncommon "common" language of literacy research. *Journal of Literacy Research, 30,* 405–433.

N. (2002, December). *Plurilingualism and partial competence: Implications for language assessment.* Presentation at the annual Language Testing Research Colloquium, Hong Kong.

enfeld, A. (1999). Looking toward the 21st century: Challenges of educational theory and practice. *Educational Researcher, 28,* 4–14.

d, A. (1998). On two metaphors for learning and the dangers of choosing just one. *Educational Researcher, 27,* 4–13.

avelson, R. J., Baxter, G. P., & Goa, X. (1993). Sampling variability of performance assessments. *Journal of Educational Measurement, 30,* 215–232.

ohamy, E. (1984). Does the testing method make a difference? The case of reading comprehension. *Language Testing, 1,* 147–170.

now, R. E. (1994). Abilities in academic tasks. In R. J. Sternberg & R. K. Wagner (Eds.), *Mind in context* (pp. 3–37). Cambridge: Cambridge University Press.

Strength through wisdom: A critique of U.S. capability. (1979). *A report to the president from the president's commission on foreign language and international studies.* Washington, DC: U.S. Government Printing Office. [Reprinted in *Modern Language Journal,* (1984), *64,* 9–57.]

Swain, M. (2001). Examining dialogue: Another approach to content specification and to validating inferences drawn from test scores. *Language Testing, 18,* 275–302.

Teachers of English to Speakers of Other Languages (TESOL). (1997). *ESL Standards for Pre-K-12 Students.* Alexandria, VA: Author.

TESOL. (2006). *Pre-K–12 English language proficiency standards.* Alexandria, VA: Author.

van Lier, L. (1989). Reeling, writhing, drawling, stretching, and fainting in coils: Oral proficiency interviews as conversation. *TESOL Quarterly, 23,* 489–508.

Wixson, K. K., Dutro, E., & Athan, R. G. (2003). The challenge of developing content standards. *Review of Educational Research, 27,* 69–107.

Young, R. F. (2000, March). *Interactional competence: Challenges for validity.* Paper presented at the annual meeting of the Language Testing Research Colloquium, Vancouver, Canada.

CPSIA information can be obtained at www.ICGtesting.com
Printed in the USA
BVOW06s2116110815

412881BV00003B/8/P